C++ LABORATORY MANUAL

CO-ADX-784

FUNDAMENTALS OF COMPUTING II

Abstraction, Data Structures, and Large Software Systems

Allen B. Tucker
Bowdoin College

Robert D. Cupper
Allegheny College

W. James Bradley
Calvin College

Richard G. Epstein
West Chester University

Charles F. Kelemen
Swarthmore College

McGRAW-HILL, INC.

New York St. Louis San Francisco Auckland Bogotá Caracas
Lisbon London Madrid Mexico City Milan Montreal New Delhi
San Juan Singapore Sydney Tokyo Toronto

FUNDAMENTALS OF COMPUTING ll
Abstraction, Data Structures, and Large Software Systems,
C++ Laboratory Manual

This book is printed on recycled, acid-free
paper containing 10% postconsumer waste .

2 3 4 5 6 7 8 9 0 FGR FGR 9 0 9 8 7 6 5

ISBN 0-07-065503-0

The editor was Eric M. Munson;
the production supervisor was Paula Flores.
Quebecor Printing/Fairfield was printer and binder.

CONTENTS

PREFACE

This laboratory manual and its accompanying software suite are designed to supplement the text *Fundamentals of Computing II: Abstraction, Data Structures, and Large Software Systems, C++ Edition* (McGraw–Hill, 1995). This manual's chapters introduce advanced elements of C++ along with an accompanying set of laboratory exercises that will develop student skills and understanding of the principles of software design.

These chapters should normally be covered in order and be coupled with their corresponding chapters in the text. Each chapter introduces appropriate new elements of C++ and related technical information, and then follows that introduction with one or more laboratory exercises that help develop student mastery of that information. Most of the exercises require students to use prewritten software from the diskette that is supplied with the *Instructor's Manual*. The software may also be obtained directly via the Internet by sending e–mail to allen@polar.bowdoin.edu. Students are encouraged to freely copy this software as needed to complete the various laboratory exercises.

Each laboratory exercise is presented as a series of steps, or parts, which are identified by the following kinds of headings:

Part 1 — Develop the Specifications

Part 2 — Develop the Program

Part 3 — Test the Program

Once students have completed these parts, they should also answer a related series of questions, which is identified by the following kind of heading:

Questions

After completing a laboratory exercise, students will normally hand in listings of their programs, the output from one or more test runs of the programs, and their answers to the accompanying questions.

Our experience finds that this laboratory suite is most effective in the setting of a "closed lab" environment. That is, students and the instructor meet on a scheduled basis for an additional 1- or 2-hour period each week, separately from the 3 hours of weekly lectures. The meeting should take place in a dedicated computer laboratory equipped with UNIX workstations (Gnu C++), PC–compatibles (Borland C++), Macintoshes (Symantec C++ or Metrowerks Code Warrior), or other machines that support C++. At least one machine should be available for every two students, and space should be arranged so that students can work in small groups at whiteboards or work tables.

During the first half hour of a lab session, the instructor may wish to present or demonstrate some technical material that is related to the exercise. The remainder of the session can be used by students to begin working on the lab exercise itself; the instructor and/or an assistant should be available throughout this period to answer questions. This overall laboratory design is similar to what students would encounter in a physics, chemistry, or biology lab, reenforcing the idea that computing is a scientific and engineering discipline as well as a mathematical one.

Many of the lab assignments will normally be completed by students working individually, and some can be completed within the scheduled lab session itself. Others, however, will not normally be completed in this amount of time; students will need to plan extra time and/or work in teams of two or three, completing these assignments outside the regularly-scheduled period and turning them in at the end of the week. Some labs are intentionally designed to be completed as *team projects*; these are marked with the prefix *(TEAM)* in the table of contents. Completion of one or more team projects gives students a valuable introduction to the style of work that the design of large software systems normally requires. In any case, lab assignments which are not completed within the scheduled lab period should be well enough understood by the end of that period that they can be completed later without major intervention from the instructor.

This laboratory manual follows the recommendations for laboratories found in the report *Computing Curricula 1991* [1], the recent ACM/IEEE–CS recommendations for undergraduate curricula in computer science and engineering. Its purpose is to support the laboratory needs of the second course, numbered C102 in curricula B, E, H, and K in that report, along with the companion text, *Fundamentals of Computing II: Abstraction, Data Structures, and Large Software Systems, C++ Edition*.

Allen B. Tucker
Robert D. Cupper
W. James Bradley
Richard G. Epstein
Charles F. Kelemen

Reference

[1]   A. Tucker (ed.), B. Barnes, R. Aiken, K. Barker, K. Bruce, J. Cain, S. Conry, G. Engel, R. Epstein, D. Lidtke, M. Mulder, J. Rogers, E. Spafford, and A. Turner, *Computing Curricula 1991*, ACM/IEEE–CS Joint Curriculum Task Force, ACM and IEEE–CS Press, New York, 1991.

MIGRATING
TO C++:
A TUTORIAL

This chapter presents the rudiments of the C++ programming language. This chapter is especially intended for those readers who learned some other language in their first course. We assume that most readers who fall in that category learned Pascal, so we shall sometimes refer to correspondences between Pascal and C++. However, this material should be useful to readers who learned some other programming language (e.g., Scheme) in their first course.

This chapter is organized in sections. Each section ends with one or more example programs that illustrate the C++ language features that are discussed in that section. This chapter ends with several programming projects that the reader can attempt in the computing laboratory.

GETTING STARTED

This section introduces the basic elements of a C++ program. These include basic input, output and arithmetic operations. Our first example program, `examp0.cxx`, applies many of these concepts.

Throughout this laboratory manual, we shall present syntax specifications for C++ language constructs as follows:

Syntax: `if-else` statement

```
if (test)
    statement-true;
else
    statement-false;
```

Keywords will be shown using a normal font and expressions that the user must provide will be shown in *italics*. These conventions shall only apply for the presentation of syntactical elements.

We shall also want to present program extracts drawn from our example programs. This will allow us to draw attention to specific issues in those programs. Here is an example of what a program extract will look like:

Extract

```
// Display final bill data.
cout << endl << endl;
cout << "The total bill comes to " << bill << ".\n";
```

All of our example programs relate to the Generic College Coffee Shop, which is named after the college or university that you are presently attending.

Identifiers

Identifiers are used to name constants, variables, functions and other entities in C++. Identifiers in C++ follow the same rules as in Pascal, except that *C++ is a case sensitive language*. Thus, the following identifiers are not identical:

coffees   Coffees   COFFEES

Identifiers are constructed from letters, digits and underscores. The first character of an identifier can either be a letter or an underscore. Identifiers that begin with an underscore are usually limited to special system functions that are provided with the particular C++ implementation that you are using.

Constants and Symbolic Constants

The basic data elements in a C++ program are constants, symbolic constants and variables. A data element has a type. We shall limit ourselves for now to two basic types:

- `int`   corresponding to the type Integer in Pascal
- `float` corresponding to the type Real in Pascal

If a data element is of the type `int`, then its value is an integral value. The rules for forming `int` constants are the same as in Pascal. The following are all `int` constants:

    -29   12   0   2   1234

If a data element is of type `float`, then its value is not restricted to an integral value. Floating point values contain a fractional part (which can be .0000...). The following are examples of C++ float constants:

    1.234 -12.3 17.0   23.000   1.2e-03   5.467e3

Symbolic constants (also called "named constants") are defined using the following syntax:

Syntax: symbolic constant definition

```
const type-name CONST-NAME1 = value1,
     CONST-NAME2 = value2,
     ....
     CONST-NAMEN = valueN;
```

A symbolic constant represents a named data element whose value cannot be changed by the programmer. By convention, the name of a symbolic constant contains upper case letters only (although digits and underscores can be used). Recall that in presenting syntax specifications, we present keywords and special symbols (such as {,), +, etc.) using normal font and everything else using *italics*. Thus, `const` is a keyword. The use of ellipses (...) in our syntax specifications indicates the presence of a repeating pattern. This is not to be confused with the use of ellipses in the C++ language, an advanced topic that is not discussed in this book.

The example program given at the end of this section (`examp0.cxx`) contains one symbolic constant definition that defines the symbolic constants `COFFEE_PRICE`, `DONUT_PRICE`, `MUFFIN_PRICE` and `TAX_RATE`. This symbolic constant definition is given below as an extract:

Extract

```
const float COFFEE_PRICE = 0.80,
      DONUT_PRICE  = 0.75,
      MUFFIN_PRICE = 1.25,
      TAX_RATE = 0.06;
```

These four symbolic constants are of type `float`. The value of `COFFEE_PRICE` is 0.80. The value of `DONUT_PRICE` is 0.75. The value of `MUFFIN_PRICE` is 1.25 and the value of `TAX_RATE` is 0.06.

Variables

Variables are defined as follows:

Syntax: variable definition

```
variable-type variable-name1, variable-name2,
      ...., variable-nameN;
```

To this point, the allowed variable types are `int` and `float`. (These are keywords, incidentally.) The name of a variable can be any identifier. For example, three definition statements are used in `examp0.cxx` to define the `int` variables `coffees`, `donuts` and `muffins`:

Extract

```
int coffees;
int donuts;
int muffins;
```

This could also have been accomplished using a single definition:

```
int coffees, donuts, muffins;
```

By convention, the name of a variable contains lower case letters only (although digits and underscores can be used). There is a technical distinction in the C++ language between a variable definition and a variable declaration. This distinction is not terribly important at this stage. It becomes more important in the construction of multi-file programs where there is a possibility that we might want to declare a variable's type in one file without instructing the compiler to allocate storage for that variable. The variable declaration is, in effect, an external reference to a variable that has its memory allocated somewhere else.   A definition not only assigns a variable a type, it is responsible for the allocation of memory for that variable.

Comments

Here is the syntax for presenting a comment in C++:

Syntax: comments

```
// text of comment
```

A comment begins with the // notation and ends at the end of the line. Thus, a comment consisting of multiple lines requires multiple uses of //. The program examp0.cxx begins with a multiple line comment that gives basic information about the program, including the programmer's name and date, and a general description of the problem.   The first five lines of that program are presented in the following extract:

Extract

```
// Program:     examp0.cxx
//
// Programmer:  J. Q. Maxwell
// Date:        Jan 12, 1993
//
```

Note that once a line contains // the rest of that line is ignored by the compiler. Most C++ experts prefer this style of comment to the old C-style comments that use /* and */ as delimiters. However, the old C-style comments are still valid and can be useful in certain situations.   For example, the old C-style comments can be used to insert comments into the middle of a line.

Functions

A C++ program consists of functions. The syntax for defining a function that contains no arguments follows:

Syntax: function definition

```
return-type function-name()
{
    statements
}
```

The return type is an identifier that gives the type of
returns. This can be either int, float, or void. The retu...
to indicate a function that does not return any value. If a return ty...
given, the type int is used by default. The name of a function is an identifier.

The first line of a function definition is called the *function header* or *function declarator*. The curly braces delimit what is called the *function body*. The function body presents any local data that is defined within the function and any statements that will execute when the function is called.

Although C++ is a block-structured language like Pascal, it is much freer in form. Thus, a function does not have special sections for declaring constants, types, variables and the executable statements within the block. All of these are contained within the C++ function body. Comments can be used to separate the data definitions from the executable code. This is shown in ex-amp0.cxx where the comment

```
// LOCAL DATA ...
```

introduces the constant and variable definitions and the comment

```
// STATEMENTS ...
```

introduces the executable code.

C++ does not allow the nesting of function definitions. That is, one cannot define a function within another function. Do not confuse this with the ability of one function to call another function, an essential capability that C++ retains. All C++ functions are on the same level of nesting in terms of the language syntax.

All symbolic constants and variables defined within a function are local to that function. This means that these data elements cannot be used by any other function except by means of argument passing. It is possible to define variables globally (or, externally, in C++ jargon), but this is considered poor style in most circumstances. Consequently, we shall not discuss externally defined variables at this time. It is quite common and acceptable, on the other hand, to define symbolic constants and user-defined types externally.

The Function main()

Every C++ program must contain a definition for the function main. Execution of a program begins with this function. If no function with this name is provided, a fatal error results. The order in which functions are presented in a program is not important. However, one must make sure that a function is declared before it is called. We shall discuss this issue further in the next section.

For simple programs, it is often the case that the function `main` is defined as a function that has a void (or empty) argument list.[1] Thus, a typical pattern for defining the function `main` is shown in the following syntax specification:

Syntax: typical layout for function `main`

```
main()
{
    // LOCAL DATA ...
    local definitions

    // STATEMENTS ...
    executable code
}
```

The `#include` preprocessor directive

Almost all programs will need to use at least one `#include` preprocessor directive. These are normally placed at the beginning of a program, right after the introductory comments. The `#include` preprocessor directive is used to "include" some specified file in your source code. The included file is pulled into your source code. This is done before your program compiles (hence, the term *preprocessor* directive). The included files typically contain information the compiler needs in order to successfully compile a program.

The most important use of the `#include` preprocessor directive is to include so-called *header files*. Many of these (such as `iostream.h`, `string.h` and `stdlib.h`) are mandated by the C++ language standard and are part of the C++ library that came with your compiler. Some header files are peculiar to a particular vendor (e.g., the `conio.h` header file of Turbo C++). By convention, the name of a header file ends with `.h`. The header files are source code files that provide declarations for constants, functions and other kinds of entities that you might need to use in a program.

The syntax for including a header file that is part of the C++ library follows:

Syntax: use of `#include` preprocessor directive

```
#include <header-file-name>
```

For example, most programs will need to include the `iostream.h` header file in order to perform input and output operations. This file is included by means of the following statement:

```
#include <iostream.h>
```

---

1. Note that some compilers, such as Turbo C++ require that `main` be declared as a `void` function, i.e.,

```
void main()
```

Note that all preprocessor directives begin with a number sign (#) and are not followed by a semi-colon. The angle brackets tell the preprocessor that this header file is part of the standard library.

The `iostream.h` header file provides definitions for the `cin` and `cout` objects that are used for input and output operations, respectively. For now, we shall view an object as a bundle of data to which operators and functions can be applied. The `iostream.h` header file provides declarations for input and output operators such as `<<` (the insertion operator, which can be applied to the `cout` object) and `>>` (the extraction operator, which can be applied to the `cin` object).

The Object `cin` and the Extraction Operator `>>`

The `cin` object represents the stream of characters coming into a program from the standard input device. Normally, this stream of characters is coming in from the keyboard. We tell a program to extract `int` or `float` data from the stream of characters coming in from the keyboard by using the extraction operator, `>>`, as follows:

Syntax: use of `cin` with `>>` operator

```
// reading in the value for one variable:
cin >> variable-name;

// reading in the value for a sequence of variables:
cin >> variable1 >> variable2 >> .... >> variableN;
```

Note that `cin` is not a keyword. It is just an identifier. Because of the use of the `iostream.h` header file, `cin` is understood to be the object defined in that file. The extraction operator (`>>`) is also declared in that header file. This operator tells the computer to extract a value for the variable that follows the operator from the input character stream. This operator can be cascaded, as shown above, to allow for the input of a sequence of values for a sequence of variables.

The most important thing to remember about the use of the `cin >>` pattern is that the computer will skip over any white space characters found in the input character stream. White space characters include space, tab, carriage return and new line. Thus, in executing the statement

```
cin >> coffees;
```

the computer will skip over any white space characters in the input character stream until it encounters the first character that is not "white space." It then attempts to extract a legal integral value from the characters that follow. It continues scanning until another white space character is encountered or it encounters an illegal character, such as a decimal point or a letter, that could not possibly be part of an integer value (since `coffees` is an `int` variable). A fatal error will occur if an illegal character is encountered.

The statement

```
cin >> coffees >> donuts >> muffins;
```

will cause the computer to extract values for the `int` variables `coffees`, do-nuts and `muffins` (in that order), by scanning the data coming in from the keyboard, skipping over any white space characters and generating a fatal error if an illegal character is encountered. Note that this description implies that the computer will process multiple lines of input in attempting to extract values for these variables since the end of line characters are considered white space.

The Object cout and the Insertion Operator <<

The `cout` object represents the output character stream, that is, the stream of characters generated by your program that normally are sent to the computer display. We can use the `cout` object to send the values of one or more expressions to the computer display, as shown below:

Syntax: use of cout with << operator

```
// sending the value of one expression to the display:
cout << expression;

// sending the value of a sequence of
// expressions to the display:
cout << expression1 << expression3 << .... << expressionN;
```

The `cout` object is defined in the `iostream.h` header file. Thus, `cout` is not a reserved word. The `<<` operator is called the insertion operator because it tells the computer to insert the values of the expressions that are provided into the output character stream.   The expressions given in the above syntax specification may be:
1. `int` or `float` constants
2. string constants, such as `"Hello, world!"`
3. `int` or `float` variables
4. expressions using arithmetic operators that yield an `int` or a `float` value.

This is not a complete list of what is possible, but it is sufficient for our immediate purposes.

The `cout <<` pattern will cause all of the output data to be written out to one line unless we tell the computer to advance to a new line. We do this by sending the new line character, denoted by `\n`, to the output stream. This can be done in one of three ways:
1. include the new line character, `\n`, in a string constant, as in `"Hello, world!\n"`
2. output the new line character by itself, as `'\n'`
3. output the value of the special identifier, `endl`, whose value is `'\n'`

(Note that double quotes delimit string constants and single quotes delimit character constants.) For example, if you want to display the values of the variables `coffees`, `donuts` and `muffins` on three separate lines one could use the following code:

```
cout << "Number of coffees: " << coffees << endl;
cout << "Number of donuts:  " << donuts  << endl;
cout << "Number of muffins: " << muffins << endl;
```

The following code:

```
cout << "Too many coffees!\n";
cout << "Too much caffeine!\n";
```

will generate the following output:

```
Too many coffees!
Too much caffeine!
```

Note the use of the new line character `\n` within the string constants in this example. The sequence `\n` within a string denotes just one character, the new line character. When this character is sent to the computer display, the output will advance to the beginning of a new line. A character that is denoted using the backslash character is called an *escape sequence*. There are several of these in C++, including `\a` for bell and `\b` for backspace.

The `cout  <<` pattern described here leaves the format of the output data to the system. You can use blanks within output strings to help make the output more readable. For example, blanks can be used to separate prompt strings from the input data or to separate output items. We shall not learn about formatting output until later.

Coordinating `cout` and `cin`

A fundamental pattern is to prompt the user for input and then to accept that input. That is accomplished by alternating the `cout  <<` and `cin  >>` patterns, as shown with the following extract from `examp0.cxx`.

Extract

```
// Get order data
cout << "Please enter number of coffees: ";
cin  >> coffees;
cout << "Please enter number of donuts:  ";
cin  >> donuts;
cout << "Please enter number of muffins: ";
cin  >> muffins;
```

The execution of this code will cause the following interaction between the user and the program. User input is shown in bold:

```
Please enter number of coffees: 2
Please enter number of donuts:  1
Please enter number of muffins: 0
```

Arithmetic Operators

The arithmetic operators in C++ resemble those used in Pascal and many other languages. The precedence rules are also similar. The arithmetic operators and their meanings are given in Table 0–1.

TABLE 0–1   C++ ARITHMETIC OPERATORS

operator:	meaning:
*	multiplication
/	division
%	modulus
+	addition
–	subtract

The *, / and % operators have higher precedence than the + and – operators. The arithmetic operators are all left associative.

The main differences between these operators and those in Pascal are the following:

1. There is no special integer division operator.   / is used to divide `ints` as well as `floats`. When an `int` is divided by an `int`, the result is an `int`. Thus, the result is the same as one would get with the Pascal **div** operator.

2. The **mod** operator of Pascal is expressed using the percent sign (%) in C++.

In mixed mode expressions (where an `int` and a `float` are combined using *, /, + or –), the `int` is coerced to a `float` before the operation is performed.[2]

The Assignment Operator

C++ considers the assignment sign (=) just another binary operator. (In addition, C++ uses the == and not the = operator for comparisons, as we shall

---

2.   Actually, a floating point constant such as 2.0 is treated as a double or double precision floating point number, as we shall see at the end of this chapter. Thus, if i is an `int` variable, then in computing i/2.0, the system will coerce i to a double and not a `float`. Similarly, if x is a float, then in computing x/2.0, the system will coerce x to a double. In other words, x/2.0 is actually a mixed mode expression.

see later.) Thus,
```
   variable = expression
```
is just an expression as is
```
   variable + expression.
```
The value of
```
   variable = expression
```
is the value that is stored in the variable on the left. For example, suppose x and y are float variables. Then, the expression
```
      x = y * y
```
is a `float`-valued expression and can be used wherever a `float` expression is permitted. The value of this expression will be the value that is assigned to x.

This feature of C++ is very useful, although one should use it judiciously. For example, it would be permissible to use the above assignment in conjunction with the `cout  <<` pattern as follows:
```
   cout << "The new value for x is " << x = y * y << endl;
```
This statement will cause x to receive a new value and then that value will be displayed.

According to the syntax rules of C++, a statement is an expression that is followed by a semi-colon. Thus,
```
      x = y * y;
```
is syntactically a statement (an assignment statement) whereas
```
      x = y * y
```
is syntactically an expression.

The assignment operator is at a lower level of precedence than the arithmetic operators given above. The assignment operator is right associative. Thus,
```
      x = y = z = 0.0;
```
is equivalent to
```
      x = (y = (z = 0.0));
```
In other words, the semantics of x = y = z = 0.0 is that z is assigned the value 0.0 and then y is assigned the value of the expression (z = 0.0), which is 0.0, and then x is assigned the value of the expression (y = (z = 0.0)), which is again 0.0.

The Arithmetic Assignment Operators

C++ contains some powerful notations that are partly responsible for its popularity. The first of these is a collection of notations that go under the rubric *arithmetic assignment operators*. These combine arithmetic operators with the assignment operator.

For example, the following pattern is very common:
```
      variable = variable + increment;
```
C++ allows us to combine the + and = operators as follows:
```
      variable += increment;
```
These two statements are completely equivalent. You should read the statement
```
      variable += increment;
```
as "add increment into variable."

In general, if *op* is an arithmetic operator, then the pattern:

```
variable op= expression
```
is always equal to
```
variable = variable op expression
```
The arithmetic assignment operators (+=, -=, *=, /=, %=) are at the same level of precedence as the assignment operator. The arithmetic assignment operators are right associative.

Example #0 Program Narrative

You now have all the information that you need to understand example #0 (examp0.cxx). This program consists of one function, which is (and must be) called main. This function begins with a section that defines the required local data:

1. The symbolic constants COFFEE_PRICE, DONUT_PRICE, MUF-FIN_PRICE and TAX_RATE. These are used to compute the total bill amount.
2. The int variables coffees, donuts and muffins. These represent a customer order at the coffee shop. The user will provide values for these variables.
3. The float variables bill and tax. The former represents the total bill amount, including the tax, and the latter is the tax amount.

The comment

```
// STATEMENTS ...
```
introduces the executable code for the main function. These statements:

1. Prompt the user for and get the order data, consisting of values for the variables coffees, donuts, and muffins.
2. Compute the total bill amount, first without the tax, and then with the tax added in.
3. Display the final bill, including the tax amount.

The code follows.

Example #0

```
// Program:         examp0.cxx
//
// This program is intended to introduce the basic structure of
// C++ functions and programs.
//
// Programmer name: J. Q. Maxwell
// Date:            Jan 12, 1993
//
// Problem description:
//
// This program computes the bill for a customer at the
// Generic Coffee Shop.  The program consists of
// four steps:
```

```
//      1. Get customer order data
//      2. Compute total bill
//      3. Display toal bill
//
// The Generic Coffee Shop menu contains the following
// items and prices:
//          coffee      $0.80
//          donut        0.75
//          muffin       1.25
//
// In addition, the state charges a 6% tax.
//


#include <iostream.h>

void main()
{
    // LOCAL DATA ...
    const float COFFEE_PRICE = 0.80,
            DONUT_PRICE  = 0.75,
            MUFFIN_PRICE = 1.25,
            TAX_RATE     = 0.06;
    int coffees;                        // number of coffees
    int donuts;                         // number of donuts
    int muffins;                        // number of muffins
    float bill;                         // total bill amount
    float tax;                          // state tax;


    // STATEMENTS ...
    // Get order data.
    cout << "Please enter number of coffees: ";
    cin  >> coffees;
    cout << "Please enter number of donuts:  ";
    cin  >> donuts;
    cout << "Please enter number of muffins: ";
    cin  >> muffins;


    // Compute total amount.
    bill =  COFFEE_PRICE * coffees
          + DONUT_PRICE * donuts
          + MUFFIN_PRICE * muffins;
    tax  = TAX_RATE * bill;
    bill += tax;        // equivalent to bill = bill + tax;


    // Display final bill data.
    cout << endl << endl;
    cout << "The total bill comes to " << bill << ".\n";
}   // end main
```

USING FUNCTIONS

This section introduces the use of functions as a means of decomposing a problem into manageable subproblems. Of particular interest is the use of function arguments and return types. These concepts are brought together in the program `exampl.cxx` that is presented at the end of this section.

Three Aspects of Functions

There are three important technical issues regarding functions in C++ that you need to understand:

1. how functions are declared
2. how functions are defined
3. how functions are called

Example #0 consisted of only the special function, `main`, which must be present in every C++ program. Now we wish to consider functions that are used to help the main function achieve its purposes. These auxiliary functions differ from the function `main` in that:

1. They must be declared, normally by means of a special declaration statement called a function prototype.
2. They will not execute unless they are called.

A simple C++ program normally consists of the function `main` plus auxiliary functions that are called by `main` either directly or indirectly. In this way, the program designer can solve a problem by decomposing the original problem into subproblems.

Arguments

The interface between a function and its calling environment is defined by a list of arguments. This defines how the calling environment passes data to the function and receives results back from the function. A function that is not declared `void` also returns a value via the function call itself.

Arguments that occur in a function call are called *actual arguments*. Arguments that occur in a function definition are called *formal arguments*. Actual arguments represent the actual data that the function uses, whereas formal arguments are used to name the actual arguments locally within the function definition.

Arguments in C++ can either be:

1. pass by value, or
2. pass by reference

Pass by value arguments, as the same suggests, are passed by value. This means that the function allocates space for the formal argument so that it may receive a copy of the actual argument. In other words, all of the values contained within the actual argument are passed to the function and the function stores these values in the space allocated for the formal argument. When changes are made to the formal argument within the function, the actual argument is not affected. Thus, pass by value is not appropriate when it is required that the function have the ability to modify the value of the actual argument. Bear in mind that the formal and actual arguments are not necessarily scalars. They might be complex structures and objects, as you shall learn later in the course.

When a function has a pass by value argument, it acts as a consumer of the data that the argument represents.

Pass by reference arguments are (as you might have guessed) passed by reference. This means that the memory allocated for the formal argument in the function is used to store the address of the actual argument. This address is called a reference. When depicted graphically, references are illustrated as pointers to the variable to which they refer. The values contained within the actual argument are not passed. When the function specifies a computation using the formal argument, the reference is automatically dereferenced. This means that the computer performs the computation using the data at the address that the reference points to. Any change to the formal argument will, in fact, occur in the actual argument. Consequently, if a function must modify an actual argument, that argument must be passed by reference.

When a function has a pass by reference formal argument, it either updates the corresponding actual argument, or it produces an initial value for that actual argument. In the latter case, we might say that the function served as a producer of the data.

The concepts of pass by value and pass by reference also occur in Pascal and other languages. In Pascal, pass by reference arguments are called **var** or varying parameters.

Function Declarations

Functions must be *declared* and *defined.* A function declaration specifies the return type of a function, its name, and the types of its formal arguments (if any). A function definition provides the function body which specifies the function's local data and the statements that will execute when the function is called. The purpose of a function declaration is to enable the compiler to check the correctness of a function call in terms of the arguments that are passed and the manner in which the return value (if any) is used. There are two ways to declare a function in C++:

1. One can use a special function declaration statement, called a *function prototype.*
2. One can use the function header (which occurs as part of a function definition) as the declaration for a function.

The use of prototypes is recommended for a variety of technical reasons. In brief, it is a good idea to separate the function declarations from the function implementations when one is building a multi-file project. Regardless of the approach that you use, when you call a function, a function declaration had better be *visible* at that point in the program. In C++, a declaration is visible from the point where the declaration occurs, forwards but not backwards in a program file.

A function prototype is an explicit function declaration statement. The syntax for a function prototype is given as follows:

Syntax: function prototype

```
return-type function-name(argument-type-list);
```

The return type indicates the type of value that the function returns. This may be `void` (if the function behaves like a Pascal procedure and does not return a value) or it may be `int`, `float` or any other appropriate type. The argument type list consists of a list of 0 or more argument types. The argument types may or may not be given with dummy argument names. The parentheses are required even if the function has no arguments.

The arguments must be specified as being either pass by value or pass by reference. Pass by value arguments are indicated by means of a type identifier only (e.g., `int` or `float`). Pass by reference arguments are indicated by means of a type identifier followed by an ampersand (`&`) (e.g., `int&` or `float&`). Note that in a function prototype one does not need to provide argument names along with the argument types. Argument names are optional and they are ignored if they are provided.

Example #1 (`examp1.cxx`) uses prototypes in the function `main`, as shown in the following extract:

Extract

```
void give_instructions();
void get_order_data(int&, int&, int&);
float compute_bill(int, int, int);
void display_bill(float);
```

These prototypes provide information that the compiler can use to assure that function calls are constructed in a correct manner. Note that no argument names are provided in these function prototypes. These particular prototypes indicate that:

1. The function `give_instructions` is a `void` function that has no arguments.
2. The function `get_order_data` is a `void` function that has three pass by reference `int` arguments.
3. The function `compute_bill` is a `float` function that has three pass by value `int` arguments.
4. The function `display_bill` is a `void` function that has one pass by value `float` argument.

The first part of a function definition (technically, that part of the function definition that precedes the function body) can also serve as a function declaration. This part of a function definition is called the *function header* or *function declarator*. A function definition has the following syntax:

Syntax: function definition including declarator

```
return-type function-name(formal-arg-list)
{
    // LOCAL DATA ...
    constant and variable definitions
```

```
     // STATEMENTS ...
     executable code
}
```

A function definition consists of two parts: a function declarator and a function body. The function body is delimited by curly braces. The function declarator has the same form as a function prototype except that formal argument names *must* be provided.

In the absence of a function prototype, the function declarator is used as the function declaration.   In this case, a function definition for function f must occur physically in a file before the definition of any function that will call the function f.

If both a function prototype and a function definition are provided, then the function header must provide the same number of arguments as the function prototype. Furthermore, the arguments in both the function header and in the prototype must match in terms of type and in terms of whether they are pass by value or pass by reference.

The following extract shows the function declarators for the functions whose prototypes were given above. Note the use of argument names and the fact that the function prototypes and the function headers match in terms of the number of arguments and their types.

Extract

```
void give_instructions() { ... }
void get_order_data(int& cof, int& don, int& muf) { ... }
float compute_bill(int cof, int don, int muf) { ... }
void display_bill(float bill) { ... }
```

In summary, the most important thing to remember concerning function declarations is that *a function declaration for a function f must be visible at all points where the function f is called*. One way to provide such a declaration for f is to use a function prototype and to place that prototype either within or before any function that intends to call f. The alternate means of accomplishing this is to provide the complete definition for f before any function that intends to call f.

The Function Body

The function body within a function definition provides the local data definitions plus the executable code for a function. The rules for defining constants and variables within a general function are the same as for the main function.   Memory is allocated for local variables and constants when the function is called.   Variables allocated in this manner are called *automatic variables*. Automatic variables are not automatically initialized, so unless we assign a value to such a variable, its value will be undefined.

A variable declared within a function may also be declared `static`. For example,

```
static float x;
```

declares x as a `static float` variable. `Static` *variables* differ from automatic variables in that `static` variables are allocated at compile-time and they are automatically initialized to zero at compile-time.   This means that the `static` variable x, cited above, would be allocated once and for all at compile-time, but its visibility would be limited to the function in which it is defined.   This means that the lifetime of the variable x would extend over the complete run of the program and is not limited to one particular execution of the function that defines it. As mentioned above, `static` variables are initialized to zero, with each type having its own notion of zero. For example, `static int` variables are initialized to 0, `static float` variables are initialized to 0.0 and `static char` variables are initialized to the string terminator character, `\0`. `Static` variables are useful, but we shall not discuss them further in this tutorial.

The following extract from `exampl.cxx` gives the complete definition for the function `get_order_data` whose prototype and function header were given above:

Extract

```
void get_order_data(int& cof, int& don, int& muf)
{
   cout << "Please enter number of coffees: ";
   cin  >> cof;
   cout << "Please enter number of donuts:  ";
   cin  >> don;
   cout << "Please enter number of muffins: ";
   cin  >> muf;
}  // end get_order_data
```

This function prompts the user for and gets `int` values that represent the number of coffees, donuts and muffins on a given coffee shop order. Note that this function has no return type and three pass by reference formal arguments. Note that no local variables are defined and that the input statements (using the `cin >>` pattern) refer to the formal arguments, `cof`, `don`, and `muf`, which are pass by reference. Thus, we are actually reading in data for the actual arguments that are provided in a function call. We shall discuss the mechanisms behind function calls shortly.

It is important to document the meaning and behavior of every function. This is done by means of comments that precede the function headers. Here is the form of documentation that we provide, in this tutorial, for functions:

Syntax: documentation for functions

```
// FUNCTION:   function-name
// PURPOSE:    description of the function's purpose
// RETURNS:    description of return value
```

```
//                   (omit for void function)
// INPUTS:           list of input arguments and their meanings
//                   (omit if no input arguments)
// OUTPUTS:          list of output arguments and their meanings
//                   (omit if no output arguments)
```

In the text, we provide a slightly different form of documentation which emphasizes the specification of function behavior by means of pre- and postconditions. At this point, we want to stress the C++ language so that you can understand the programs in the text and write your own programs, so we are de-emphasizing formal specifications for the time being.

The `return` Statement

The `return` statement takes the following form in a non-`void` function:

Syntax: the `return` statement in a non-`void` function

```
return expression;
```

The type of *expression* must be the same as the return type of the function. This might require type casting *expression* in some cases. This form of the `return` statement has the following semantics: The expression is evaluated and its value is returned as the return value of the function. Execution of the function terminates and control passes back to the point in the calling environment (i.e., the calling function) from which the function was called. A function that returns a value must terminate with the execution of this form of the `return` statement. The calling function has the option of either using the value that is returned or ignoring it.

The `return` statement takes the following form in a `void` function:

Syntax: the `return` statement in a `void` function

```
return;
```

A `void` function need not terminate with the execution of the `return` statement, but the `return` statement can be used to force termination before one reaches the final curly brace in the function body. If the final curly brace is encountered before a `return` statement is encountered, the equivalent of a `return` statement is executed automatically. None of the `void` functions given in `exampl.cxx` utilize the `return` statement. Each of these functions terminates when the last statement in the function body is finished executing.

Function calls

A function call can follow one of several patterns. Two of these are given below:

Syntax: two kinds of function calls

```
// calling a void function or calling
// a function but ignoring its return value
function-name(actual-arg-list);

// calling a function and using its return
// value (in this case by storing that value
// in a variable)
variable = function-name(actual-arg-list);
```

Void functions must always be called using the first of the above patterns. This function call causes the function *function–name* to execute with the indicated actual arguments. Functions that return a value can be called with either pattern. However, if the first pattern is used, the value returned by the function is lost and cannot be utilized by the calling program. The second pattern actually is intended to suggest any situation in which the value returned by a function is being utilized. This is not necessarily done in an assignment statement. Moreover, a function that returns a value of type *t* can be used wherever an expression of type *t* is appropriate.

The main function in examp1.cxx contains four function calls. These are shown below:

Extract

```
give_instructions();
get_order_data(coffees, donuts, muffins);
total_bill = compute_bill(coffees, donuts, muffins);
display_bill(total_bill);
```

The first, second and fourth function calls follow the first pattern since the functions involved are void functions. The third function call follows the second pattern since the value returned by the function compute_bill is being stored in the variable total_bill.

 The above function calls clearly reflect the overall logic of the main function. It:

1. Presents the user with instructions by calling give_instructions.
2. Gets the order data from the user by calling get_order_data. This function passes back the order data using the pass by actual arguments coffees, donuts and muffins.
3. Computes the total bill, by calling compute_bill, and stores the bill amount in the variable total_bill. The main function passes the order data (coffees, donuts and muffins) that is needed to compute the total bill.
4. Displays the final bill data by calling display_bill. The total bill amount is passed to the function via the argument total_bill.

The complete code for examp1.cxx follows:

Example #1

```
// Program:          exampl.cxx
//
// Programmer name: J. Q. Maxwell
// Date:            Jan 22, 1993
//
// Problem description:
//
// This program computes the bill for a customer at the
// Generic Coffee Shop.  The program consists of
// four steps:
//     1. Give user instructions
//     2. Get customer order data
//     3. Compute total bill
//     4. Display toal bill
//
// The Generic Coffee Shop menu contains the following
// items and prices:
//        coffee      $0.80
//        donut        0.75
//        muffin       1.25
//
// In addition, the state charges a 6% tax.
//


#include <iostream.h>


void main()
{
    // FUNCTION PROTOTYPES ...
    void give_instructions();        // GIVE USER INSTRUCTIONS
    void get_order_data(int&, int&, int&);
              // GET ORDER AMOUNTS FOR
              // COFFEES, DONUTS, MUFFINS
    float compute_bill(int, int, int);
    void display_bill(float);


    // LOCAL DATA ...
    int coffees;                     // INPUT: Number of coffees
    int donuts;                      // INPUT: Number of donuts
    int muffins;                     // INPUT: Number of muffins
    float total_bill;                // OUTPUT:  Total bill amount


    // STATEMENTS ...
    give_instructions();
    get_order_data(coffees, donuts, muffins);
    total_bill = compute_bill(coffees, donuts, muffins);
    display_bill(total_bill);
} // end main
```

```cpp
// FUNCTION:  give_instructions
// PURPOSE:   Give user instructions
void give_instructions()
{
    cout  << "This program computes a customer bill for the  "
          << endl
          << "Generic Coffee Shop.  Enter customer order" << endl
          << "data when prompted." << endl;
}   // end give_instructions


// FUNCTION:  get_order_data
// PURPOSE:   Get order amounts for coffees, donuts, muffins
// INPUTS:
//   none
// OUTPUTS:
//   cof       number of coffees
//   don       number of donuts
//   muf       number of muffins
void get_order_data(int& cof, int& don, int& muf)
{
    cout << "Please enter number of coffees: ";
    cin  >> cof;
    cout << "Please enter number of donuts:   ";
    cin  >> don;
    cout << "Please enter number of muffins: ";
    cin  >> muf;
}   // end get_order_data


// FUNCTION:   compute_bill
// PURPOSE:    Return total bill amount based upon order data
// RETURNS:    float, the total bill amount
// INPUTS:
//   cof       number of coffees
//   don       number of donuts
//   muf       number of muffins
// OUTPUTS:
//   none
float compute_bill(int cof, int don, int muf)
{
    // LOCAL DATA ...
    const float COFFEE_PRICE = 0.80,
                DONUT_PRICE  = 0.75,
                MUFFIN_PRICE = 1.25,
                TAX_RATE     = 0.06;
    float bill;                     // total bill amount
    float tax;                      // state tax;


    bill = COFFEE_PRICE * cof
         + DONUT_PRICE * don
         + MUFFIN_PRICE * muf;
    tax  = TAX_RATE * bill;
    bill += tax;        // equivalent to bill = bill + tax;
    return bill;
}   // end compute_bill
```

```
// FUNCTION:    display_bill
// PURPOSE:     Display total bill amount
// INPUTS:
//   bill       total bill amount
// OUTPUTS:
//   none
void display_bill(float bill)
{
   cout << endl << endl;
   cout << "The total bill comes to " << bill << ".\n";
}  // display_bill
```

LOGICAL EXPRESSIONS AND DECISION STRUCTURES

This section presents the program, examp2.cxx. This program introduces control structures that are used to determine the flow of control in a program. In addition, we introduce logical expressions and operators and several features that will enable us to gain more control over the appearance of displayed data.

The Type char

A variable of type char can only store one character. The following program code shows the definition of a char symbolic constant called QUIT and a char variable called ch. The assignment statement assigns the value of QUIT to ch.

```
const char QUIT = 'Q';
char ch;
ch = QUIT;
```

char variables can be read in using the cin >> pattern and can be displayed using the cout << pattern. In particular, when the computer executes the statement:

```
cin >> ch;
```

where ch is a char variable, all white space characters are skipped over until a non-white space character is encountered in the input character stream. That first non-white space character will become the value for ch.

Note that char constants are delimited by single quotation marks and that string constants are delimited by double quotation marks. Thus, 'Q' is not the same as "Q". The former ('Q') is of type char and the latter ("Q") is of type string (or, array of char). Strings are implemented as arrays of chars. A string is always stored with a string terminator character (denoted by \0) at the end of the string. Thus, the string "Q" requires two bytes of the computer's memory: one byte for the character 'Q' and one byte for the string terminator character, \0. The character 'Q' requires just one byte of the computer's memory.

Logical Values

There is no special boolean (or logical) type in C++. Instead, *any non-zero value corresponds to true and a zero value corresponds to false*. Decisions are made by testing variables and expressions for being in the state of having a zero or a non-zero value. In order to capture the idea of a Pascal boolean variable, the C++ programmer would declare an `int` variable with the convention that 1 represents true and 0 represents false. However, it is important to bear in mind that insofar as logical tests are concerned (for example, in a `while` loop or in an `if` statement), any non-zero value is considered "true."

Comparison Operators

Comparison operators are used to compare numbers and characters. There are six comparison operators and these are all at a lower level of precedence than the arithmetic operators but at a higher level of precedence than the assignment and arithmetic assignment operators. However, the six comparison operators are divided into two groupings: the relational operators and the equality operators. The relational operators have higher precedence than the equality operators. All six comparison operators are left associative. The four relational operators and their meanings are shown in Table 0–2:

TABLE 0–2   RELATIONAL OPERATORS AND THEIR MEANINGS

operator:	meaning:
<	less than
<=	less than or equal to
>	greater than
>=	greater than or equal to

The two equality operators and their meanings are given in Table 0–3:

TABLE 0–3   EQUALITY RELATIONS AND THEIR MEANINGS

operator:	meaning:
==	equal to
!=	not equal to

A very common error is to use = instead of == to check for equality. This error is not only common, it is downright dangerous, because this is a semantical and not a syntactical error.   In other words, in most circumstances where you use = in lieu of ==, no error message will appear and your program will not produce the correct results.

The comparison operators return a value of 1 if the result of the comparison is true and 0 if the result of the comparison is false. Note that the comparison operators do not return any non-zero value as representing true, but the value of 1, specifically.

Suppose we have the following definitions for the variables j, k, ch1 and ch2:

```
int j = 3, k = 5;
char ch1 = 'Q', ch2 = 'q';
```

Note that in defining a variable we can also initialize it. Given these definitions and assuming that j, k, ch1 and ch2 have the values shown, then the expressions on the left column of Table 0–4 have the values shown on the right:

TABLE 0–4   EXAMPLE LOGICAL EXPRESSIONS AND THEIR VALUES

expression:	value:
j == k	0
j != k	1
j < k	1
j >= k	0
j = k	5 (do you see why?)
ch1 > 'A'	1
ch1 = ch2	'q' (do you see why?)

Note that the expression j = k resolves to (i.e., evaluates to) 5, *and thus j = k is interpreted as being true when used as a logical* test. Observe that j == k is false, but j = k is true, but both are perfectly acceptable as test conditions in a loop or in an if statement.   This should convince you that using the assignment operator in lieu of the equality operator in a program can be disastrous!

Note that all of the comparison operators return a value of 1 for true and 0 for false, but that any expression, even those that do not involve the comparison operators, can be considered as a logical test in a control structure (such as a loop or an if statement).

Compound Statements

The curly braces play a role in C++ analogous to the role of the **begin** – **end** reserved words in Pascal. We have already seen how the curly braces delimit the function body in a function definition. More generally, curly braces delimit what is called a *compound statement* with a function body being a special case of this concept. Each compound statement in C++ defines a scope in which new identifiers (constants and variables, for example), can be defined. This is not true of compound statements in Pascal.

When we give a syntax specification for a control structure, any reference to "statement" in that specification indicates that either a simple statement or a compound statement can be inserted at that point. A simple statement is an expression followed by a semi-colon. A compound statement is a sequence of 0 or more statements delimited by curly braces.

The if Statement

The if statement in C++ corresponds to the **if-then** statement of Pascal. It allows the program to specify a course of action to be taken if a certain logical test evaluates to true (i.e., any non-zero value). Here is the syntax specification for the C++ if statement:

Syntax: the if statement

```
if (test)
    statement
```

The semantics of the if statement should be familiar to you: if the logical test evaluates to true (any non-zero value), then *statement* will execute. Otherwise, *statement* is skipped.

The following code segment assumes that the variable ch is a char variable that has received some value:

```
if (ch == 'Q')
{
    cout << "The user decided to quit.\n";
    cout << "This was a wise choice.\n";
}
```

In this example, if ch equals 'Q', the message
```
    The user decided to quit.
    This was a wise choice.
```
will appear at the computer display. If ch has any other value, then no message will appear (based upon this code segment alone). Note that there is no semi-colon after the last curly brace but that *the semi-colon after the second* cout *is mandatory*.

The following code segment is not equivalent to the previous one despite the deceptive indentation scheme:

```
if (ch == 'Q')
    cout << "The user decided to quit. \n";
    cout << "This was a wise choice. \n";
```

This code segment will display
```
The user decided to quit.
This was a wise choice.
```
if ch equals 'Q' and it will display
```
This was a wise choice.
```
if ch has any other value. Only the statement
```
cout << "The user decided to quit. \n";
```
is under the control of the if statement.

The if-else statement

The if-else statement of C++ corresponds to the **if-then-else** state-ment of Pascal. It allows the programmer to choose among two alternative courses of action. Here is the syntax specification for this control structure:

Syntax: the if-else statement

```
if (test)
    statement-t
else
    statement-f
```

The semantics of this construct should be familiar to you.   If the logical test evaluates to true (any non-zero value), then *statement-t* will execute. If the log-ical test evaluates to false (zero), then *statement-f* will execute. Either *state-ment-t* or *statement-f*, but not both, will execute given this construction.
Consider the following code segment:

```
if (ch == 'Q')
    cout << "The user entered Q. \n";
else
    cout << "The user did not enter Q. \n";
```

The above code will generate the output
```
The user entered Q.
```
if the variable ch has the value 'Q' and the message
```
The user did not enter Q.
```
if ch has any other value. Note that the semi-colons that mark the end of the two cout statements are required.
The following code segment is equivalent to the previous. Note that no semi-colon follows the first compound statement in this example (i.e., there is no semi-colon immediately before the else). Also note that a compound statement may contain just one statement or even no statements.

```
if (ch == 'Q')
{
    cout << "The user entered Q. \n";
}
```

```
else
{
    cout << "The user did not enter Q. \n";
}
```

The Multiple Alternative Decision Pattern

C++, like Pascal, allows `if` and `if-else` statements to be nested one within the other. This requires a rule for deciding which `if` an `else` belongs to. That rule is that an `else` is matched with the nearest, unmatched `if`. Every `else` must be matched with some `if`. Otherwise, there is a syntax error.

A common pattern using nested `if-else` statements is represented by the following pseudo-code:

```
if test-1 then do statement-1
else if test-2 then do statement-2
else if ....
else if test-n then do statement-n
else do statement-f.
```

The logic here is that we evaluate a sequence of logical tests (`test-1`, `test-2`, ...). As soon as we encounter a test that evaluates to true (non-zero), we execute the corresponding statement (`statement-1`, `statement-2`, ...) and then we exit the structure. If all of the tests are false, we do `statement-f`. Sometimes, the last `else` is omitted, and there is no `statement-f`. If `statement-f` is provided, then one and only one of the statements `statement-1`, `statement-2`, ..., `statement-n`, `statement-f` will execute. Of course, some or all of these statements may be compound statements.

The above pseudo-code is captured by the following syntax specification:

Syntax: multiple alternative decision pattern

```
if (test-1)
    statement-1
else if (test-2)
    statement-2
else if ...
     ...
else if (test-n)
     statement-n
else
     statement-f
```

For example, suppose the `char` variable `grade` contains a student's letter grade (`'A'`, `'B'`, ...). The following code will display an appropriate message based upon the value of `grade`:

```
if (grade == 'A')
    cout << "Excellent\n";
else if (grade == 'B')
```

```
      cout << "Good\n";
else if (grade == 'C')
      cout << "Fair\n";
else if (grade == 'D')
      cout << "Poor\n";
else if (grade == 'F')
      cout << "Very poor\n";
else
      cout << "Illegal grade value\n";
```

Note that the message "Illegal grade value" will be displayed if grade has a value other than A, B, C, D, or F.

Logical Operators

Logical operators are used to combine values in order to generate new logical values. There are three logical operators. The not operator (!) is a unary operator that is higher in precedence than any operator discussed thus far. The and (&&) and or (||) operators are lower in precedence than equality and inequality, but higher in precedence than the assignment and arithmetic assignment operators. The operator && has a higher precedence than the operator ||. The operators && and || are left associative and ! is right associative.

The ! (not) operator is a unary operator. If x represents some logical value, the truth value of !x is the opposite of the truth value of x. Thus, if x is true (any non-zero value), the expression !x will evaluate to false (0). If x is false (i.e., 0), then !x will evaluate to the specific non-zero value 1, which represents true. The semantics of the ! (not) operator is given by in Table 0–5:

TABLE 0–5   THE ! (NOT) OPERATOR

value of operand, x:	!x
non-zero	0
0	1

Note that the value of !x is always 0 or 1, regardless of the value of x. Furthermore, if x is a variable, computing !x does not change the value of x.

The && (logical and) operator is binary. If x1 and x2 denote the operands for &&, then the truth table of Table 0–6 shows how the value of x1 && x2 is determined (when x1 represents the left operand, and x2 the right). The above truth table indicates that if x1 is non-zero, then the computer will evaluate x2 in order to determine the value of x1 && x2. If x2 is non-zero, x1 && x2 will evaluate to 1. If x2 is 0, x1 && x2 will evaluate to 0. However, if x1 is zero, the code generated will not evaluate x2. Instead, x1 && x2 will evaluate to 0 regardless of the value of x2. The notation --- used for the value of x2 in the third row of the above table is communicating the fact that the && operator is *short-circuited* in C++. This means that the expression x2 will not be evaluated at all if the value of x1 is false.

TABLE 0–6   THE && (LOGICAL AND) OPERATOR

value of x1:	value of x2:	x1 && x2
non-zero	non-zero	1
non-zero	0	0
0	---	0

The || (logical or) operator is also short-circuited, as indicated by the following truth table shown as Table 0–7:

TABLE 0–7   THE || (LOGICAL OR) OPERATOR

value of x1:	value of x2:	x1 || x2
non-zero	---	1
0	non-zero	1
0	0	0

If the value of x1 is non-zero, then evaluation is short-circuited and x2 will not be evaluated at all. The value of x1 || x2 in such a case will be 1. If the value of x1 is 0, then the value of x1 || x2 will depend upon the value of x2, as shown in the table.

One must be careful to verify that one's logic is correct even if the evaluation of an expression involving && or || is short-circuited. For example, consider the following expression:

```
(x == y) && (z != get_data())
```

Suppose x, y and z are float variables and that get_data is a float function that reads in a float value from the keyboard and returns that float value. If x does not equal y, the function get_data will not be called. If it is important that the function get_data *always* be called at this point, then some construction other than the one shown above would be required.

One must be careful to use && and not &, || and not |. This is because & and | are also C++ binary operators. These operators (& and |) denote the bitwise AND and OR operators, respectively. These are low-level C++ operators that work with variables on a bit by bit basis. Wherever the expression x1 && x2 makes sense to the compiler, so does the expression x1 & x2 (assuming the types we have learned thus far) and these two expressions do not have the same semantics. The situation is similar to the situation with respect to the possible use of = in lieu of ==.

The program `examp2.cxx` (presented at the end of this section) reflects the fact that customers at the Generic College Coffee Shop are offered discounts based upon whether they are faculty members, students, senior citizens or just regular folks. The function `compute_discount_data` in that program computes a discount amount (`da`) and a discount rate (`dr`) based upon knowledge of the bill amount (`bill`) and the customer discount code (`dc`). The customer discount code (`dc`) is a char variable whose value determines the kind of discount that applies. The letter `'f'` indicates a faculty discount. The letter `'s'` indicates a student discount. The letter `'g'` indicates a senior citizen discount (`'g'` stands for golden years) and any other letter indicates that no discount applies. No distinction is made between upper case and lower case letters in evaluating the discount rate. For example, `'f'` and `'F'` are treated as being identical. The following extract from `examp2.cxx` contains the code for the function `compute_discount_data`. Note the use of the || operator.

Extract: the function `compute_discount_data`

```
// FUNCTION:   compute_discount_data
// PURPOSE:    To return the discount rate and the discount amount
// INPUTS:
//    dc       discount code
//    bill     total bill    (including tax)
// OUTPUTS:
//    da       discount amount
//    dr       discount rate
void compute_discount_data(char dc, float bill, float& da, float&
dr)
{
   // LOCAL DATA ...
   const float FAC_DISCR = 0.20,
           STU_DISCR = 0.10,
           SEN_DISCR = 0.05;


   if (dc == 'f' || dc == 'F')
   {
      dr = FAC_DISCR;
   }
   else if (dc == 's' || dc == 'S')
   {
      dr = STU_DISCR;
   }
   else if (dc == 'g' || dc == 'G')
   {
      dr = SEN_DISCR;
   }
   else
      dr = 0.0;


   da = bill * dr;
}  // end compute_discount_data
```

The `switch` and `break` Statements

The C++ `switch` statement offers an alternate means of implementing the multiple alternative decision pattern. The C++ `switch` statement bears some resemblance to the Pascal **case** statement. However, there are important differences between the C++ `switch` and the Pascal **case**.

A common pattern for the use of the `switch` statement is shown in the following syntax specification:

Syntax: common `switch` statement pattern

```
switch (selector)
{
   case label-1:
       statement-seq-1;
       break;
   case label-2:
       statement-seq-2;
       break;
   ...
   case label-n:
       statement-seq-n;
       break;
   default:
       statement-seq-d;
}
```

The labels (*label–1*, ...) are called *case labels*. Note the following about the use of the `switch`:

1. The `switch` selector must be an *ordinal variable*. An ordinal variable is a variable whose type is an ordinal type. The ordinal types that we have learned thus far are `int` and `char`. The type `float` is not ordinal nor are character `string` types. In general, an ordinal type is any type for which the notion of a successor makes sense. Thus, the successor of 3 is unambiguously 4, but what is the successor of 3.14? Is it 3.15 or 3.141 or 3.14000 or what?
2. The `case` labels must be given as single ordinal constants whose type matches that of the selector. In particular, case labels cannot be lists or ranges of values.
3. The statement sequences given in the syntax specification (*statement–seq–1*, ...) represent any sequence of 0 or more statements. These statement sequences need not be delimited by curly braces.
4. The use of the `break` statement is essential in order to cause the program to break out of the `switch` after the execution of the appropriate statement sequence.

The `switch` statement sketched in the above syntax specification is identical in behavior to the following code that uses nested `if-else` statements in lieu of a `switch`:

```
if (selector == label-1)
    {
```

```
        statement-seq-1;
    }
    else if (selector == label-2)
    {
        statement-seq-2;
    }
    else if ...

    ...
    else if (selector == label-n)
    {
        statement-seq-n;
    }
    else
    {
        statement-seq-d;
    }
```

In many situations, the use of the switch statement results in code that is more clear than corresponding code that uses nested if-else statements.

The default clause in the switch is optional and may be omitted. In that case, if the selector does not match any of the case labels, none of the statement sequences (*statement–seq–1*, ...) will execute. There is no need to include a break statement after the default statement sequence, because execution will flow out of the switch at this point.

Consider the following sketch for a switch statement:

```
switch (selector)
{
    case label-1:
        statement-seq-1;
    case label-2:
        statement-seq-2;
        break;
    ...
    case label-n:
        statement-seq-n;
        break;
    default:
        statement-seq-d;
}
```

This differs from our original syntax specification in that there is no break statement after *statement–seq–1*. What are the implications of having omitted that break statement?

First, let us observe that this is not a syntax error nor is it necessarily a semantical (or logical error). In general, once C++ finds a case label that matches the switch selector, it will execute all statement sequences in the rest of the switch, ignoring subsequent case and default labels, until a break statement is encountered. It is the break statement that causes the flow of control to break out of the switch once a match is made. Consequently, in our new example, if the selector matches the first case label (*label–1*), the following statement sequences will execute before the flow of execution leaves the

```
switch:
    statement–seq–1;
    statement–seq–2;
```
The label *label–2* is completely ignored in this case.

These semantic considerations allow us to construct `switch` statements that organize `case` labels into groups. This will allow us to associate a given statement sequence with a set of `case` labels rather than just a single `case` label. All we need to do in order to capture this effect is to list a sequence of labels without any intervening statement sequences or breaks. The following syntax specification suggests this pattern (and can be generalized further):

Syntax: `switch` with `case` label groupings

```
switch (selector)
{
    case label-1a:
    case label-1b:
        statement-seq-1;
        break;
    case label-2a:
    case label-2b:
        statement-seq-2;
        break;
    ...
    case label-na:
    case label-nb:
        statement-seq-n;
        break;
    default:
        statement-seq-d;
}
```

This latest `switch` pattern is equivalent to the following pattern using nested `if-else` statements:

```
        if (selector == label-1a || selector == label-1b)
        {
            statement-seq-1;
        }
        else if (selector == label-2a || selector == label-2b)
        {
            statement-seq-2;
        }
        else if ...

        ...
        else if (selector == label-na || selector == label-nb)
        {
            statement-seq-n;
        }
        else
        {
            statement-seq-d;
        }
```

We can now offer an alternative implementation for the function `compute_discount_data` that was presented earlier. In this new version, which is actually used in `examp2.cxx`, the `switch` statement is used in lieu of nested `if-else` statements:

```
// FUNCTION:   compute_discount_data
// PURPOSE:    To return the discount rate and the discount amount
// INPUTS:
//    dc       discount code
//    bill     total bill    (including tax)
// OUTPUTS:
//    da       discount amount
//    dr       discount rate
void compute_discount_data(char dc, float bill, float& da,
         float& dr)
{
   // LOCAL DATA ...
   const float FAC_DISCR = 0.20,
           STU_DISCR = 0.10,
           SEN_DISCR = 0.05;


   switch (dc)
   {
     case 'f':
     case 'F':
     dr = FAC_DISCR;
     break;
      case 's':
      case 'S':
      dr = STU_DISCR;
      break;
      case 'g':
      case 'G':
      dr = SEN_DISCR;
      break;
      default:
      dr = 0.0;
   }
   da = bill * dr;
}  // end compute_discount_data
```

Explicit Type Conversions

We have mentioned that C++ automatically coerces types when mixed-mode expressions are evaluated. For example, when an `int` variable is multiplied by a `float` variable, the `int` is coerced to a `float` before the multiplication is performed. Consider the expression

```
j * x
```

where j is an `int` and x is a `float`. In evaluating this expression, the system will coerce j to a `float` value before performing the multiplication with x.

Here is a detailed explanation of what we mean when we say "the system will coerce j to a `float` before performing the multiplication with x": In evaluating this expression, the system will retrieve the value of j (an int) and the value of x (a float) from the computer memory. The system will then convert the value of the copy that it has of j to a float value. If the value of j is 5, then the copy of j is converted to 5.0. Note that this does not change the value of j in the computer's memory, not does it change the type of j. *The coercion is performed in the computer's arithmetic logic unit in preparation for the floating point multiplication operation.*

The conversion of j to a float in the above example was implicit in the semantics of the expression j * x. Sometimes, we want a type conversion to be explicit, either because the compiler demands that we do this or for the sake of clarity. This is accomplished by applying a type casting operator to the expression that we want to convert. The type casting operator has the same name as the type to which we are converting. Thus, the expression j * x is equivalent to the following expression which uses an explicit type casting operator:

```
float(j) * x
```

The notation float(j) indicates that a type casting operator is being applied to a copy of the variable j before the multiplication is performed. It can be argued that even when explicit type casting is not necessary, it is preferred to implicit conversions in that explicit type casting alerts the reader to the fact that a type conversion is taking place.

We can also type cast a float to an int. In this case the fractional part of the float number is lost. For example, if we want to multiply j by the integral part of x, we would use the expression:

```
j * int(x)
```

If x has the value 3.94, then int(x) has the value 3. Note that the fractional part of x is truncated and not rounded. If you want to round a float value, you need to apply the round function whose prototype is provided by the math.h header file. Thus, the value of round(3.94) is 4.

The type casting operators (float(), int(), etc.) are at the same level of precedence as a function call, which is the highest level of precedence in C++. Like function calls, the type casting operators are left associative.[3]

Type coercion also occurs if the type of the expression on the right of an assignment operation is different from the type of the variable on the left. For example, if j is an int and x is a float, then the assignment

```
j = x
```

is equivalent to

```
j = int(x).
```

That is, in the former case, the value of x is implicitly coerced to an int by truncation and in the latter case, the conversion is explicitly done by means of type casting. Similarly, the assignment

```
x = j
```

---

3.   C-style type casting is still valid. For example, in lieu of j * int(x) we would write j * (int) x. This type of type casting operation is at the same level of precedence as logical not (!), which is one step below the precedence of function application. In general, the new C++ style of type casting, shown above, is preferred.

would coerce the value of j to a float. The coerced value would then be stored in x.

The Functions setw and setprecision

The iomanip.h header file provides function prototypes for two functions that are useful for formatting output. These are the functions setw and set-precision.

The setprecision function is used to control the number of digits that will be displayed to the right of the decimal point when a float value is displayed using the cout << pattern. This function is called a manipulator since it manipulates the way data is displayed at the computer screen.

One uses the setprecision function by calling it in the context of the cout << pattern, as shown in the following syntax specification:

Syntax: use of setprecision manipulator

```
cout << item-1 << ....
    << setprecision(int-arg)
    << .... << item-n;
```

This pattern will cause all float values that are displayed after the call to setprecision to be displayed with at most int-arg digits to the right of the decimal point, where int-arg is an integer.[4]

The setw function is another function provided by the iomanip.h header file. This function is used to manipulate the field width of the item that follows it in the cout << pattern. This function differs from setprecision in that it does not permanently alter the behavior of the cout object. Instead, it sets the field width for the item that immediately follows it in the cout << pattern. The following syntax specification shows how setw is used:

Syntax: use of setw manipulator

```
cout << item-1 << ....
    << setw(int-arg) << item-k
    << ....  << item-n;
```

Given the pattern shown above, the value of item-k will be displayed in a field whose width is int-arg. All other items will be displayed using the default field widths (i.e., they are not affected by the use of setw). If the value of item-k cannot be adequately represented in a field of width int-arg, then the effect of the setw manipulator is over-ridden and the correct value is displayed.

---

4. However, we have found that the GNU G++ compiler interprets setprecision differently. In GNU G++, setprecision determines the precision one gets when one displays a float value. By precision we mean the total number of digits that are displayed regardless of the position of the decimal point.

The following extract from the program examp2.cxx shows the function
display_disc_bill. This function displays the total bill amount (before
the discount is subtracted out), the discount rate, and the discount amount.
Note the use of setprecision(2) to set the precision as appropriate for the
display of dollars and cents. This precision is in effect for all subsequent displays of float values (namely, for the display of bill, da, and bill - da).
Also note that the float value dr * 100 is type cast to an int so that the
discount rate can be displayed as an integral percentage.

Extract: the function display_disc_bill

```
// FUNCTION:    display_disc_bill
// PURPOSE:     Display total bill amount, discount rate,
//              discount amount and discounted bill
// INPUTS:
//    bill      total bill amount
//    da        discount amount
//    dr        discount rate
// OUTPUTS:
//    none
void display_disc_bill(float bill, float da, float dr)
{
   cout << endl << endl;
   cout << "The total bill comes to $" << setprecision(4)
        << bill << endl
     << "The discount rate was "    << int(dr * 100) << "%" << endl
     << "The discount amount was $"   << da << endl
     << "The discounted bill amount is $" << bill - da << endl;
}   // display_disc_bill
```

Example #2

Here is the code for the program examp2.cxx. Note that the code for the
functions compute_discount_data and display_disc_bill have been
omitted since they were given as extracts earlier in the text.

```
// Program:         examp2.cxx
//
// Programmer name: J. Q. Maxwell
//   Date:          Jan 22, 1993
//
//   Problem description:
//
// This program computes the bill for a customer at the
// Generic Coffee Shop.  The program consists of
// five steps:
//      1. Give user instructions
//      2. Get customer order data, including discount code
//      3. Compute total bill
//      4. Compute discount amount
//      5. Display total bill, including discount amount
```

```
//
// The Generic Coffee Shop menu contains the following
// items and prices:
//        coffee        $0.80
//        donut          0.75
//        muffin         1.25
//
// In addition, the state charges a 6% tax.
//
// The following special discounts are offered:
//        faculty       20%
//        students      10%
//        seniors        5%
// Only one discount applies per customer


#include <iostream.h>
#include <iomanip.h>              // for setprecision


void main()
{
    // FUNCTION PROTOTYPES ...
    void give_instructions();
    void get_order_data(int&, int&, int&, char&);
    float compute_bill(int, int, int);
    void compute_discount_data(char, float, float&, float&);
    void display_disc_bill(float, float, float);


    // LOCAL DATA ...
    int coffees;                 // INPUT: Number of coffees
    int donuts;                  // INPUT: Number of donuts
    int muffins;                 // INPUT: Number of muffins
    char disc_code;              // INPUT: Discount code
    float total_bill;            // OUTPUT:  Total bill amount
    float disc_amount;           // OUTPUT:  Discount amount
    float disc_rate;             // OUTPUT:  Discount rate


    // STATEMENTS ...
    give_instructions();
    get_order_data(coffees, donuts, muffins, disc_code);
    total_bill = compute_bill(coffees, donuts, muffins);
    compute_discount_data(disc_code, total_bill,
        disc_amount, disc_rate);
    display_disc_bill(total_bill, disc_amount, disc_rate);
}   // end main


// FUNCTION:  give_instructions
// PURPOSE:   Give user instructions
void give_instructions()
{
    cout << "This program computes a customer bill for the  "
        << endl
```

```
                   << "West Chester Coffee Shop.  Enter customer order" << endl
                   << "data when prompted." << endl;
      }   // end give_instructions


      // FUNCTION:   get_order_data
      // PURPOSE:    Get order amounts for coffees, donuts, muffins
      //             and get a discount code
      // INPUTS:
      //   none
      // OUTPUTS:
      //   cof       number of coffees
      //   don       number of donuts
      //   muf       number of muffins
      //   dc        discount code
      void get_order_data(int& cof, int& don, int& muf, char& dc)
      {
         cout << "Please enter number of coffees: ";
         cin  >> cof;
         cout << "Please enter number of donuts:  ";
         cin  >> don;
         cout << "Please enter number of muffins: ";
         cin  >> muf;
         cout << "Please enter one of the following discount codes: "
              << endl;
         cout  << "           f - faculty" << endl
               << "           s - student" << endl
               << "           g - golden"  << endl
               << "           n - none"    << endl;
         cin  >> dc;
      }   // end get_order_data


      // FUNCTION:    compute_bill
      // PURPOSE:     Return total bill amount based upon order data
      // RETURNS:     float, the total bill amount
      // INPUTS:
      //   cof       number of coffees
      //   don       number of donuts
      //   muf       number of muffins
      // OUTPUTS:
      //   none
      float compute_bill(int cof, int don, int muf)
      {
         // LOCAL DATA ...
         const float COFFEE_PRICE = 0.80,
                 DONUT_PRICE  = 0.75,
                 MUFFIN_PRICE = 1.25,
                 TAX_RATE     = 0.06;
         float bill;                 // total bill amount
         float tax;                  // state tax;
         bill = COFFEE_PRICE * cof
              + DONUT_PRICE * don
              + MUFFIN_PRICE * muf;
         tax  = TAX_RATE * bill;
         bill += tax;      // equivalent to bill = bill + tax;
         return bill;
      }   // end compute_bill
```

>>>> THE FUNCTION `compute_discount_data` GOES HERE.
>>>> This was presented in a program extract.

>>>> FUNCTION `display_discount_bill` GOES HERE.
>>>> This was presented in a program extract.

LOOPS

This section introduces three control structures available in C++ for constructing loops:

1. the `while` statement
2. the `for` statement
3. the `do-while` statement

The `while` is hardly distinguishable from the Pascal **while-do** statement. The `do-while` resembles the Pascal **repeat-until**. However, the `for` loop in C++ is much more flexible and powerful than the **for** statement in Pascal. The example programs `examp3.cxx`, `examp4.cxx` and `examp5.cxx` illustrate the use of these C++ looping constructs.

We shall introduce the `while` loop first and then we shall define the semantics of the `for` loop in terms of the `while` loop. Finally, we shall introduce the `do-while` loop.

The `while` Statement

The `while` statement is used to implement indefinite repetition. The syntax for the `while` statement is given in the following syntax specification:

Syntax: the `while` statement

```
while (test)
    statement
```

The statement within a `while` can either be a simple statement or a compound statement. The semantics for the `while` is as follows: the computer will evaluate the expression, *test*. If *test* evaluates to any non-zero value (i.e., true), then *statement* will execute and then *test* will be evaluated again to see if the looping process should continue. If *test* evaluates to 0, *statement* does not execute and the loop terminates. Thus, *statement* executes over and over again so long as *test* evaluates to a non-zero value.

For example, the following code segment will compute the sum of the integers 1 + 2 + ... + num, where num is a value input from the user:

Example

```
int sum, count, num;
cout << "Enter a number: ";
```

```
cin  >> num;
count = 1;
sum    = 0;
while (count <= num)
{
    sum += count;
    count += 1;
}
```

Initialization of Variables

Variables can be initialized at the point where they are defined. For example, the following definitions initialize the `float` variable `sum` to 0.0 and the `int` variable `index` to 0. Note that the `float` variable `x` is not initialized:

```
float sum = 0.0, x;
int index = 0;
```

Increment and Decrement Operators

We have already seen how C++ provides arithmetic assignment operators in order to allow programs to capture the pattern

```
        var = var op expr
```

more succinctly. The following patterns are also common:

```
        var = var + 1;    // increment var
        var = var - 1;    // decrement var
```

C++ provides the increment and decrement operators in order to express these patterns in a succinct notation. These notations are:

```
        var++;    // equivalent to var = var + 1;
        var--;    // equivalent to var = var - 1;
```

The increment and decrement operators have two forms: a postfix form and a prefix form. The postfix form is the one that we have already presented. In the prefix form, the operator appears before the variable that it is applied to:

```
        ++var;       // equivalent to var = var + 1;
        --var;       // equivalent to var = var - 1;
```

Observe that *the statement*

```
        ++var;
```

appears to be equivalent to *the statement*

```
        var++;
```

However, *the expressions* ++var and var++ are not equivalent! The semantics of var++ is:

"use the value of var and then increment var"

whereas the semantics of ++var is:

"increment var and then use the value of var."

This distinction is important when the increment and decrement operators are used in expressions that involve other operators. Consider the expression

```
sum += count++
```
Since the postfix form of the increment operator is being used, this is equivalent to:
```
(sum += count, count = count + 1, sum)
```
where the comma operator (,) is the C++ operator that has the *absolute lowest precedence*. The value of this expression is the value of `sum`, the last expression in the sequence. Thus, `count++` means "use `count` and then increment it." The semantics of the comma operator are defined as follows. The expression
```
expr1, expr2, expr3
```
is evaluated by evaluating `expr1`, then `expr2` and finally `expr3`. The value of the expression is the value of `expr3`.

The expression
```
sum += ++count
```
(in which the prefix form of the increment operator is being used) is equivalent to
```
(count = count + 1, sum += count)
```
Thus, `++count` means "increment `count` before using it."

These same semantic considerations apply in distinguishing between the prefix and postfix forms of the decrement operator.

The increment and decrement operators are right associative and are at the same level of precedence as logical not (!). Thus, among the operators that we have seen thus far, increment and decrement have the highest precedence. Only type casting and function application have a higher precedence.

In the case of increment and decrement, the meaning of the higher precedence is a little bit strange. Consider the expression
```
var1 op var2++
```
where `op` is at a lower precedence than `++`. This expression is equivalent to:
```
(temp = var1 op var2, var2 = var2 + 1, temp)
```
where `temp` is a temporary variable of the same type as `var1`. Thus, one might be justified in asking in what sense `++` has higher precedence than `op`, since the operation `op` is applied before the incrementing of `var2`. The answer is that `++` has higher precedence in the sense that `++` is appalied to just `var2`, not the result of `(var1 op var2)`.

The `for` Loop

The `for` loop is indicative of the expressive power of C++ (and C). The semantics of the `for` loop can be given in terms of a `while` loop, so technically, the `for` loop does not add to the capabilities of the C++ language. However, the `for` loop represents a very succinct notation that once mastered is preferable to the use of the `while` in many situations. One must be careful, however, not to write incomprehensible code, which amounts to an abuse of the power that the `for` loop offers.

Here is the syntax specification of the `for` statement:

Syntax: the `for` statement

```
for (initialization step ; test ; update step)
    statement
```

The statement under the control of the `for` is called the loop body.

The semantics of the above `for` loop can be given in terms of the `while` loop as follows:

```
initialization step;
while (test)
{
    statement;
    update step;
}
```

The `for` loop is generally preferred because all of the loop control information is bundled together at one convenient location.

In using the `for` loop, one or more of the following may be omitted:

1. the initialization step
2. the test
3. the update step

For example, the following pattern is permitted and represents an infinite loop:

```
for (;;)
    statement
```

This is not a useless construct so long as one provides a means of exiting the loop. This can be accomplished, for example, by a conditional execution of the `break` statement within the loop (as we shall soon demonstrate).

It is quite common to see the initialization step omitted:

```
for (; test ; update step)
    statement
```

If we leave out the initialization step and the update step, we end up with a construct that is identical to a `while`:

```
for (; test ;)
    statement
```

Other omission patterns are less common, but permissible. The semantics of a `for` is always consistent with the semantics given above (in terms of the `while` statement).

Scope of Variables

It is permissible to define C++ variables anywhere in a source code file. Variables defined outside any function are called *external* and are discouraged since they represent global variables. The scope of an external variable (and all external declarations and definitions) is from the point in the file at which it is defined, forwards, but not backwards in that file.   In particular, an external variable is global to all functions whose definitions occur later in the file.

It is permissible to define new variables anywhere in a function definition and locally within any compound statement. The exact location where a variable is defined determines its scope. The scope of a variable defined within a function definition is the compound statement (or, block) in which it is defined and all blocks within the scope of that block. If a variable is defined in the middle of a block, its scope is limited to the point at which it is defined, forward and not backward, in that block. A variable defined in an inner block is not visible in a more outer block.

Consider the following function definition:

```
int e;
void func(int a, int b)
{
    // LOCAL DATA ...
    int c;
        // a, b, c and e visible;  d is not
    while (...)
    {
    // begin a more inner block
    int d;
        // a, b, c, d, and e visible
    } // end inner block
    ... // a, b, c and e visible; d is not
} // end func
```

In this case, the variable e is an external variable, and is global to the function, func. The function body defines a block and the function formal arguments (a and b in our example) are visible throughout this block. The variable c is also visible throughout the function, since it is defined at the beginning of the function's outermost block. The variable d, however, declared within an inner block, is only visible within that block.   Note that the block in which d is defined is the loop body of a while statement.

It is not unusual to declare a for loop index within the for statement itself. This can be defended if the loop index has no special meaning outside of the loop. For example, a statement might begin as:

```
for (int i = 0 ; i < n ; i++)
{ ... }
```

Here, the variable i is being defined and initialized within the for statement. It is only visible within the block in which the for statement resides.[5]

We can express our earlier integer sum example using the for loop as follows:

```
int sum = 0, num;
cout << "Enter a number: ";
cin  >> num;
for (int count = 1; count <= num; count++)
{
    sum += count;
}
```

The function process_order_data can be used to illustrate the concept of scope both for variable definitions and for function declarations. This function is given below as an extract. Note that function prototypes for get_order_data and compute_bill are declared locally within this function. The prototypes are given here rather than externally (e.g., at the beginning of the program file) since this is the only function that calls these particular functions. It would have been acceptable to declare the prototypes more globally. The variables coffees, donuts, muffins and cur_order are local to this function and are not accessible outside of this function. Note that the for loop defines an int variable i that is visible from the for statement forward in the function.

Extract: the function process_order_data

```
// FUNCTION:   process_order_data
// PURPOSE:    Processes order data in a sentinel loop, returning
//             the best order amount, the least order amount, and
//             the number of orders.
// INPUTS:
//    max_ord  largest order amount, initially 0.0
//    min_ord  smallest order amount, initially 1000.0
// OUTPUTS:
//    max_ord  largest order amount
//    min_ord  smallest order amount
//    num_ord  number of orders
```

---

5.   The following (apparently sensible) pattern was not allowed using Turbo C++ version 2.0, but it was allowed on the other compilers that we tested:
```
for (int i = 0; i < n ; i++)
{
    . . .
  for (int j = 0; j < m; j++)
  {
    . . . .
  }   // end inner for
  . . . .
}   // end outer for
```
The Turbo C++ compiler objected to the definition for j in the inner loop.

```
void process_order_data(float& max_ord, float& min_ord, int&
num_ord)
{
    // FUNCTION PROTOTYPES ...
    void get_order_data(int&, int&, int&);
    float compute_bill(int, int, int);


    // LOCAL DATA ...
    int coffees;                 // number of coffees on an order
    int donuts;                  // number of donuts on an order
    int muffins;                 // number of muffins on an order
    float cur_order;             // current order amount


    // STATEMENTS ...
    cout << "How many orders need to be processed? ";
    cin  >> num_ord;


    for (int i = 0; i < num_ord; i++)
    {
        // Get order data for next order and
         // update max-min variables
        get_order_data(coffees, donuts, muffins);
        cur_order = compute_bill(coffees, donuts, muffins);
        if (cur_order > max_ord)
      max_ord = cur_order;
        if (cur_order < min_ord) // else would be wrong here. why?
      min_ord = cur_order;
    }
// a fix for no orders
    if (num_ord == 0)
       min_ord = 0.0;
}   // end process_order_data
```

Observations on Example #3

The complete code for example #3 (examp3.cxx) is given at the end of this section, along with the code for examp4.cxx and examp5.cxx. Before we discuss issues pertinent to the latter two programs, let us complete our discussion of all issues relating to example #3.

This program keeps track of the best and worst customers at the Generic College Coffee Shop. The manner in which total bill amounts are computed for this example is a bit different from some of our earlier examples (in particular, examp1.cxx and examp2.cxx) in that no customer discount is being applied. The main function calls the following functions:

1. give_instructions, a void function which gives the user instructions,
2. process_order_data, the void function whose definition was shown above, which processes order data in a loop, returning the largest

and smallest bill amounts as well as the total number of orders processed,

3. `display_maxmin`, a `void` function which displays the largest order amount, the smallest order amount and the total number of orders.

The function `process_order_data` was presented earlier as an extract. It asks the user for the number of orders and then uses a `for` loop to get the data for that many orders. It calls two functions in order to accomplish this task:

1. `get_order_data`, a `void` function which gets the specific order details for a given order (e.g., the number of coffees and donuts),

2. `compute_bill`, a `float` function that returns the total bill amount (including the state tax, but not including any discount considerations).

You might want to study the code for `examp3.cxx` before continuing on with the rest of this section.

Using the `break` Statement in an "Endless" `for`

We mentioned that when the `for` statement takes the form:

```
for (;;)
    statement
```

it represents an "endless" loop. In order for this construct to be correct (assuming that you do not want an endless loop in a program), the loop body must provide some mechanism for leaving the loop. This can be accomplished by means of the `break` statement. For example, the following code is equivalent to the code that was given earlier (in several differing versions) for computing the value of $1 + 2 + ... +$ num:

```
int sum = 0, count = 1, num;
cout << "Enter a number: ";
cin  >> num;
for (;;)
{
    if (count > num) break;
    sum += count;
    count++;
}
```

This code is less clear (in the opinion of the authors) than the implementation that was given earlier that used the `for` loop replete with initialization, test and update steps. This current example illustrates how one can jump out of an endless `for` loop by means of the conditional execution of a `break` statement.

When the `break` statement executes within a `for` loop body, the computer jumps out of the `for` loop and resumes execution with the statement following the loop. In the above example, if `count > num`, then the loop will terminate.

Example #4 (`examp4.cxx`) illustrates the use of the `break` to jump out of an endless `for`. The code for `examp4.cxx` is found after the code for `examp3.cxx` at the end of this section. Note that in `examp4.cpxx` the conditional execution of the `break` occurs in the middle of the `for` loop body and not at the beginning. The `for` loop in `examp4.cxx` contains a `switch` statement which also uses the `break` statement. Note that when a `break` executes within a `switch` within a `for` loop, the `break` causes the termination of the `switch` and not of the `for` loop. In general, `break` will cause the computer to terminate the execution of the "nearest" `switch` or loop (regardless of whether the loop is implemented using a `for`, a `while` or a `do-while`).   You might want to study `examp4.cxx` at this time.

The `ctype.h` header file

Let us now turn our attention to the new features that are introduced in example #5 (`examp5.cxx`).   The code for `examp5.cxx` is given at the end of this section immediately after the code for `examp4.cxx`. First, note that `examp5.cxx` uses the `ctype.h` header file.   This header file provides function declarations (in the form of prototypes) for functions that are useful for handling characters. These functions either test characters for certain characteristics or they manipulate individual characters in some way.   A list of the `ctype.h` functions that are especially useful is provided in Table 0–8. All of these functions take an argument of type `char`.

TABLE 0–8   C++ CHARACTER TESTING FUNCTIONS

function name:	semantics:
`isalnum`	returns true if argument is letter or digit
`isalpha`	returns true if argument is alphabetic
`isdigit`	returns true if argument is decimal digit (0–9)
`islower`	returns true if argument is lower case letter
`isspace`	returns true if argument is a white space character (space, carriage return, tab, new line)
`isupper`	returns true if argument is upper case letter
`isxdigit`	returns true if argument is a hexadecimal digit (0–9, a–f, A–F)
`tolower`	if argument is an upper case letter, returns the lower case version of that letter; otherwise returns the argument unchanged
`toupper`	if argument is a lower case letter, returns the upper case version of that letter; otherwise returns the argument unchanged

Please note that all of the above functions whose semantics is given as follows: "Returns true if argument is ...." will return false if the stated condition on the argument is not satisfied. For example, isalnum will return false if its argument is neither a letter nor a digit.

The do-while Statement

The syntax for the do-while statement is given as follows:

Syntax: do-while statement

```
do
    statement;
while (test);
```

Note that *statement* in the above syntax specification can either be a simple statement or a compound statement. The semantics of the do-while is that the execution of *statement* occurs at least once. After each execution of *statement*, *test* is evaluated. If *test* is non-zero (true), then *statement* executes again. Otherwise, execution of the loop terminates. For example, we could use the following code to compute 1 + 2 + ... + num so long as num is at least 1:

```
int sum = 0, count = 1, num;
cout << "Enter a number (must be at least 1): ";
cin  >> num;
do
{
    sum += count;
    count++;
} while (count <= num);
```

The continue Statement

The continue statement is used to skip over the remaining portion of a loop body without necessarily terminating the loop. This applies regardless of whether we are discussing a loop that is implemented using a for, a while or a do-while. This always forces the loop test to be re-evaluated and this will determine whether the loop will continue executing. This differs from the break which forces a jump completely out of the loop.

Here is a sketch of the do-while loop that is used in examp5.cxx. This loop uses a continue to jump over the switch if the user enters an illegal menu choice (the legal choices being c, d, m or q). Pseudocode (shown using italics and enclosed in square brackets) is used to indicate parts of the loop that we do not wish to present in detail at this point:

```
do
{
    [get value for item]
    item = toupper(item);
```

```
    if (!legal_choice(item))
    {
        [display error message]
        continue;
    }
    // assert: item is legal choice
    switch(item)
    {
        [implementation of switch]
    }
} while (item != 'Q');
```

In the above code, after the user enters his or her choice, the function `le-gal_choice` is called to determine whether the choice entered was a legal one or not. If this function returns 1, the choice was legal. If this function returns 0, the choice was illegal. If the choice was illegal, we want to skip over the rest of the `do-while` loop body and set up for the next execution of the loop body. This is accomplished by means of the `continue` statement.

Note that the pattern:

```
    if (!test) statement
```

is equivalent to saying "if `test` is zero (not true), then execute statement." The above is equivalent to the following code that uses an explicit comparison with 0:

```
    if (test == 0) statement
```

C++ programmers tend to prefer the first pattern (using `!test`) as opposed to the second (using `test == 0`).

You should study the code for `examp5.cxx` that is given at the end of this section.

Example #3

```
// Program:          examp3.cxx
//
// Programmer name: J. Q. Maxwell
// Date:            Jan 26, 1993
//
// Problem description:
//
// This program computes the largest and smallest bills
// for customers at the Generic Coffee Shop on a
// given day.  The program consists of the following
// steps.
//     1. Give user instructions
//     2. Process customer data in a for loop,
//        keeping track of the smallest and largest bills.
//     3. Display the largest and smallest total bill
//        amounts. Also, display the total number of
```

```
//          orders.
//
// The Generic Coffee Shop menu contains the following
// items and prices:
//          coffee        $0.80
//          donut          0.75
//          muffin         1.25
//
// In addition, the state charges a 6% tax.
//


#include <iostream.h>
#include <iomanip.h>              // for setprecision


void main()
{
    // FUNCTION PROTOTYPES ...
    void give_instructions();
    void process_order_data(float&, float&, int&);
    void display_maxmin(float, float, int);


    // LOCAL DATA ...
    float max_order = 0.0;          // largest order amount
    float min_order = 1000.0;       // smallest order amount
    int   num_ord;                  // number of orders


    // STATEMENTS ...
    give_instructions();
    process_order_data(max_order, min_order, num_ord);
    display_maxmin(max_order, min_order, num_ord);
}


>>>
>>> definition of give_instructions goes here
>>>


>>>
>>> definition of process_order_data goes here
>>> this was presented earlier as an extract
>>>


>>>
>>> definition for get_order_data goes here
>>> this was given earlier in exampl.cxx
>>>


>>>
>>> definition of compute_bill goes here
>>> this was given earlier in exampl.cxx
>>>
```

```
// FUNCTION:    display_maxmin
// PURPOSE:     Displays the maximum and minimum bills and
//              the total number of orders
// INPUTS:
//   max_ord  largest order
//   min_ord  smallest order
//   num_ord  number of orders
// OUTPUTS:
//   none
void display_maxmin(float max_ord, float min_ord, int num_ord)
{
   cout << endl << endl;
   cout << "Here are the results for today's orders: " << endl;
   cout << "Largest order was  $ " << setprecision(4) << max_ord
<< endl;
   cout << "Smallest order was $ " << min_ord << endl;
   cout << "Number of orders was " << num_ord << endl;
}  // end display_maxmin
```

Example #4

```
// Program:        examp4.cxx
//
// Programmer name: J. Q. Maxwell
// Date:            Feb 4, 1993
//
// Description:
//
// This program computes the amount due for an order at the
// Generic Coffee Shop.  Data for an order is entered as follows:

// The user will be prompted with a menu of possible items:
//       (C)offee  (D)onut   (M)uffin   (Q)uit
// If the user enters Q (for quit), the order is completed and
// order summary data will be displayed.  Otherwise, the user
// will be asked to specify the number of items of the type
// indicated on the order.  There is no restriction on the
// number of timesthe user can enter a particular item code.
//
// Order summary data consists of:
//     Total number of coffees ordered
//     Total number of donuts ordered
//     Total number of muffins ordered
//     Total amount due
//
// Here are the current item prices:
//     coffee        $0.80
//     donut          0.75
//     muffin         1.25
//
#include <iostream.h>
#include <iomanip.h>

void main()
{
```

```cpp
// LOCAL DATA ...
const float COFFEE_PRICE = 0.80,
            DONUT_PRICE  = 0.75,
            MUFFIN_PRICE = 1.25;
int num;    // number of a particular item ordered
            // (e.g., number of coffees)
char item;              // item chosen (c, d, m or q(uit))
int total_coff = 0;   // total number of coffees
int total_don  = 0;   // total number of donuts
int total_muff = 0;   // total number of muffins
float total_due;      // total bill amount


// STATEMENTS ...
// Get data until user says "quit".
for (;;)       // endless for loop
{
   cout << "Enter item code (c, d, m, q): ";
   cin  >> item;
   if (item == 'q' || item == 'Q') break;     // exit loop
   switch (item)
   {
   case 'c':
   case 'C':
      cout << "Number of coffees: ";
      cin  >> num;
      total_coff += num;
      break;
   case 'd':
   case 'D':
      cout << "Number of donuts: ";
      cin  >> num;
      total_don += num;
      break;
   case 'm':
   case 'M':
      cout << "Number of muffins: ";
      cin  >> num;
      total_muff += num;
      break;
   default:
      cout << "Illegal code.  Try again!" << endl;
   }  // end switch
}  // end for


// Compute total amount due.
total_due = total_coff * COFFEE_PRICE
        + total_don  * DONUT_PRICE
        + total_muff * MUFFIN_PRICE;


// Report out final results.
cout << endl << endl;
cout    << "Total number of coffees ordered:   "
        << total_coff << endl
        << "Total number of donuts ordered:    "
```

```
                    << total_don  << endl
                    << "Total number of muffins ordered:   "
                    << total_muff << endl;
          cout << endl;
          cout << "Total amount due:  $" << setprecision(4)
            << total_due << endl;
      }   // end main
```

Example #5

```
// Program:            examp5.cxx
//
// Programmer name: J. Q. Maxwell
// Date:              Feb 4, 1993
//
// Description:
//
// This program computes the amount due for an order at
// the Generic Coffee Shop.  An order is entered as follows:
// The user will be prompted with a menu of possible items:
//       (C)offee  (D)onut   (M)uffin   (Q)uit
// If the user enters Q (for quit), the order is completed
// and order summary data will be displayed.  Otherwise,
// the user will be asked to specify the number of items
// of the particular type on the order.
//
// There is no restriction on the number of times the user
// can enter a particular item code.
//
// Order summary data consists of:
//      Total number of coffees ordered
//      Total number of donuts ordered
//      Total number of muffins ordered
//      Total amount due
//
// Here are the current item prices:
//      coffee        $0.80
//      donut          0.75
//      muffin         1.25
#include <iostream.h>
#include <iomanip.h>
#include <ctype.h>      // for toupper


void main()
{
    // FUNCTION PROTOTYPE ...
    int legal_choice(char);


    // LOCAL DATA ...
    const float COFFEE_PRICE = 0.80,
            DONUT_PRICE  = 0.75,
```

```cpp
                  MUFFIN_PRICE = 1.25;
int num;                // number of particular item ordered
char item;              // item chosen (c, d, m or q(uit))
int total_coff = 0;  // total number of coffees
int total_don  = 0;  // total number of donuts
int total_muff = 0;  // total number of muffins
float total_due;     // total bill amount


// STATEMENTS ...
// Get data until user says "quit".
do
{
   cout << "Enter item code (c, d, m, q): ";
   cin  >> item;
   item = toupper(item);
   if (!legal_choice(item))
   {
   // display error message; jump to loop test
   cout << "Illegal code. Try again!" << endl;
   continue;
   }
   // assert: item is legal choice
   switch (item)
   {
   case 'C':
      cout << "Number of coffees: ";
      cin  >> num;
      total_coff += num;
      break;
   case 'D':
      cout << "Number of donuts: ";
      cin  >> num;
      total_don += num;
      break;
   case 'M':
      cout << "Number of muffins: ";
      cin  >> num;
      total_muff += num;
      break;
   }   // end switch
} while (item != 'Q');


// Compute total amount due.
total_due = total_coff * COFFEE_PRICE
       + total_don  * DONUT_PRICE
       + total_muff * MUFFIN_PRICE;


// Report out final results.
cout << endl << endl;
cout  << "Total number of coffees ordered:   "
       << total_coff << endl
       << "Total number of donuts ordered:    "
       << total_don  << endl
       << "Total number of muffins ordered:   "
```

```
            << total_muff << endl;
     cout << endl;
     cout << "Total amount due:  $" << setprecision(4)
       << total_due << endl;
}   // end main


// FUNCTION:     legal_choice
// PURPOSE:      Determines whether item code is legal choice.
// RETURNS:      1 if item is C, D, M, or Q, 0 otherwise
// PRE:          if item is a letter, it is an upper case letter
// INPUTS:
//     item       item code
// OUTPUTS:
//     None
int legal_choice(char item)
{
    return ( item == 'C' || item == 'D' || item == 'M'
          || item == 'Q');
}
```

ADDITIONAL SCALAR TYPES

This section introduces enumerated types and some additional scalar types that are available in C++. Example #6 (examp6.cxx) at the end of this section illustrates the use of enumerated types.

Enumerated Types

Enumerated types in C++ are similar to enumerated types in Pascal. The major differences relate to the issue of *type safety*. In general, C++ is more forgiving if we violate the integrity of a type than is Pascal. (In other words, C++ is less *type safe*.) C++, on the other hand, is more stringent in enforcing type safety than its predecessor, C. We shall explore the idea of type safety in some detail in this section, especially as the issue relates to enumerated types.

The following syntax specification shows how one declares an enumerated type whose name is *type-name*:

Syntax: declaring an enumerated type

```
enum type-name {enumerated-constant-list};
```

Type-name is a user-defined type as opposed to the standard types (int, float, char, etc.) that are provided by C++. The fact that *type-name* is a user-defined type implies that one may define variables to be of this type within the scope of this declaration. The enumerated constant list can take various forms (as we shall see) but it is essentially a list of identifiers. These identifiers represent the sole legal values that variables of this user-defined type may be assigned.

The following code segment shows the declarations for two enumerated types, called `day` and `veggie`:

```
enum day {sunday, monday, tuesday, wednesday, thursday,
        friday, saturday};
enum veggie {spinach, broccoli, onion, carrot};
```

Within the scope of these declarations, one can define variables to be of the types `day` and `veggie`, as shown in the following code segment:

```
day today = sunday, tomorrow = monday;
veggie veg1, veg2;
```

What are the implications of the fact that the variable `today` is of type `day`? In principle, the values of the variable `today` are limited to the seven values given in the declaration of the type `day`, namely: `sunday`, `monday`, `tuesday`, `wednesday`, `thursday`, `friday`, and `saturday`. Any assignment of a value of another type would be flagged by the compiler in the form of a compiler warning.[6] For example,

```
        today = carrot;
```
would be flagged, as would:
```
        veg1 = sunday;
```
In the first case the (Turbo C++) compiler will warn that you are "trying to assign a `veggie` to a `day`" and in the second case, the compiler will warn that you are "trying to assign a `day` to a `veggie`." However, the compiler will only warn you if you attempt to make an assignment that violates the type rules. The compiler will not complain if you try to do something which seems outrageous, such as comparing veggies and days. For example, the apparently meaningless comparison

```
        today < veg1
```
will not cause the (Turbo C++) compiler to issue a warning!

This behavior can be explained by the fact that C++ inherits from standard C the idea that an enumerated constant is actually an `int` in disguise. In our declaration for the type `day`, `sunday` is a symbol for 0, `monday` is a symbol for 1, etc. Similarly, `spinach` is a symbol for 0, `broccoli` is a symbol for 1, etc. Thus, the expression

```
        today < veg1
```
causes the compiler to coerce both `today` and `veg1` to the type `int`. Then, the comparison operator is performed relative to the two `int`s that `today` and `veg1` represent. (For example, `sunday < carrot` is true, whereas `friday < spinach` is 0 or false.)

Can you explain the following (Turbo C++) compiler warning (assuming that `veg` is of type `veggie`)?

```
        statement:  veg = broccoli + sunday;
```

6. In fact, different compilers have different properties in terms of the type safety issues for enumerated types. You might want to experiment with your compiler. Our discussion is based upon Turbo C++. Symantec C++ has similar properties. GNU G++ seems to provide less type safety than the other two compilers.

warning: `int` assigned to a `veggie`

The evaluation of `broccoli + sunday` causes `broccoli` and `sunday` to be coerced to type `int`. The two `int`s (0 and 1) are added and the result (1) is stored in `veg`. The value of `veg` will become 1 (which is equivalent to `broccoli`), but the compiler gives the programmer fair warning that something seems to be awry in this program.

Can you explain the following (Turbo C++) compiler warning (assuming that `today` is of type `day`)?

statement: `for (today = monday; today <= friday; today++)`
            `.... // whatever`

warning: `int` assigned to a `day`

In this case the culprit is the expression `today++`. This is equivalent to

```
today = today + 1
```

In computing `today + 1`, `today` is coerced to an `int` and, thus, the result of `today + 1` is an `int`. Thus, we are attempting to assign an `int` to a `day`. The correct way to use an enumerated type in a `for` loop such as this is as follows:

```
for (today = monday; today <= friday; today =
    day(today + 1))
      ...... // whatever
```

Note that the loop update step involves computing `today + 1`, which evaluates to an `int`, and then type casting that `int` to a `day`, so that it can be assigned to the variable `today`. Note the use of explicit type casting in this case.

Explicit type casting makes the update step in the above `for` loop acceptable to the compiler. The compiler checks this sort of thing at compile-time, that is, before the program actually executes. Thus, the compiler will not detect a situation in which the value of

```
day(int-expression)
```

is not a legal value of type `day`. The programmer must be aware of this sort of possibility (which is a bit of an anomaly). For example, the output from the following code:

```
for (today = monday; today <= saturday;
    today = day(today + 1))
    {
          cout << "Today is " << today << endl;
    }
    cout << "Final value is " << today << endl;
```

will be:

```
Today is 1
Today is 2
Today is 3
Today is 4
Today is 5
Today is 6
Final value is 7
```

Note that `today` is assigned the value 7, which is not one of the legal values (since `saturday` is equal to 6), but there is no run-time protection against this sort of error. The update statement

```
today = day(today + 1)
```

satisfies the type safety criteria imposed by the compiler.

The above example also illustrates that when one displays the value of an enumerated type, an `int` appears at the computer display. The input and output of enumerated types is discussed in the next subsection.

One can modify the default assignment of values to enumerated constants (namely, that the first enumerated constant has value 0 and that each successive constant has a value one greater than the previous) by explicit assignments to the constants, as in the following alternative declarations for the type `day`:

```
enum day {sunday = 1, monday, tuesday, wednesday, thursday,
    friday, saturday};
    // monday is 2, tuesday is 3, etc.

enum day {sunday = 0, saturday = 0, monday = 1, tuesday = 1,
    wednesday = 1, thursday = 1, friday = 1};
    // weekend days are 0; weekday days are 1
```

Input and Output of Enumerated Types

The anomalous `for` loop example, given above, in which the value of 7 is assigned to a variable of type `day`, also illustrates that values of an enumerated type are displayed as `int` values.   By contrast, values of an enumerated type cannot be read in, even as `int`s.   For example, the following code (in Turbo C++):

```
today = monday;
cin >> today;
cout << "Today is " << today;
```

will produce the output

```
    Today is 1
```

regardless of the value the user enters for the variable `today`.   The value entered for an enumerated type is simply ignored. Consequently, it is usually the case that special functions are written for the purpose of reading in values of an enumerated type and for displaying those values.

One such function is used in `examp6.cxx` to output values of an enumerated type, `customer_type`, which is declared as follows:

```
    enum customer_type {faculty, student, senior, regular};
```

This type is used to represent four kinds of customers at the Generic College Coffee Shop: faculty, who get a 20% discount, students, who get a 10% discount, senior citizens, who get a 5% discount, and ordinary folks, who do not get a discount.

The function `display_cust_type` in `examp6.cxx` is used to display the customer type as a string embedded within a message, such as:

```
    The customer's discount status is FACULTY
```
The function `display_cust_type` takes one input argument, `ctype`, which is of type `customer_type`, and uses a switch statement to convert the value of `ctype` to an appropriate output message. Here is the code for the function `display_cust_type`:

Extract: the function `display_cust_type`

```
// FUNCTION:    display_cust_type
// PURPOSE:     To display a string that corresponds
//              to customer type
// INPUTS:
//    ctype     customer type (faculty, student, senior, regular)
// OUTPUTS:
//    None
void display_cust_type(customer_type ctype)
{
   cout << "This customer's discount status is ";
   switch (ctype)
   {
     case faculty:
     cout << "FACULTY";
     break;
     case student:
     cout << "STUDENT";
     break;
     case senior:
     cout << "SENIOR";
     break;
     case regular:
     cout << "*** NO DISCOUNT APPLIES ***";
     // no other possibilities
   }  // end switch
   cout << endl;
}  // end display_cust_type
```

In the function `main` of `examp6.cxx`, the variable `cust_status` is declared to be of type `customer_type`. The value of `cust_status` is set by means of the following assignment:

```
        cust_status = convert_to_type(disc_code);
```
The function `convert_to_type` takes a character code (passed as the argument `dc`) and returns the `customer_type` value that corresponds to that code. This illustrates that one way in which the value for an enumerated type can be gotten from the user is to ask the user to enter a code and then to have the program convert that code to a value of an enumerated type. The definition of `convert_to_type` follows:

Extract: the function `convert_to_type`

```
// FUNCTION:    convert_to_type
// PURPOSE:     Converts character code to a customer type
// RETURNS:     A customer_type
```

```
//              (faculty, student, senior, regular)
// PRE:         character code is an upper case letter
// POST:        return value is one of:
//              {faculty, student, senior, regular}
// INPUTS
//     dc       discount code
// OUTPUTS
//     None
customer_type convert_to_type(char dc)
{
    customer_type ctype;
    switch (dc)
    {
      case 'F':
      ctype = faculty;
      break;
       case 'S':
      ctype = student;
      break;
       case 'G':
      ctype = senior;
      break;
       default:
      ctype = regular;
    }  // end switch
    return ctype;
}    // end convert_to_type
```

Before reading the rest of this section, you might want to skip ahead to the discussion of example #6 (examp6.cxx) that is found at the end of this section. The code for examp6.cxx immediately follows that discussion.

Additional Integer Types

At this point we wish to mention additional C++ types that you might find useful. The type int is just one of many integer types available in C++. The integer types differ with respect to two dimensions:

1. The number of bytes used in the computer's memory to represent variables and constants of that type, and
2. Whether the type supports negative as well as non-negative values.

The integer types that support both negative and non-negative values are:

1. char
2. short int (or, just: short)
3. int
4. long int (or, just: long)

You might be surprised to see the type char in this list. But, insofar as C++ is concerned, characters are represented by integer values in the range –128 and 127. These values can be represented by one byte of the computer's memory (using eight bit binary numbers and what is called two's complement representations for negative values). The values 0 through 127 are used to encode the standard ASCII character set. When you execute the statement:

```
cout << ch;
```
where `ch` is a char variable, the `<<` operator is defined in such a way that `ch` will be displayed as an ASCII character and not as an integer. Similarly, when you read in character data using
```
cin >> ch;
```
the `>>` operator is defined so as to accept an ASCII character as input, but to store the ASCII character as a one byte binary code in the computer's memory.

Compiler implementors are free to implement the signed integer types consistent with the following constraints:

1. `char` values occupy one byte of memory
2. `short int` values occupy at least two bytes of memory
3. `int` values occupy at least as many bytes as `short int` values
4. `long int` values occupy at least four bytes of memory and no fewer bytes than `int` values

One can qualify any integer type as being `unsigned`. This has the effect of causing the computer to interpret the bit pattern that represents the unsigned integer as a binary number and not as a two's complement number. Thus, `unsigned` integers can be used to represent values that are zero or greater. They cannot be used to represent negative values. The largest absolute value of an `unsigned int` is about twice that of a signed integer. For example, legal values for the type `unsigned char` are 0 through 255.

The `limits.h` header file provides data concerning the implementation of the various integer types for a particular compiler. This data is presented in the form of symbolic constants that you can access and display. A list of some of those symbolic constants along with their meanings is given in Table 0–9.

Another way to get a handle on how integers and other types are represented is to use the `sizeof` function. The `sizeof` function may be applied to a type, a variable or a constant. It returns an integer that gives the number of bytes occupied by a data element of the relevant type. Here are some sample calls to `sizeof`:

```
sizeof(unsigned char)
    // bytes required to store an unsigned char
sizeof(ch)
    // bytes required to store the variable ch
sizeof(1)
    // bytes required to store the int 1
```

TABLE 0–9   INTEGER TYPE DATA FROM `limits.h`

symbolic constant:	meaning:
CHAR_MAX	maximum char value
CHAR_MIN	minimum char value
UCHAR_MAX	maximum unsigned char value
SHRT_MAX	maximum short value
SHRT_MIN	minimum short value
USHRT_MAX	maximum unsigned short value
INT_MAX	maximum int value
INT_MIN	minimum int value
UINT_MAX	maximum unsigned int value
LONG_MAX	maximum long value
LONG_MIN	minimum long value
ULONG_MAX	maximum unsigned long value

It is the programmer's responsibility to assure that type coercion among integer types is not producing erroneous values. For example, suppose we have:

```
char ch1;
unsigned char ch2;
```
The assignments
```
ch2 = (unsigned char) 230;
ch1 = ch2;
```
will cause the value of `ch2` to be coerced to a `char` value before it can be stored in `ch1`. However, there is no sensible `char` value that corresponds to the number 230 in the ASCII character set. Consequently, the value assigned to `ch1` will be unreliable. This is not the sort of error that the compiler will catch. Also note that we are explicitly type casting 230 as an `unsigned char` in order to store it in the variable `ch2`. However, even if we omitted the explicit type casting, the assignment
```
ch2 = 230;
```
would have the same effect.

Additional `Float` Types

C++ supports three `float` types:
1. `float`

2. `double`
3. `long double`

There is no distinction between signed and unsigned `float` types (all `float` types support negative values). Language implementors are constrained to follow the following guidelines:

1. a `float` value must occupy at least four bytes
2. a `double` value must occupy at least six bytes and at least as many bytes as a `float`
3. a `long double` must occupy at least as many bytes as a `double`

The `float.h` header file defines symbolic constants which specify the limits for the `float` types in your system. These include the following:

TABLE 0–10   SYMBOLIC CONSTANTS FOR FLOAT TYPE LIMITS

symbolic constant:	meaning:
`FLT_DIG`	minimum number of significant digits for a float
`DBL_DIG`	minimum number of significant digits for a double
`LDBL_DIG`	minimum number of significant digits for a long double
`FLT_MAX_10_EXP`	maximum float exponent (base 10)
`DBL_MAX_10_EXP`	maximum double exponent (base 10)
`LDBL_MAX_10_EXP`	maximum long double exponent (base 10)
`FLT_MIN_10_EXP`	minimum float exponent (base 10)
`DBL_MIN_10_EXP`	minimum double exponent (base 10)
`LDBL_MIN_10_EXP`	minimum long double exponent (base 10)

More About Type Conversions

C++ will attempt type coercion in the following situations:
1. When a value of one type is assigned to a variable of another.
2. When a binary operation is mixed mode; that is, when a binary operation involves operands of different types.
3. When a function is passed a value of one type, but expects a value of another.

It is important to understand when these automatic type conversions are safe and when they may introduce errors into a program.

Consider type conversions in an assignment, such as:

```
variable = expression
```

In this case, the compiler attempts to coerce the value of the expression on the right to the type of the variable on the left. This coercion will succeed so long as both variable and expression are one of the integer or float types that we have been discussing. There is no problem if the variable type provides greater precision than the expression type. For example,

```
doubleVariable = floatExpression
```

will not cause any trouble. The value of the `float` expression is converted to a double, which just means that the `double` variable provides some extra bytes for the representation of the value of the `float` expression. However,

```
floatVariable = doubleExpression
```

can be troublesome in two regards. First, there can be a loss of precision, which is only troublesome if that loss of precision is relevant to the problem being solved. Second, the value of the `double` expression may be out of the range of values that the `float` variable can represent. In other words, the exponent for the `double` expression may either be more positive or more negative than a `float` variable allows. In this case, the behavior of the program is (in principle) unpredictable. Another way of stating this is that different compilers may handle the situation differently, but, in general, the results produced by the program will be unreliable.

The above analysis applies to all situations in which the variable on the left cannot accommodate the range of values of the expression on the right. Thus, an assignment of the form

```
intVariable = longExpression
```

will cause erroneous results if the value of the long expression is either less than the value of `INT_MIN` or greater than the value of `INT_MAX`. Errors can also result if one attempts to store an unsigned integer value to a signed integer variable:

```
intVariable = unsignedIntExpression
```

Problems can also arise when a `float` expression is assigned to an integer variable; for example:

```
intVariable = doubleExpression
```

This may result in the loss of precision due to the loss of the fractional part of the value of the `double` expression. It may also be the case that the truncated value of the `double` expression is out of the range of values that can be stored in an `int` variable.

In evaluating expressions, C++ follows rather complicated rules which determine the coercions from one type to another. The first general rule is that all integer types (`char`, `unsigned  char`, `short  int`, `unsigned  short  int`) that are stored with fewer bytes than an `int` (a determination which is compiler–dependent) are coerced to `int` before being operated upon. This rule is referred to as the *integral promotion rule*. For example, if `first`, `second`, and `third` are of type `unsigned  char`, then the assignment

```
third = first + second;
```

is computed as follows: `first` and `second` are coerced to `int`, the addition is performed, and then the result is coerced back to an `unsigned char`.

The other rules are quite complicated. The general guidance is:

1. If either operand is type `long double`, the other operand is converted to `long double`.
2. Otherwise, if either operand is `double`, the other operand is coerced to `double`.
3. Otherwise, if either operand is `float`, the other operand is coerced to `float`.
4. Otherwise, the operands are integer types and the integral promotion rule is applied (`short ints` to `int`).
5. (If we get to this point, both operands are integral types.) If either operand is `unsigned long`, then the other operand is coerced to `unsigned long`.
6. Otherwise, if one operand is `long int` and the other is `unsigned int`, the following rule applies: if `long` can represent possible unsigned `int` values, `unsigned int` is coerced to `long`.
7. Otherwise, both operands are coerced to `unsigned long`.
8. Otherwise, if either operand is `long`, the other is converted to `long`.
9. Otherwise, if either operand is `unsigned int`, the other is converted to `unsigned int`.
10. If the compiler reaches this rule, both operands should be `int`.

Integer and `Float` Constants

Integer constants are stored as `int` values unless:

1. The value is too large to store in `sizeof(int)` bytes, or
2. The value is given with the suffix L (or, the lower case letter, l; but L is preferred since it will not be confused with the number 1).

For example, the constant `1060` is stored as an `int`, but the constant `1060L` is stored as a `long int`.

`Float` constants are stored as `double` values by default. Hence, the constant `9.0` is actually stored as a `double` and not as a `float`. If you want to store `9.0` as a `float` (and not as a `double`), you must use the suffix F (or, f), as in: `9.0F`. If you want to store `9.0` as a `long double`, you must use the suffix L (or, l), as in: `9.0L`.

Consequently, the mixed mode expression:

```
9.0/2
```

actually involves the division of a `double` by an `int`. This will cause the `int` to be coerced to a `double`.

Remarks Concerning Example #6

This program is similar to `examp1.cxx` and `examp2.cxx` in that a state tax is again being applied and customer discounts are in effect. However, in this case, a variable `cust_status` whose type is the enumeration type, `custom-`

er_type, is used to encode the kind of discount to which a customer is entitled.

Example #6

```
// Program:           examp6.cxx
//
// Programmer name: J. Q. Maxwell
// Date:             Jan 22, 1993
//
// Problem description:
//
// This program computes the bill for a customer at the
// Generic Coffee Shop.  The program consists of
// six steps:
//     1. Give user instructions
//     2. Get customer order data, including discount code
//     3. Determine discount type
//     4. Compute total bill
//     5. Compute discount amount
//     6. Display total bill, including discount type
//
// The Generic Coffee Shop menu contains the following
// items and prices:
//         coffee      $0.80
//         donut        0.75
//         muffin       1.25
//
// In addition, the state charges a 6% tax.
//
// The following special discounts are offered:
//         faculty      20%
//         students     10%
//         seniors       5%
// Only one discount applies per customer


#include <iostream.h>
#include <iomanip.h>          // for setprecision
#include <ctype.h>            // for toupper


// GLOBAL TYPE DEFINITION ...
enum customer_type {faculty, student, senior, regular};


void main()
{
    // FUNCTION PROTOTYPES ...
    void give_instructions();
    void get_order_data(int&, int&, int&, char&);
    customer_type convert_to_type(char);
    float compute_bill(int, int, int);
```

```
        void compute_discount_data(customer_type, float,
              float&, float&);
        void display_disc_bill(customer_type, float, float, float);



        // LOCAL DATA ...
        int coffees;                        // INPUT: Number of coffees
        int donuts;                         // INPUT: Number of donuts
        int muffins;                        // INPUT: Number of muffins
        char disc_code;                     // INPUT: Discount code
        customer_type cust_status;          // OUTPUT:  Type of customer
        float total_bill;                   // OUTPUT:  Total bill amount
        float disc_amount;                  // OUTPUT:  Discount amount
        float disc_rate;                    // OUTPUT:  Discount rate



        // STATEMENTS ...
        give_instructions();
        get_order_data(coffees, donuts, muffins, disc_code);
        cust_status = convert_to_type(disc_code);
        total_bill = compute_bill(coffees, donuts, muffins);
        compute_discount_data(cust_status, total_bill,
              disc_amount, disc_rate);
        display_disc_bill(cust_status, total_bill,
              disc_amount, disc_rate);
    }   // end main



    >>>
    >>> definition for give_instructions goes here
    >>>



    // FUNCTION:   get_order_data
    // PURPOSE:    Get order amounts for coffees, donuts, muffins
    //             and get a discount code
    // INPUTS:
    //    none
    // OUTPUTS:
    //    cof       number of coffees
    //    don       number of donuts
    //    muf       number of muffins
    //    dc        discount code
    void get_order_data(int& cof, int& don, int& muf, char& dc)
    {
        cout << "Please enter number of coffees: ";
        cin  >> cof;
        cout << "Please enter number of donuts:  ";
        cin  >> don;
        cout << "Please enter number of muffins: ";
        cin  >> muf;
        cout << "Please enter one of the following discount codes: "
            << endl;
        cout  << "          f - faculty" << endl
              << "          s - student" << endl
              << "          g - golden"  << endl
```

```
               << "          n - none"     << endl;
     cin  >> dc;
     dc = toupper(dc);
  }  // end get_order_data


  >>>
  >>> definition of convert_to_type goes here
  >>> this function was presented earlier as
  >>> an extract
  >>>


  >>>
  >>> definition of compute_bill goes here
  >>> this function was presented in exampl.cxx
  >>>


  // FUNCTION:  compute_discount_data
  // PURPOSE:   To return the discount rate and the discount amount
  // INPUTS:
  //    ctype   customer type (faculty, student, senior, regular)
  //    bill    total bill   (including tax)
  // OUTPUTS:
  //    da      discount amount
  //    dr      discount rate
  void compute_discount_data(customer_type ctype,
          float bill, float& da, float& dr)
  {
     // LOCAL DATA ...
     const float FAC_DISCR = 0.20,
             STU_DISCR = 0.10,
             SEN_DISCR = 0.05;


     switch (ctype)
     {
       case faculty:
       dr = FAC_DISCR;
       break;
        case student:
       dr = STU_DISCR;
       break;
        case senior:
       dr = SEN_DISCR;
       break;
        case regular:
       dr = 0.0;
        // no other possibilities
     }  // end switch
     da = bill * dr;
  }  // end compute_discount_data


  // FUNCTION:   display_disc_bill
  // PURPOSE:    Display total bill amount, discount rate,
```

```
//              discount amount and discounted bill
// INPUTS:
//   ctype     customer type (faculty, student, senior, regular)
//   bill      total bill amount
//   da        discount amount
//   dr        discount rate
// OUTPUTS:
//   none
void display_disc_bill(customer_type ctype, float bill, float da,
float dr)
{
   // FUNCTION PROTOTYPE ...
   void display_cust_type(customer_type);


   cout << endl << endl;
   cout << "The total bill comes to $" << setprecision(4)
        << bill << endl;
   display_cust_type(ctype);
   cout  << "The discount rate was "   << int(dr * 100)
        << "%" << endl
        << "The discount amount was $"  << da << endl
        << "The discounted bill amount is $" << bill - da
        << endl;
}  // display_disc_bill


>>>
>>> definition of display_cust_type goes here
>>> this was presented earlier as an extract
>>>
```

ARRAYS AND STRINGS

This section presents the final C++ example in our C++ tutorial, example #7 (examp7.cxx).   This will provide all of the requisite C++ knowledge that you will need to understand the Searcher program given in Chapter 0 of the text.   In particular, example #7 introduces arrays and strings.

Defining and Manipulating Arrays

An array is a linear sequence of elements all of the same type. The elements are called *components* and the type is called the *component type* of the array. The following syntax specification illustrates how an array is defined in C++ :

Syntax: defining an array

```
component-type array-name[dimension];
```

The above pattern defines an array whose name is *array-name* and whose component type is *component-type*. The symbol *dimension* is a positive integer constant (or positive integral expression whose value can be determined at compile time) which indicates the number of components that the array contains. This constant is called the *dimension of the array* and it determines the range of indices that can be used to access array components.

The individual components of an array can be referenced by means of *array references*. An array reference has the following form:

array–name[index]

The index may be given as an integer constant, variable or expression. One can consider an array of dimension N as a collection of N variables. A valid array reference can be viewed as the name of one of these N variables. Array components are indexed starting with the value 0. Thus, the last valid index in an array whose dimension is N is always N − 1. Any index outside of this range of values, 0 through N − 1, is not a valid index. However, the run-time environment will not alert you to the fact that an array index might be out of range.

Consider the following definitions:

```
const int MAXSIZE   = 20;
const int MAXSTRING = 30;
int a[10], e;          // a is an array, but e is not
float f[MAXSIZE];      // MAXSIZE is a constant
char str[MAXSTRING];   // MAXSTRING is a constant
```

In the above definitions, a is an array whose dimension is 10. Thus, the legal array references for this array are a[0], a[1], ..., a[9]. These can be considered the names of the ten variables of type int that constitute the array a.

Note that arrays and scalar variables can be defined in the same definition. The variable e is not an array but a simple integer. In the above definitions, the array f has dimension MAXSIZE, a constant, and the array str has the dimension MAXSTRING. (Later we shall see that an array of characters is considered a string.) The array f can be viewed as consisting of the float variables f[0], f[1], ..., f[19] and the array str can be viewed as consisting of the char variables str[0], str[1], ..., str[29].

Since a valid array reference is just a variable whose type is the component type of the array, it (the array reference) can be used wherever a variable of that type is permitted. For example, a[i] is an int, so long as the value of i is between 0 and 9, and a[i] can be used wherever an int is appropriate. As another example, f[j] is a float, so long as j is within the range 0–19, and can be used wherever a float is appropriate. Care must be taken, however, to assure that the index that is provided in an array reference is within range.

The following examples show the use of array references for the array a:

```
// use of array references in comparisons
if (a[i] < a[j]) { .... }

// use of array references in cin and cout patterns
cin >> a[i];
```

```
cout << a[i];

// use of array references on left and right hand sides
// of an assignment
a[i] = 10;
x = a[i]
y = a[i] * a[j];

// calling a function, passing array components
// as actual arguments.
int sum_first_three(int, int, int);
     // function prototype
x = sum_first_three(a[0],a[1],a[2]);
     // function call
```

Each of these examples can be understood if one just reminds oneself that a valid reference to the array a is just a variable whose type is int.

Arrays as Function Arguments

Entire arrays can be passed as function arguments. Passing an array as an argument is not the same as passing an array component as an argument. We need to discuss:

1. how array arguments are declared in function prototypes,
2. how array arguments are defined in function definitions,
3. how arrays are passed as actual arguments.

A function prototype indicates that an argument is an array whose component type is *t* using the notation:

```
t[]
```

For example, here is the function prototype for an int function array_sum that computes the sum of a specified number of array components in an array of integers, starting with the first:

```
int array_sum(int[], int);
```

Here the first argument is an array of integers and the second argument is an int which specifies how many array components are to be included in the sum.

A function definition, unlike a function prototype, must provide names for its arguments. The syntax for indicating that the argument *arg* is an array whose component type is *t* is the following:

```
t arg[]
```

Here is the function declarator for the function array_sum whose prototype was given earlier:

```
int array_sum(int x[], int n) { .... }
```

Here is the complete definition for the function array_sum:

```
int array_sum(int x[], int n)
{

   // LOCAL DATA ...
   int sum = 0;
```

```
    // STATEMENTS ...
    for (int i = 0; i < n; i++)
    {
        sum += x[i];
    }
    return sum;
} // end array_sum
```

Note that the name of the array argument, x, is used within the body of the function as if it were an array that is defined locally. Thus, x[i] in the function body refers to the component of the actual argument array whose index is i, regardless of the name of the actual argument array.

In fact, all array arguments are pass by reference arguments. In the above example, when the function array_sum is called, the space allocated for the argument x will be sufficient to store the address of the actual argument array. For example, suppose the actual argument, say big_array, is an array of 1,000 integers. The memory allocated for the formal argument, x, will only be sufficient to store the address of big_array as opposed to a copy of big_array itself. Thus, x is a reference to that array and not a copy of the array. This is why we said that an array argument declared in this way is a pass by reference argument.

Syntactically, we pass an array as an actual argument by using the name of the array in the appropriate slot in the actual argument list. For example, suppose a is an array of integers, as defined earlier, and that asum is an int variable. Then we could call the function array_sum to compute the sum of a[0] through a[9], storing the result in asum, as follows:

```
    asum = array_sum(a, 10);
```

This illustrates an important point that we shall elaborate upon in greater detail in Chapter 2 of the text: when the name of an array is used by itself in an expression, the name is interpreted as the base address of the array. Thus, what we are actually passing to the function array_sum is the base address of the array a. This address is stored in the memory allocated for the formal argument, x.

Strings in C++

A string is an array whose component type is char. In an earlier example, we defined a string variable str as an array of char:

```
    char str[MAXSTRING];
```

Here MAXSTRING was a symbolic constant which gave the maximum length of the string. The value of MAXSTRING is 30 and thus the legal array references for str are str[0], str[1], ..., str[29].

Our usual intention is to use string variables (such as str) with one or more of the functions that are declared in the string.h header file. These functions require that the last character in a string be the special string terminator character, \0.[7] This is because C++, unlike Pascal, does not store the length of a string as a byte within the memory allocated for the string. For example, in Turbo Pascal, the declaration

       var PasStr: String[20];

causes 21 bytes of memory to be allocated, 20 bytes for the string itself and 1 byte to record the length of the string (in this case, that byte will always have a value between 0 and 20). The variable PasStr can store up to 20 characters.

In C++ if you want to define a string capable of storing 20 characters, you must define that string as an array of 21 characters, because you must allocate one byte for the string terminator character.

Some of the functions that are declared in the string.h header file are given in Table 0–11. In each case we give a brief description of what the function does.

TABLE 0–11   STRING FUNCTIONS FROM string.h

function call:	semantics:
strcpy(string1, string2)	copies string2 to string1
strcmp(string1, string2)	compares string1 and string2
strlen(string)	returns the length of a string
strchr(string, character)	used to search a string for a given character
strcat(string1, string2)	string1 = string1 concatenated with string2

Here are some important facts concerning the use of these functions:

1. You must use strcpy instead of the assignment sign to copy one string to another. Suppose s1 and s2 are string variables. A very common error is to attempt to use the incorrect

       s1 = s2;

   instead of the correct:

       strcpy(s1, s2);

2. The strcmp function returns 0 if string1 is equal to string2, a negative value if string1 comes before string2 in lexicographical order and a positive value if string1 comes after string2 in lexicographical order. Suppose s1 and s2 are strings. Then the following expression is true (1) if and only if s1 and s2 are identical:

       !strcmp(s1, s2)

3. The function strlen returns the length of a string *not including the string terminator character*. You might view strlen as counting the

7. Like the new line character, \n, the string terminator character is just a single character that is denoted using an escape sequence.

number of characters in a string before the string terminator character is encountered.

4. The `strchr` function actually returns a pointer to a character (i.e., the address of a character). For the time being we can view `strchr` as returning false (0, or the `NULL` pointer) if the string given as the first argument does not contain any occurrences of the character given as the second argument. If the character is found, this function returns a true value (i.e., non-zero); namely, the address in the string where that character is found.

5. In concatenating `string2` onto `string1`, the `strcat` function overwrites the string terminator character contained in `string1`. Care must be taken that enough space is allocated for `string1` to contain the concatenated strings, or else the system will overwrite information already stored after the end of `string1` in the computer's memory.

A String Type and Two String Functions

Many of the examples in chapters 0 – 2 of the text refer to a type `string` that is declared as follows:

```
const int MAXSTRING = 21;
const int LINESIZE  = 80;
typedef char string[MAXSTRING];
```

The `typedef` statement declares `string` as a user-defined type which is an array of `MAXSTRING` characters. Wherever this declaration is visible, the programmer can declare variables to be of type `string`.

A useful function, which appears in many examples in this text, is the `read_string` function which reads in a string from the keyboard. This function is used in `examp7.cxx` and is reproduced in the following extract:

Extract: the function `read_string`

```
// FUNCTION: read_string(char str[], int len)
// PURPOSE:Reads at most len characters from input stream
//     and stores them as str.  Extra characters are
//     ignored.  Inserts null character into str.
// INPUTS:
//     len  maximum number of chars to read into str
// OUTPUTS:
//     str  the string that was read in
void read_string(char str[], int len)
{
    cin.getline(str, len);
    if (cin.gcount() == len - 1)
    {
        cin.ignore(LINESIZE, '\n');
    }
}  // end read_string
```

Understanding this function requires that you understand that `cin` is an object. The `cin` object corresponds to the keyboard. Since we have not discussed objects formally as yet, we will just say that we can apply functions to objects. When we apply a function to an object, the object changes its state or performs some service for us. Thus, the application of a function to the `cin` object might cause the `cin` object to perform some input processing. If `obj` is an object and if `func` is a function with no arguments, then the syntax for applying `func` to `obj` is:

```
obj.func()
```

This expression is valid only if `func` is a function that can be applied to `obj` according to the rules of the language.

Suppose `str` is an array of characters (e.g., a variable of type `string`). Then, we can ask `cin` to read data into `str` by applying the `getline` function, as follows:

```
cin.getline(str, len);
```

The `getline` function, like the `cin` object, is provided by the `iostream.h` header file. This call to the `getline` function will read in up to `len - 1` characters into the array of characters, `str`, and it will place the string terminator character at the end of the string. We are responsible for assuring that the value of `len` is not too large (for otherwise, we will be reading in data outside of the bounds of the string). The `getline` function will read in characters until either `len - 1` characters have been read or the end of line character is encountered.

However, it is possible that the user has typed in more than `len - 1` characters. In that case, there are some unread characters still in the input character stream that must be ignored in order for us to go on to the next input line.   In other words, we need to tell the system to ignore any extraneous characters that the user might have typed. In order to determine how many characters were read in during the last application of `getline` to `cin`, we must apply the function `gcount` to `cin`. This will return a count of the number of characters that were read in by the previous application of `getline`. If the value returned by `gcount` is `len - 1`, then *there is at least one extraneous character that needs to be ignored*.[8] This is accomplished by applying the `ignore` function to the `cin` object. We assume that the maximum number of characters that might possibly need to be ignored is `LINESIZE` or 80.

Another string-oriented function provided in `examp7.cxx` is `upper_case`. This illustrates character by character processing of an array of characters. This function takes a string argument and converts all lower case letters to upper case using the `toupper` function.

---

8.   Do you see why? At the very least we have the one (on UNIX) or two (in DOS) characters that mark the end of the line. These must be ignored so that the input processing stream is set to the beginning of the next line.

Extract: the function `upper_case`

```
// FUNCTION: upper_case(char str[])
// PURPOSE:Converts all letters in string to upper case
// PRE:  str contains the string terminator character
// POST: str is the original string with all lower case
//      letters replaced by upper case
// INPUTS:
//    str   string to be capitalized
// OUTPUTS:
//    str   capitalized string
void upper_case(char str[])
{
    for (int i = 0; i < strlen(str); i++)
        str[i] = toupper(str[i]);
}   // end upper_case
```

Synopsis of Example #7

This program will display the names and total bill amounts for those customers whose bills are above average. Two arrays are used:
1.   cust_name, an array whose component type is string
2.   cust_amt, an array whose component type is float

The cust_name array is kept in correspondence with the cust_amt array, so that cust_name[i] is the name for the customer whose total bill amount is cust_amt[i].

The main function calls three functions:
1.   getall_order_data
2.   compute_average
3.   display_best_customers

The function getall_order_data is responsible for filling in the arrays cust_name and cust_amt with data and for determining the value of num_cust, an int variable that records the total number of customers. It reads in customer data in a sentinel loop and computes the total bill amount for each customer. When the user enters a customer name of "*", the loop terminates. The function compute_average then computes the average of the total bill amounts. The function display_best_customers displays the names and total bill amounts for all customers whose total bill amounts were greater than the average.

The function getall_order_data is pivotal and is extracted here for special attention:

Extract: function `getall_order_data`

```
// FUNCTION:  getall_order_data
// PURPOSE:   Get order data from user, filling in array cname
//         with customer names, camt with bill amounts and
//         determining ncust, the number of customers.
```

```
// PRE:        None
// POST:       ncust <= MAX_CUST; any attempt to read
//         in more data will fail
// OUTPUTS:
//    cname        array of customer names
//    camt         array of bill amounts
//    ncust        number of customers
void getall_order_data(string cname[],
          float camt[],
          int& ncust)
{
   // FUNCTION PROTOTYPES ...
   void read_order(string, int&, int&, int&, char&);
   customer_type convert_to_type(char);
   float compute_bill(int, int, int);
   float compute_discount(customer_type, float);


   // LOCAL DATA ...
   string cur_name;      // current order: name of customer
   int num_coffee;    //           number of coffees
   int num_donut;     //           number of donuts
   int num_muffin;    //           number of muffins
   char cust_code;    //           customer discount code
   customer_type cust_status; //  customer discount type
   float bill;           //  total bill (w/o discount)
   int ind = 0;          //  array index


   // Read in order data until SENTINEL is
   // entered for customer name
   do
   {
     if (ind > 0)
     cin.ignore(LINESIZE,'\n');
     read_order(cur_name, num_coffee, num_donut,
       num_muffin, cust_code);
       // get current order data
     if (!is_sentinel(cur_name))
     {
     if(ind < MAX_CUST)
     {
        // still room in array for another customer
        strcpy(cname[ind], cur_name);
        cust_status = convert_to_type(cust_code);
        bill = compute_bill(num_coffee, num_donut, num_muffin);
        bill -= compute_discount(cust_status, bill);
        camt[ind++] = bill;
     }
     else
     {
        // no more room; issue warning; terminate input
        cout << "\aOnly " << MAX_CUST
        << " customers can be processed\n"
        << "Last customer ignored\n";
        break;  // exit loop
     }  // end if-else
```

```
      }  // end if
   } while (!is_sentinel(cur_name));
   ncust = ind;
}  // end getall_order_data
```

This function uses a `do-while` statement to implement the sentinel loop. The first order of business within the `do-while` is to call the `read_order` function, which reads in order data for one customer (i.e., the customer name, numbers of coffees, muffins and donuts, and customer discount code). However, if the user enters the sentinel for the customer name, `read_order` will not request the rest of the order data, but will return with the value of `cur_name` equal to the sentinel value.   The function `getall_order_data` will use the `is_sentinel` function to check to see if `read_order` has returned the sentinel or is returning valid customer data.   If `is_sentinel` returns true, the loop will terminate. Otherwise, the function tests to see if there is room for more data in the arrays. If there is no more room (`ind  >= MAX_CUST`) the loop will terminate with an appropriate error message.

The code for `examp7.cxx` follows.

Example #7

```
// Program:    examp7.cxx
//
// Programmer name:  J. Q. Maxwell
// Date:     Feb 14, 1993
//
// Problem description:
//
// This program processes customer order data at the Generic
// College Coffee Shop and yields the names and total bill
// amounts for those customers whose bills are above the
// average.
//
// The Generic College Coffee Shop continues to sell coffee,
// muffins, donuts and offer the following discounts:
// faculty = 20%, students = 10%, seniors = 5%.  There is
// a 6% state tax. ee examp6.cxx for pricing details.
//


#include <iostream.h>
#include <iomanip.h>
#include <string.h>
#include <ctype.h>


// STRING TYPE, RELATED CONSTANTS AND FUNCTION PROTOTYPES
const int MAXSTRING = 21;       // thus, max strlen is 20
const int LINESIZE  = 80;       // maxium number of chars in
                                // input line
typedef char string[MAXSTRING];// string is now a type
```

```
void upper_case(char[]);          // useful function for upper
                                  // casing all chars in a string
void read_string(char[], int);    // reads in string with at most
                                  // int chars.



// OTHER GLOBAL CONSTANT DEFINITIONS AND TYPE DECLARATIONS ...
enum customer_type {faculty, student, senior, regular};
const int MAX_CUST = 25;
const char SENTINEL = '*';



// GLOBAL FUNCTION DEFINITIONS ...
int is_sentinel(string str)
   { return int(strchr(str, SENTINEL)); }
        // return TRUE  (1) if str CONTAINS the sentinel charater
        // return FALSE (0) otherwise
     // Note: compiler forced us to typecast strchr result
     // so that return value is an int and not a pointer.



// MAIN FUNCTION ...
void main()
{
   // FUNCTION PROTOTYPES ...
   void getall_order_data(string[], float[], int&);
   float compute_average(float[], int);
   void display_best_customers(string[], float[], int, float);


   // LOCAL DATA ...
   string cust_name[MAX_CUST]; // array of customer names
   float  cust_amt[MAX_CUST];  // array of customer order
                               // amounts
   int num_cust;               // number of customers
   float average_amt;          // average order amount


   // STATEMENTS ...
   getall_order_data(cust_name, cust_amt, num_cust);
   average_amt = compute_average(cust_amt, num_cust);
   display_best_customers(cust_name, cust_amt,
        num_cust, average_amt);
} // end main



// FUNCTION DEFINITIONS ...


>>>
>>> definition for getall_order_data goes here
>>> this function was presented earlier as an
>>> extract.
>>>
```

```cpp
// FUNCTION:   read_order
// PURPOSE:    Prompts user for and gets valid order data or
//             a sentinel value for customer name.
// PRE:        None
// POST:       ccode is returned as an upper case char
// OUTPUTS:
//    cname      customer name
//    ncof       number of coffees
//    ndon       number of donuts
//    nmuff      number of muffins
//    ccode      customer discount code
void read_order(string cname, int& ncof, int& ndon, int& nmuff,
char& ccode)
{
    // STATEMENTS ...
    cout << endl << endl;
    cout << "Enter customer name or " << SENTINEL << ": ";
    read_string(cname, MAXSTRING);
    upper_case(cname);
    if (!is_sentinel(cname))
    {
        // Get rest of customer data.
        cout << "Enter number of coffees: ";
        cin  >> ncof;
        cout << "Enter number of donuts:  ";
        cin  >> ndon;
        cout << "Enter number of muffins: ";
        cin  >> nmuff;
        cout << "Please one of the following discount codes: "
             << endl;
        cout << "          f - faculty" << endl
          << "           s - student" << endl
          << "           g - golden"  << endl
          << "           n - none"    << endl;
        cin  >> ccode;
        ccode = toupper(ccode);
    } // end if
}   // end read_order



>>>
>>> definition for convert_to_type goes here
>>> this was given earlier, in examp7.cxx
>>>



>>>
>>> definition for compute_bill goes here
>>> this was given earlier, in examp1.cxx
>>>



// FUNCTION:   compute_discount
// PURPOSE:    To compute the discount amount based upon the total
//             bill and customer type
// RETURNS:    The discount amount
// INPUTS:
```

```
//    ctype   customer type (faculty, student, senior, reg
//    bill    total bill   (including tax)
float compute_discount(customer_type ctype, float bill)
{
   // LOCAL DATA ...
   const float FAC_DISCR = 0.20,
           STU_DISCR = 0.10,
           SEN_DISCR = 0.05;
   float da;   // discount amount


   // STATEMENTS ...
   switch (ctype)
   {
     case faculty:
     da = FAC_DISCR * bill;
     break;
      case student:
     da = STU_DISCR * bill;
     break;
      case senior:
     da = SEN_DISCR * bill;
     break;
      case regular:
     da = 0.0;
      // no other possibilities
   }   // end switch
   return da;
}   // end compute_discount



// FUNCTION:  compute average
// PURPOSE:To compute the average of the bill amounts in the
//         array camt
// RETURNS:A float, the average bill amount
// INPUTS:
//    camt an array of bill amounts
//    ncustnumber of amounts in the array
float compute_average(float camt[], int ncust)
{
    // LOCAL DATA ...
    float sum = 0.0;


    // STATEMENTS ...
    for (int i = 0; i < ncust; i++)
     sum += camt[i];
    return sum / float(ncust);
} // end compute_average



// FUNCTION:  display_best_customers
// PURPOSE:Displays customer names and bill amounts for
//          orders that were above the average.
// INPUTS:
//    cnamean array of customer names
```

```
//     camt an array of bill amounts
//     ncustnumber of amounts in the array
//     ave_amt average of bill amounts in array camt
void display_best_customers(string cname[],
     float camt[],
     int ncust,
     float ave_amt)
{
     // STATEMENTS ...
     cout << endl << endl;
     cout << "Here is the data for the best customers: "
          << endl << endl;
     for (int i = 0; i < ncust; i++)
     {
     if (camt[i] > ave_amt)
     {
          cout << "Customer name: "
          << cname[i] << endl;
          cout << "Bill amount: $: "
          << setprecision(4) << camt[i] << endl;
          cout << endl;

     }
     }
}   // end display_best_customers


//
//STRING FUNCTIONS read_string AND upper_case
//


>>>
>>> definition for function read_string goes here
>>> this was presented earlier as an extract
>>>

>>>
>>> definition for function upper_case goes here
>>> this was presented earlier as an extract
>>>
```

LABORATORY EXERCISES

This section presents three laboratory exercises that relate to the material presented in this tutorial and in Chapter 0 of the text.

LABORATORY EXERCISE—CONGRESSIONAL PAC MONEY

This programming project is similar to the Searcher program presented in the text. In solving this problem, you should give clear specifications (pre- and postconditions) for each function that your problem solution requires.

The problem: Congressman Foghorn is running for re-election.   To help matters along, he has decided to sponsor the legislation of any person or organization that donates at least $10,000.00 to his campaign.   Congressman Foghorn has hired you to develop a program to keep track of donations.[9]   Your program will read contributor information, sort it into alphabetical order by contributor name, and process requests for information pertaining to particular contributors.   In addition, Congressman Foghorn will be able to get a complete and alphabetical listing of contributors at the computer screen.

Each contributor will be identified by the following information:

contributor name:	a string of up to 30 characters
contribution amount:	in dollars and cents
favorite legislation	a string of up to 75 characters

The program will run in three phases, as described below.

Part 1 — The data entry phase

During this phase, the user (normally a clerk in Foghorn's office) will enter contributor information from the keyboard. The user will be prompted for the contributor name (last name first), contribution amount, and favorite legislation as the following example suggests (user inputs are underlined):

---

9.   Since this is a "pretend" situation, you need not worry about the possible legal and ethical implications of working on this program.   In real life, you might want to avoid working for someone with the ethics of a Congressman Foghorn.

```
Please enter the requested information when prompted.
Enter names in the form last name, first name.
Enter an asterisk (*) in lieu of a name to end data entry.

Name:          Loman, Willy
Amount:        34000.00
Legislation:   Salesman Retirement Fund

Enter an asterisk (*) in lieu of a name to end data entry.

Name:          Seaver, Tom
Amount:        54000.00
Legislation:   Curveball Improvement Act

Enter an asterisk (*) in lieu of a name to end data entry.

Name:          Vanilli, Milli
Amount:        25.00

******** MESSAGE: DID NOT CONTRIBUTE ENOUGH
******** CONTRIBUTOR NOT ENTERED INTO DATABASE

Enter an asterisk (*) in lieu of a name to end data entry.

Name:          Schickele, Peter
Amount:        84000.00
Legislation:   Outrageous Music Preservation Act

Enter an asterisk (*) in lieu of a name to end data entry.

Name:          *
```

Here are some important facts about data entry:

1. The data will be entered in a sentinel loop with an asterisk as the sentinel value. Once an asterisk is entered, no more data entry occurs.
2. If a person contributes less than $10,000.00, the program catches this and does not permit a favorite legislation entry for that person. In addition, the data for that person is not stored in the arrays, where only "big-time" contributor data is kept. The user is informed that the data has not been stored in the database.
3. The data for big-time contributors (those who contribute more than $10,000.00) will be stored in three arrays: one for contributor names, one for campaign contributions, and one for favorite pieces of legislation.
4. You may assume that there are no more than 50 big-time contributors. You may also assume that no name occurs more than once in the input.

Part 2 — Sorting the contributor information

The contributor information will be sorted alphabetically by contributor name. You may use the bubblesort algorithm and you may assume no more than 50 contributors will be stored in the array.

Part 3 — Information retrieval

During this phase, the user will be able to find out the contribution amount and favorite legislation for individual contributors. The user will be prompted to enter a search key. If the user enters ALL, that will cause a complete listing of contributors and contribution amounts to occur. Again, an asterisk (*) will be used as a sentinel signal. An example of the interaction between the user and the program during this phase follows:

```
Please enter a search key when prompted.
Enter ALL to see all contributors and asterisk (*) to halt:

Search key:     Seaver, Tom

Amount:         54000.00
Legislation:    Curveball Improvement Act

Search key:     Pooh, Winnie T.

****** NOT LISTED AS BIG-TIME CONTRIBUTOR

Search key:     ALL

Loman, Willy       34000.00
Schickele, Peter   84000.00
Seaver, Tom        54000.00

Search key:     *

******    YOU ARE LEAVING THE FOGHORN
******    CONTRIBUTOR DATABASE PROGRAM
```

Worksheet for Laboratory Exercise —
Congressional PAC Money

```
/* -- Program name:
   -- Programmer:
   -- Date:
   -- ** Overview
           .
           .
           .
                    */

#include < ... >

// GLOBAL CONSTANTS AND TYPEDEF'S

// GLOBAL FUNCTION PROTOTYPES


main()
{
   // FUNCTION PROTOTYPES


   // LOCAL DATA


   // STATEMENTS




}
// Function:
// Purpose:
// Pre:
// Post:
return-type function-name1(formal arguments)
{



}// end function-name1

   .
   .
   .
```

LABORATORY EXERCISE—CALCULATI...

This project has two pu...
provide some practice with the ...
Chapter 0 of the text.

The text uses the example of ...
grades for a class of students. In ...
out some statistical analysis on a se...

The grades can be scores on one t...
Specifically, the input is a list of grade...
since only summaries are being produ...
tegers. A typical input dialogue would ...

```
Enter a list of grades, one per li
90
85
74
100
95
81
69
83
90
-1
```

Note the use of the negative input value as a sentinel to mark the end of the input.

The output consists of five descriptive statistics:

- mean—what we commonly call the "average"—the sum of the grades divided by their count;
- median—the "middle" grade—a value such that half the grades are above it, half below;
- mode—the grade that occurs the most often; in case of ties, all are modes;
- standard deviation—a measure of how spread out the grades are; the formula is given below;
- range—another measure of spread, found by subtracting the smallest score from the largest.

The output also consists of one of two optional displays—either a frequency table or a histogram. Thus for the given input data, the output dialogue could look like this:

```
Mean: 85.2
Median: 85Modes: 90
Standard deviation: 9.3
Range: 31
Do you want the frequency table (F) or histogram (H)?: F
    Score     Frequency
    69        1
    74        1
```

```
                  1
              1   1
                  2
       95     1
      100     1
```

Alternatively, if the histogram had been selected, it might look like this:

```
      60-69     *
      70-79     *
      80-89     ***
      90-100    ****
```

Part 1 — Decompose the Problem

Begin to solve this problem by applying the concept of top-down design. Draw a structure chart for your solution. When you are done, arrange with another student in the lab to conduct a "structured walk-through" on each other's design. If you are unfamiliar with the concept of structured walk-throughs, read the discussion in Chapter 8 of the main text. After the walk-through, make whatever corrections need to be made in your design.

Part 2 — Develop the Specifications

Using the guidelines given in Chapter 0 of the main text, develop input and output specifications for each of the functions in your design. When you are done, walk through your specifications with another student.

Part 3 — Develop the Program

Now begin to write the program. The best way is to use the "code a little, test a little" principle. That is, rather than writing your entire program then testing it all at once, test after each function. There are two ways to do this: top-down or bottom-up. In top-down development, you code the main function first, then add the other functions one at a time, working down the structure chart. In bottom-up testing, you start at the bottom of the structure chart, write those functions first, test them and work up. Since bottom-up development requires writing drivers for each function, we recommend that you use the top-down approach. Thus you would start by writing your main function and "stubs" for each function that gets called in turn. For instance, suppose the body of your main function looks like this:

```
main()
{
    // FUNCTION PROTOTYPES ...
    void a(float, float, float);
    void b(int, int, int, int, int);
    void c(string);
    void d();
```

```
    // LOCAL DATA ...
    float x, y, z;
    int l, m, n, o, p;

    // STATEMENTS ...
    a(x,y,z);
    b(l,m,n,o,p);
    c("what_me_worry");
    d();
}
```

A stub for the function a might look like this:

```
void a(float x, float y, float x)
{
    cout << "We made it to function a!" << endl;
}    // stub a
```

Stubs for b, c and d would be coded similarly. Thus running the main function the first time tests two things: whether or not the function interfaces are correct and whether the functions are invoked in the proper sequence.

Once your main function is successfully developed and tested, begin to add the additional, completed functions one at a time. Its usually best to code output first, then input, and finally processing. This is because once you have the output function working (passing it some dummy data), you have a way to display the results of the input and processing functions when testing them.

Here are a few hints for calculating the statistics.
- The easiest way to create the frequency table is to use an array with dimension 101 (i.e., an array with indices 0 through 100). Initialize this array to zeroes. To process, say, a grade of 90, increment the value stored in location 90 by 1. Continue in this fashion.
- Once you have the frequency table, the rest of the statistics are easy to find. Suppose the number, n, of grades is odd. If the list of grades were sorted, the median would be found in location $\frac{(n + 1)}{2}$; the data in this location can be found without sorting; however, use a loop which sums the values in the frequency table from one end or the other until $\frac{(n + 1)}{2}$ is reached.   If n is even, the median is the value midway between the value in location $\frac{(n + 1)}{2}$ and the value in location $\frac{n}{2}$ in the sorted list. Once again this can be found from the frequency table without sorting. Likewise the mode can be read directly from the frequency table.
- The formula for the standard deviation is:

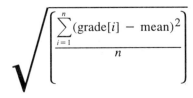

$$\sqrt{\left[\frac{\sum_{i=1}^{n}(\text{grade}[i] - \text{mean})^2}{n}\right]}$$

Questions

1. Indicate how the structure chart was helpful to you in the design phase of this project.
2. Did the walk-throughs catch any design or specification errors for you? If so, what would the consequences of not catching those errors have been? How much longer would it have taken you to find them without conducting the walk-through? If no errors were caught, answer the previous question imagining you had errors.
3. Did the "code a little, test a little" principle described here work for you? How might the process of testing and debugging have been more difficult without it?

Worksheet for Laboratory Exercise —
Calculating Descriptive Statistics

```
/* -- Program name:
   -- Programmer:
   -- Date:
   -- ** Overview
          .
          .                                    */

#include < ... >

// GLOBAL CONSTANTS AND TYPEDEF'S

// GLOBAL FUNCTION PROTOTYPES


main()
{
   // FUNCTION PROTOTYPES

   // LOCAL DATA

   // STATEMENTS




}
// Function:
// Purpose:
// Pre:
// Post:
return-type function-name1(formal arguments)
{


}// end function-name1

   .
   .
   .
```

Notes for Answers to Questions

1.

2.

3.

LABORATORY EXERCISE—THE GRADEBOOK PROBLEM

Given a list of student names, with three test scores for each name, develop a program that computes and displays the average of these scores for each student. A sample of typical input and output for one run of this program is shown below.

Name	score1	score2	score3	Average
Backus	75	85	95	85.0
Wirth	85	85	85	85.0
Turing	90	85	80	85.0
Gries	86	84	85	85.0
von Neumann	91	82	82	85.0
McCarthy	70	85	100	85.0
Lovelace	55	100	100	85.0
Church	80	80	95	85.0
Markov	90	90	75	85.0
Hopper	70	90	95	85.0
Naur	84	84	87	85.0

Here, the input appears in the first four columns and the output appears in the last column. An interactive program for this problem should provide suitable prompts and headings so that the input is entered correctly and the output is well-documented.

Part 1 — Write the Specifications

Write pre- and postconditions that describe the set of all possible inputs and corresponding outputs for this program.

Part 2 — Develop the Program

Write a complete C++ program that solves this problem.

Part 3 — Run the Program

Run the program using the above sample input, and be sure that it gives the correct output. Rerun the program with other alternative inputs.

Questions

1. How would your program be affected if either the size of the input set or the number of tests per student were unknown? That is, the set might contain scores for 11 students or it might contain scores for 1100 students. It might contain 3 test scores per student or it might contain 13.

2. Suppose that the program had to account for the possibility of one or more missing scores for any student, and we used the convention that a dash 9–0 means "grade missing." How would your specifications and your program be modified to accommodate this variation?

Worksheet for Laboratory Exercise —
The Gradebook Problem

```
/* -- Program name:
   -- Programmer:
   -- Date:
   -- ** Overview
          .
          .
          .
                   */

#include < ... >

// GLOBAL CONSTANTS AND TYPEDEF'S

// GLOBAL FUNCTION PROTOTYPES


main()
{
    //FUNCTION PROTOTYPES

    //LOCAL DATA

    //STATEMENTS




}
//Function:
//Purpose:
//Pre:
//Post:
return-type function-name1(formal arguments)
{


}// end function-name1

    .
    .
    .
```

Notes for Answers to Questions

1.

2.

The searcher Program
C++ Code Listing

```
/* -- Program name: Searcher


   -- Programmer:    Student programmer
   -- Date:          June 1, 1993


   -- ** Overview
   -- This program allows the user to enter student data for
   -- all students in a class.  It then allows the user to
   -- access each student's final average.


   -- The program begins by presenting the user with
   -- instructions.


   -- It then asks the user to enter the number of students in
   -- the class (an integer).


   -- It then asks the user to enter the grade data for that
   -- many students.  For each student, the following data is
   -- entered:


   --   STUDENT NAME          (a string)
   --     FIRST HOURLY SCORE  (a float)
   --     SECOND HOURLY SCORE (a float)
   --     FINAL EXAM SCORE    (a float)


   -- The program uses this information to compute a final
   -- average for each student.  The student's name and final
   -- average are then stored in parallel arrays.


   -- Once all of the student data for the class has been
   -- entered, the data in the parallel arrays is sorted
   -- alphabetically by student name.


   -- Finally, the program enters a "process requests" phase
   -- that allows the user to enter student names in a loop.
```

```
        -- For each student name entered, the program will either
        -- display that student's final average or, if no such
        -- student is contained in the name array, the program
        -- will display an appropriate error message.


        -- The user can terminate this process by entering an
        -- asterisk (*) in lieu of a student name.


        -- ** Warnings
        -- This program does virtually no integrity checks on the
        -- input data.  Any character other than Y will be treated
        -- as an N.  Exam scores are not checked for being
        -- in range (say 0 to 100).                 */


#include <iostream.h>
#include <string.h>


// GLOBAL CONSTANTS AND TYPEDEF'S ...
const int MAXCLASS = 50;    // maximum number of students in class
const int MAXSTRING = 20;   // maximum student name length
const int LINESIZE  = 80;   // maximum length of input line
typedef char string[MAXSTRING];


// GLOBAL FUNCTION PROTOTYPE ...
void read_string(char*, int);


void main()
{
    // FUNCTION PROTOTYPES ...
    void give_instructions();
    void get_class_data(string[], float[], int&);
    void sort_by_name(string[], float[], int);
    void process_requests(string[], float[], int);


    // LOCAL DATA ...
    string stu_names[MAXCLASS];      // list of student names
    float stu_averages[MAXCLASS];    // list of student averages
    int class_size;


    // STATEMENTS ...
    give_instructions();
    get_class_data(stu_names, stu_averages, class_size);
    sort_by_name(stu_names, stu_averages, class_size);
    process_requests(stu_names, stu_averages, class_size);
}


// Function: give_instructions
// Purpose:  Gives the user instructions
```

```cpp
// Pre:        output = empty
// Post:       output contains instructions for program use
void give_instructions()
{
   cout << "This program will ask you to enter student data\n";
   cout << "It will then sort the student names and final\n";
   cout << "averages alphabetically by name.  Then, it will\n";
   cout << "allow you to request computed averages for \
           particular\n";
   cout << "students." << endl << endl << endl;
   cout << "Press any key, then enter to continue: ";
   cin.get();
   cin.ignore(LINESIZE, '\n');
   cout << endl;
} // end give_instructions()


// Function: get_class_data
// Purpose:  Gets the student names and averages for
//           students in a class.
// Pre:      input = N (N repetitions of:
//               aName FHScore SHScore FScore)
// Post:     class_size = N
//               and for all i in [1..class_size] :
//                        stu_names[i-1] = i-th aName
//               and for all i in [1..class_size] :
//                  stu_averages[i-1] =
//                  weighted average determined by
//                  (i-th FHScore i-th SHScore i-th FScore)
void get_class_data(string stu_names[], float stu_averages[],
int& class_size)
{
   // FUNCTION PROTOTYPES ...
   void get_student_data(char*, float&, float&, float&);
   float compute_average(float, float, float);


   // LOCAL DATA ...
   string  student_name;
   float   first_hourly, second_hourly, final_exam;


   // STATEMENTS ...
   cout << "How many students are in the class? ";
   cin  >> class_size;
   cin.ignore(LINESIZE, '\n');    // go to beginning of next line


   for (int i = 0; i < class_size; i++)
   {
     get_student_data(student_name, first_hourly, second_hourly,
      final_exam);
     stu_averages[i] = compute_average(first_hourly,
         second_hourly, final_exam);
     strcpy(stu_names[i], student_name);
   }
} // end get_class_data
```

```
// Function: get_student_data
// Purpose:  Prompts the user for and gets all data for one
//           student.
// Pre:      input = aName FHScore SHScore restOfData
// Post:     input = restOfData and student_name = aName
//               and first_hourly = FHScore
//               and second_hourly = SHScore
//               and final_exam = FScore


void get_student_data(char* student_name, float& first_hourly,
    float& second_hourly, float& final_exam)
{
   // STATEMENTS ...
   cout << "Please enter the student's name: ";
   read_string(student_name, MAXSTRING);
   cout << "Please enter an exam score when prompted:\n";
   cout << "First hourly score: ";
   cin  >> first_hourly;
   cout << "Second hourly score: ";
   cin  >> second_hourly;
   cout << "Final exam score: ";
   cin  >> final_exam;
   cin.ignore(LINESIZE, '\n');    // next input on new line
   cout << endl << endl;
} // end get_student_data


// Function: compute_average
// Purpose:  Returns a student's final average
// Pre:      first_hourly, second_hourly and final_exam
//           are defined
// Post:     compute_average = maximum of ((0.25 * (first_hourly
//                      + second_hourly)
//                      + 0.50 * final_exam), 0)
float compute_average(float first_hourly, float second_hourly,
         float final_exam)
{
   // LOCAL DATA ...
   const float WEIGHT1 = 0.25,
           WEIGHT2 = 0.25,
           WEIGHTF = 0.50;
   float tent_average;   // tentative average


   // statements
   tent_average = WEIGHT1 * first_hourly
     + WEIGHT2 * second_hourly
     + WEIGHTF * final_exam;
   if (tent_average < 0.0) tent_average = 0.0;
   return (tent_average);
} // end compute_average


// Function: sort_by_name
// Purpose:  Bubblesorts the array stu_names alphabetically,
```

```
//                   keeping the array stu_averages in the proper
//                   correspondence
// Notation:         old(a) --> b will mean that the memory cell a was
//                   mapped to the memory cell b in a permutation.
// Pre:              class_size >= 0 and
//                   for all i in [1..class_size] :
//                   stu_names[i-1], stu_averages[i-1] are defined
// Post:             stu_names is a permutation of old(stu_names) and
//                   stu_averages is a permutation of
//                   old(stu_averages) and
//                   for all i, j in [1..class_size-1] :
//                   (if old(stu_names[i-1]) --> stu_names[j-1]  then
//                   old(stu_averages[i-1]) --> stu_averages[j-1])
//                   and
//                   for all i in [1..class_size - 1] :
//                      stunames[i-1] < stunames[i]
void sort_by_name(string stu_names[], float stu_averages[], int
class_size)
{
   // LOCAL DATA ...
   enum {false, true} done = false;
   string tname;
   float tfloat;
   int limit = class_size - 1;



   // STATEMENTS ...
   // outer loop
   for (int pass = 1; !done && (pass <= limit); pass++)
   {
      done = true;
      // inner loop
      for (int i = 0; i < (class_size - pass); i++)
      {
      if (strcmp(stu_names[i], stu_names[i+1]) > 0)
      {
         strcpy(tname, stu_names[i]);
         strcpy(stu_names[i], stu_names[i+1]);
         strcpy(stu_names[i+1], tname);
         tfloat = stu_averages[i];
         stu_averages[i]   = stu_averages[i+1];
         stu_averages[i+1] = tfloat;
         done = false;
      }
      } // inner loop
   } // outer loop
} // end sort_by_name



// Function: process_requests
// Purpose:  Processes user requests for student final averages.
// Pre:      input = (repetitions of aName) '*'
//               and output = oldStuff
// Post:     searchkey = '*' and input = empty
//             oldstuff = oldstuff \n
//                (repetitions of : student grade report
//                    for i-th aName)
```

```cpp
void process_requests(string stu_names[], float stu_averages[],
     int class_size)
{
   // FUNCTION PROTOTYPE ...
   int search(string, string[], int);



   // LOCAL DATA ...
   const int SENTINEL = '*';
   string search_key;
   int location;



   // STATEMENTS ...
   cout << endl << "Begin searching phase ... " << endl;
   cout << "Please enter a student's name or *: ";
   read_string(search_key, MAXSTRING);
   while (search_key[0] != SENTINEL)
   {
      location = search(search_key, stu_names, class_size);
      if (location != -1)
      cout << "This student's average is "
           << stu_averages[location] << endl;
      else
      cout << "No student in this class has that name.\n";
       cout << "Please enter a student's name or *: ";
       read_string(search_key, MAXSTRING);
   }
   // hang up program
   cout << "Press any key to exit: ";
   cin.get();
} // end process_requests


// Function: search()
// Purpose:  Performs a linear search on the array stu_names
//           using the key search_key.  Returns location of found
//           element in the array stu_names or -1 if the search
//           fails.
// Pre:      class_size >= 0 and search_key is defined and
//            stu_names is sorted in ascending order
// Post:     ((there exists i in [1..class_size) :
//                search_key = stu_names[i-1] ^ search_key = i)
//           or
//           ((for all i in [1..class_size) :
//                search_key != stu_names[i-1] ^ search_key = -1)
int search(string search_key, string stu_names[], int class_size)
{
   // LOCAL DATA ...
   int index = 0;
   enum {found, not_found_yet} status = not_found_yet;


   // statements
   while ((status == not_found_yet) && (index < class_size))
   {
```

```
            if (!strcmp(stu_names[index], search_key))
            {
        status = found;
            }
            else
            {
        index++;
            }
      } // while


      if (status == found)
         return(index);
      else
         return(-1);
} // end search



// Function:    read_string
// Purpose:     To read an input string from the keyboard.  This
//              function will truncate excess characters so that
//              the input stream position will be at the beginning
//              of the next line
// Define:      M = MAXSTRING
// Pre:         input = c1 c2 .... cN \n restOfInput, where
//              each cj is a character and N >= 0
// Post:        input = restOfInput and
//                  ((N > M ^ str = c1 c2 .... cM) or
//                   (N < M ^ str = c1 c2 .... cN))


void read_string(char* str, int len)
{
   cin.getline(str, len);
   if (cin.gcount() ==  len - 1)
   {
      cin.ignore(LINESIZE, '\n');
   }
}  // end read_string
```

SOFTWARE DEVELOPMENT
WITH OBJECTS

This chapter presents the syntax and semantics of all C++ language features that are introduced in Chapter 1 of the text. These features include classes, data members and member functions, constructors and destructors, objects and the application of functions to objects. In addition, we introduce structures and their use. Most of our examples are "extracts" from the `Student` and `Section` classes that are discussed in the main text. You will find the source code for these classes and the `ObjSearcher` program in an appendix at the end of this manual.

`class` DECLARATIONS

A `class` declaration declares a type. A variable whose type is a class is called an object. A class may *inherit* properties of one or more base classes. We shall not discuss inheritance until Chapter 2. Here is a syntax specification for declaring a class that does not inherit properties from any other class:

Syntax: a simple `class` declaration[1]

```
class class-name
{
   private:
      // DATA MEMBERS ...
      data member declarations

   public:
      // MEMBER FUNCTIONS ...
      member function declarations
};  // end class-name
```

---

1. For those readers who skipped Chapter 0, in presenting a syntax specification we use normal type to indicate key words and information that is invariant and italics to indicate information that the programmer must provide.

The above syntax specification shows the declaration of a class, *class-name* that contains some *private data members* and some *public member functions*.

Syntactically, a data member declaration has the same form as a variable definition. A member function declaration has the same form as a function prototype.

The declaration for the Student class is shown in Figure 1–1 below.

Extract: declaration for the class Student

```
class Student
{
    private:
        // data members
        string student_name;
        float   first_hourly, second_hourly,
         final_exam, average;


    public:
        // member functions
        // constructor - destructor
        Student();
        ~Student();


        // access
        char* get_name();


        // modify
        void set_name(string);
        void read_in();
        void compute_average();


        // display
        void display_average();
}; // Student class
```

FIGURE 1–1 C++ declaration for the Student class.

The Student class contains five data members: student_name, first_hourly, second_hourly, final_exam, and average. Note that the data members are private and that their declarations take the same form (syntactically) as variable definitions.

The privacy of the Student class data members implies that these data members are only visible within the definition of Student class member functions. A function that is not a Student class member function is not permitted to access these data members directly.

The above declaration for Student indicates that it has seven public member functions. These include the constructor Student and the destructor

~Student. In addition, we have the function `get_name` that is used to access the name of a `Student`, the functions `set_name`, `read_in` and compute_average that modify `Student` data members in various ways and the function `display_average` that will display information about a `Student`. Member function declarations are actually function prototypes and the syntactic rules for declaring a member function are the same as for providing a function prototype. For convenience, we group member functions into "categories" that reflect their use. The category names appear as comments in the class declaration. In the case of the `Student class` declaration we have the following member function categories:

1. constructor – destructor
2. access
3. modify
4. display

The fact that the member functions are public has the following significance. In any source code file in which a `Student` object is defined, the member functions can be applied to that `Student` object. We shall have more to say about how functions are applied to objects a little later.

`class` declarations are usually provided in a separate file, called a header file. An implementation file where a variable that belongs to a given class is defined should include the header file that provides the declaration for that class. For example, the `Student class` declaration shown above is contained in the `student.h` header file. A program that needs to declare `Student` objects should include the `student.h` header file using the `#include` preprocessor directive.

DEFINING AND USING OBJECTS

The example of Figure 1–2 shows a small program that defines a `Student` object and applies functions to it.

```
#include "student.h"

main()
{
    // LOCAL DATA ...
    Student stu;

    // STATEMENTS ...
    stu.read_in();
    stu.compute_average();
    stu.display_average();
}   // end main
```

FIGURE 1–2   A simple program using an object.

The `Student` class member function definitions are provided in a file called student.cxx.[2] The presence of that file is not reflected in the above main program file. The main program file only needs to include the `student.h` header file that contains the declaration for the `Student` class. This header file provides sufficient information for this main program file to compile as an autonomous unit. For example, the header file tells the compiler how much space needs to be allocated for a `Student` object and it also allows the compiler to check that all of the function calls (actually, function applications to the `Student` object) are constructed in the correct manner.[3]

Note that the #include preprocessor directive in the above program took the form:

```
#include "student.h"
```

and not the form:

```
#include <student.h>
```

This is because the `student.h` file is not part of the standard collection of header files that is provided with the C++ compiler. The quotes as opposed to the brackets tell the compiler to look for the `student.h` file in the current working directory.

The program of Figure 1–2 illustrates how objects are defined and used in a program. We define an object as follows:

Syntax: defining an object

```
class-name object-name;
```

At first glance this looks like an ordinary variable definition and it is to the extent that this definition causes the system to allocate space for an object whose type is *class-name* and whose name is *object-name*. The space allocated for *object-name* includes space for all of its data members. *However, a major difference between an ordinary variable definition and an object definition is that the latter causes the automatic application of a constructor to the object that is defined.* For example, the definition

```
Student stu;
```

not only causes space to be allocated for the `Student` object whose name is `stu`, it also causes the `Student` class constructor, called `Student`, to be applied to that object. A constructor is just a function that is automatically applied when an object is created. In many simple programs, a constructor either does nothing at all, or it will initialize some data members.

---

2. The suffix `.cxx` is used in the UNIX environment. In Turbo C++, the proper suffix is `.cpp`.

3. This form of program organization is termed a "project" in Turbo C++ and Symantec C++. The UNIX environment allows one to provide multiple files when calling the G++ compiler. More sophisticated project management capabilities are provided by the UNIX `make` utility.

Another distinction between an ordinary variable and an object is the following: when the system leaves the scope of an object's definition, the destructor for that object's class is automatically applied to that object. In the case of the object `stu` in the example of Figure 1–2, we leave the scope of that object's definition when we leave the function `main`. At this point, the `Student` class destructor, called `~Student`, is applied to the object. In many simple programs, a destructor does nothing interesting. However, when we learn about dynamic memory allocation, the significance of destructors will become evident.

Usually, the application of a constructor or of a destructor to an object is automatic. However, other functions must be applied explicitly, using the following syntax:

Syntax: applying a function to an object

```
object-name. function-name(actual-arg-list)
```

Suppose `object-name` belongs to the class `class-name`. Suppose further that we are not within the definition of a member function for the class `class-name`. Then, in order for the above function application to be correct, `function-name` must be a `public` member function of the class `class-name`. The specification public appears in the function declaration as shown in Figure 1–1. Since C++ uses function overloading, the actual identity of a function in a function call is determined by its name *and* its list of argument types.

In the above syntax specification, `function-name(actual-arg-list)` is called a *message* and `object-name` is called the *receiver* of that message.

Three functions are explicitly applied to the object `stu` in the simple program example of Figure 1–2. These function applications occur in the following statements:

```
stu.read_in();
stu.compute_average();
stu.display_average();
```

These statements apply the functions `read_in`, `compute_average` and `display_average` (in turn) to the object, `stu`. The function `read_in` prompts the user for and gets data for the object, `stu`. The function `compute_average` computes the value of `average`, a private `Student` class data member. Finally, the `display_average` function displays the value of the `average` data member. Note that no arguments are passed in these function calls.

Syntactically,

```
object-name. function-name(actual-arg-list)
```

is an expression. The type of this expression is the return type of function-name.

MEMBER FUNCTION DEFINITIONS

We shall now discuss member function definitions. Member function definitions (also called implementations) are normally provided in a .cxx file that is part of a project.[4]   For example, the declaration for the `Student` class is provided in the file `student.h`, but the definitions for the `Student` class member functions are provided in the file `student.cxx`.

Constructors

A constructor is a special kind of function that is automatically applied to an object when the object is created.   The syntax for defining a constructor is straightforward.

Syntax: definition of a constructor

```
class-name::class-name(formal-arg-list)
{
    statements
}
```

The name of a constructor is the name of its class.   Note the use of scope resolution

```
    class-name::
```

in order to indicate that the function being defined is a member of the indicated class.   The operator :: is called the *scope resolution operator*. The constructor without any arguments is called the default constructor. Such a constructor must be declared and defined for a class *class-name* if:

1. The class *class-name* has at least one constructor that has one or more arguments, and
2. The class *class-name* is going to be used to define array variables whose component type is *class-name*.

The form of an object definition determines which constructor is applied when several are available. For example, suppose a class `CL` has two constructors as indicated in the following class declaration sketch:

```
class CL
{
    private:
        ....

    public:
        CL();    // constructor without arguments
        CL(float, float);
                 // constructor with two float arguments
        ....
};  // end CL
```

---

4.   Turbo C++ uses `.cpp` for this kind of file.

The definition

```
CL obj1, obj2(0.0, -1.0);
```

will cause the CL constructor that has no arguments to be applied to obj1 and the CL constructor that has two float arguments to be applied to obj2. Note again that an object definition always involves the application of a constructor to the object being defined.

The following extract presents the definition of the unique Student class constructor:

Extract: **Student class** constructor

```
// Constructor:  Student()
// Purpose:      To initialize the receiver object
// Pre:          None
// Post:         Initializes the receiver object with
//               student_name = " "
Student::Student()
{
   strcpy(student_name, " ");
} // end Student::Student()
```

This constructor initializes the value of student_name to the empty string and does not initialize the other Student data members. *Note that we are not initializing* student_name *for the entire class, but for the particular* Student *object to which this constructor is being applied at a given point in time.* For example, the definition

```
Student stu;
```

causes the above constructor to be applied to the object called stu and this will cause the data member called student_name contained within that object to be initialized to the empty string.

Destructors

A class is only permitted to have one destructor and that destructor is not permitted to have any arguments. Here is a syntax specification for defining a destructor:

Syntax: definition of a destructor

```
class-name::~class-name()
{
    statements
}
```

The name of a destructor for a class is ~ followed by the name of the class. Note the use of scope resolution in the destructor header.

The following extract shows the Student class destructor, ~Student:

Extract: Student class destructor

```
// Destructor:  ~Student()
// Purpose:     Destroys the receiver object
// Pre:         The receiver object is initialized
// Post:        The receiver object is destroyed
Student::~Student()
{
    ;   // no dynamic storage to be deallocated
} // end Student::~Student()
```

This destructor does nothing very interesting. The system will create default constructors and destructors if you do not declare and define them explicitly, but including explicit constructors and destructors makes class declarations more clean and more clear.

Other Member Function Definitions

Here is the syntax specification for defining a member function:

Syntax: member function definition

```
return-type class-name::function-name(formal-arg-list)
{
    // LOCAL DATA ...
    local data definitions

    // STATEMENTS ...
    executable code
}
```

The above construct defines a member function *function-name* that was declared in the declaration for the class *class-name*. An error will occur if this function has not already been identified as a member function in the class declaration. Note the use of scope resolution in order to inform the compiler that this definition is for the particular function called *function-name* that is a member of the class *class-name*.

A member function is (when all is said and done) just a function. Thus, the rules for specifying the return type and the formal arguments are the same as for ordinary functions. Arguments may be declared as pass by value or pass by reference. A member function can contain local data definitions. The most important difference between the implementation of a member function versus an ordinary function is that a member function can refer to all of the private members of the class to which it belongs. In practice, when a member function is applied to an object, the member function thus has access to all of the private data members of that object.

This point can be illustrated by considering the definitions for the Student class member functions set_name and compute_average. Here is the definition for Student::set_name:

Extract: definition for `Student::set_name`

```
// Function: Student::set_name()
// Purpose:  Sets the receiver object's name to aName
// Pre:      The receiver is intialized and aName = aString
// Post:     student_name = aString
void Student::set_name(string aName)
{
   strcpy(student_name, aName);
} // end Student::set_name()
```

Note that this is a void function. A `string` argument, `aName`, is being passed into the function. The value of `aName` is being copied into a `string` called `student_name`. Where is `student_name` located? The variable `student_name` refers to the `student_name` data member of the `Student` class object that this function is being applied to in a particular call to this function. For example, if we have:

```
Student stu;
stu.set_name("Doe, Jane");
```

then `student_name` in the function definition refers to the `student_name` data member within the object `stu`.

The variables `first_hourly`, `second_hourly`, and `final_exam` in the definition for `Student::compute_average` are data members of the `Student` object to which the function is being applied in a particular function call:

Extract: definition for `Student::compute_average`

```
// Function: Student::compute_average()
// Purpose:  To compute the receiver's average based upon
//           the exam scores and exam weights
// Pre:      first_hourly, seond_hourly, and final_exam
//           are defined
// Post:     average = WEIGHT1 * first_hourly + WEIGHT2 * second_hourly
//               + WEIGHTF * final_exam
void Student::compute_average()
{
   // LOCAL DATA ...
   const float WEIGHT1 = 0.25,
           WEIGHT2 = 0.25,
           WEIGHTF = 0.50;


   // STATEMENTS ...
   average = WEIGHT1 * first_hourly
     + WEIGHT2 * second_hourly
     + WEIGHTF * final_exam;
} // Student::compute_average()
```

THE VARIABLE `this`

It is sometimes necessary to refer to the receiver object explicitly in a member function. At other times, an explicit reference to the receiver object can make code easier to read. The variable `this` is the implicit first argument of every member function. The variable `this` only makes sense in the context of a member function. It contains the address of the receiver object and is thus a pointer to the receiver object. (We shall discuss pointers in detail in Chapter 2 of the text and in Chapter 2 of this manual.) In order to use the variable `this`, we must dereference it, as explained below.

Suppose `dmember` is a data member of a class `CL`. Then, any member function of `CL` can refer to `dmember` as:

```
dmember
```

or as

```
this -> dmember
```

In the first case, we just have the ordinary reference to a data member such as we have seen in previous examples. In the latter case, we are referencing `dmember` by specifically dereferencing the variable `this`, which is a pointer to the receiver object. The pattern

```
this -> dmember
```

can be read as "the data member `dmember` of the object that `this` points to." Since `this` is always used in a member function, `this` is always a pointer to the object to which the member function is being applied. Thus, the above pattern can also be read as "the data member `dmember` of the object to which *this* function is being applied." However, this explanation having been given, we do not recommend that you use the variable `this` in this manner.

Suppose `memfunc` is a member function of a class `CL`. Let us assume that `memfunc` has no arguments. It does not matter whether `memfunc` is `private`, `protected`[5] or `public`. Within the definition of any member function of the class `CL`, we can apply `memfunc` to the receiver object using the notation

```
memfunc()
```

or the notation

```
this -> memfunc()
```

This pattern can be read as follows: "Apply the function `memfunc` to the object that the function that we are defining is being applied to."

Some people argue that the variable `this` should only be used when necessary, but we feel that it can make the code easier to read. Consider the function `Section::read_in` which is reproduced in the following extract. The use of the variable `this` is shown in **boldface** for emphasis.

Extract: definition of `Section::read_in`

```
// Function:  Section::read_in()
// Purpose:   To read in all of the data for the
//            receiver section.
// Define:    inputPattern = aName FHScore SHScore FScore
// Define:    the notation c[i].Student::read_in()
//            means that the function read_in()
//            has been applied to the Student c[i].
//            This implies that the post condition for
```

5. Protected members become important when we discuss inheritance in the next chapter.

```
//                   Student::read_in() applies.
// Pre:        The receiver is initialized class_size = 0 and
//                input = N (N repetitions of: inputPattern)
//                and N <= MAXCLASS
// Post:       class_size = N and N <= MAXCLASS and
//                 for all i in [1..class_size] :
//                        c[i-1].Student::read_in()
void Section::read_in()
{
    // LOCAL DATA ...
    Student astudent;
    int num;



    // STATEMENTS ...
    cout << "How many students are in the class? ";
    cin  >> num;
    for (int i = 0; i < num; i++)
    {
        cin.ignore(LINESIZE, '\n');// go to beginning of next line
        astudent.read_in();
        this -> add_student(astudent);  // increments class_size
    }
} // Section::read_in()
```

The explicit use of the variable `this` in `Section::read_in` is intended to make it easier for the human reader to see that the function that is being called is `Section::add_student` and not some stand-alone version of `add_student`. Furthermore, the use of the variable `this` makes it clear that `Section::add_student` is being applied to the receiver object.

There are cases in which the use of the variable `this` is not optional. A typical case would be a member function of a class `CL` whose return type is `CL`. For example, the definition of such a function might look as follows:

```
CL CL::memfunc()
{
    ....
    return *this;
}   // end CL::memfunc
```

The first `CL` in the function header is the return type, which is the same type as the class to which this function belongs. That is, this function returns a `CL` object. The second `CL` in the function header is used for scope resolution. This second `CL` identifies this as the definition for the function `memfunc` that is a member of the class `CL`. It is not uncommon for a function like this to return an updated version of the receiver object. That is accomplished by means of the statement:

```
        return *this;
```

The notation `*this` can be read as "the object to which the variable `this` points." Thus, in this case, we are returning the receiver object as the value of the function.

ARRAYS OF OBJECTS

In defining an array of objects, one must be aware of how constructors and destructors are applied. Otherwise, arrays of objects pose no special problems. Suppose CL is a class and a function f defines an array of CL objects as follows:

```
void f()
{
    // LOCAL DATA ...
    CL arr[10];
    ....
}  // end f
```

The definition for arr in the function f causes space to be allocated for ten CL objects. The important point to bear in mind is that this will cause the default constructor (the one with no arguments) for the CL class to be applied to each of these ten objects. When the system leaves the scope of the definition of the array arr (i.e., when we exit the function, f), the system will apply the destructor ~CL to each of the ten objects in the array.

Once we understand the idea of an array reference, as introduced in Chapter 0 of this manual, then we know what we need to know about using an array of objects. A reference of the form arr[i] (using the above example) is of type CL. Thus, we can apply to arr[i] any public member function that belongs to the class CL. If memfunc is such a function, the notation

```
arr[i].memfunc()
```

means "apply memfunc to the object arr[i] that belongs to the class CL." We are assuming here that the function CL::memfunc takes no arguments.

Chapter 1 of the text introduces the Section class. Each object in this class contains an array of Student objects. Here is the declaration for the class Section:

Extract: declaration of class Section

```
class Section
{
    private:
        // data members
        Student c[MAXCLASS];
        int class_size;


    public:
        // member functions
        // constructor - destructor
        Section();
        ~Section();


        // access
        Student search(string);
```

```
        // modify
        void read_in();
        void add_student(Student);
        void compute_averages();
        void sort_by_name();
};   // Section class
```

It is important to realize that a class declaration does not define any objects and, thus, does not cause any memory to be allocated. Memory is allocated when a function is entered that has a definition of the form:

```
    Section sec;
```

This particular definition will cause the allocation of enough space to represent one Section object. One Section object contains an array c that contains MAXCLASS (50) Student objects. The array c is a data member of the class Section. Once memory has been allocated for the object sec, the Section class constructor is applied to sec and the default Student class constructor is applied to each of the Student objects (c[0], c[1], ... etc.) contained within sec. When we leave the scope of the definition of sec, the Student class destructor is applied to each of the Student objects contained within sec (c[0], c[1], ... etc.) and then the Section class destructor is applied to sec itself.

SPECIFICATIONS FOR AN OBJECT-ORIENTED DESIGN

It is desirable to introduce a standard format for specifying classes and their member functions. You may use this style of documentation whenever you are given the task of developing an object-oriented design and we shall use this style in presenting some of the lab exercises in this laboratory manual.

Our standard format groups the public member functions of a class into categories. The most common categories are:
1. Constructor(s) and the destructor
2. Access functions; used to access data members
3. Modify functions; used to modify data members
4. Display functions; used to display information about the receiver at the computer display
5. Testing functions; used to test the receiver for being in some specific state, yielding a result of true or false

The following syntax specification shows how the specifications for a class can be laid out in a header file. Information that the programmer must provide is presented using *italics*. This format can be expanded to accommodate other C++ constructs, such as protected members, private member functions and inheritance. Note that we are not describing a C++ language construct here but a format for presenting commentary associated with a class.

Syntax: format for documenting a `class`

```
// Specifications for the class class-name
//
```

```
// Purpose of class:
//     description
//
// Private members:
// Data members:
//     data member types, names and meanings
//
// Public members:
// Member functions:
// Constructors - destructor
//
// Constructor:   class-name(arg-list)
// Purpose:       description
// Pre:           precondition
// Post:          postcondition
//
// Destructor:    ~class-name()
// Purpose:       description
// Pre:           precondition
// Post:          postcondition
//
// access:
//
// Function:      class-name::function-name(arg-list)
// Purpose:       description
// Pre:           precondition
// Post:          postcondition
//
```

The following example shows part of the specification for the class Student, using the above format:

```
// Specifications for the class Student
//
// Purpose of class:
//     A Student object encodes information about an
//     individual student, including the student's name
//     and exam scores
//
// Private members:
// Data members:
//       string    student_name name of student
//       float     first_hourly first hourly exam score
//       float     second_hourly second hourly exam score
//       float     final_exam   final exam score
//       float     average      final average (weighted average
//                                   of exam scores)
//
// Public members:
// Member functions:
// Constructors - destructor
//
// Constructor:  Student()
// Purpose:      To initialize the receiver object
// Pre:          None
// Post:         Initializes the receiver object with
```

```
//                      student_name = " "
//
// Destructor:  ~Student()
// Purpose:     Destroys the receiver object
// Pre:         The receiver object is initialized
// Post:        The receiver object is destroyed
//
// access:
//
// Function:    Student::get_name()
// Purpose:     To return the name of the receiver object
// Pre:         student_name = aName
// Post:        get_name = aName
//
// modify:
//
// Function:    Student::set_name()
// Purpose:     Sets the receiver object's name to aName
// Pre:         The receiver is initialized and aName = aString
// Post:        student_name = aString
//
// ... and so forth
```

ORGANIZING C++ PROGRAMS AS PROJECTS

This section describes how C++ programs can be organized as projects. We present descriptions of projects in three C++ environments:
1. Turbo C++ for IBM compatible computers,
2. Symantec C++ for Apple MacIntosh computers, and
3. GNU C++ for UNIX systems.

Project organization is essential for managing the complexity of large programs. The basic features of project organization in C++ are as follows:
1. Class declarations and function prototypes are presented in .h or header files.
2. Member function and stand-alone function definitions are presented in .cxx (.cpp in Symantec and Turbo C++) or implementation files.
3. Implementation files can be separately compiled and are in some sense autonomous units insofar as the compiler is concerned.
4. Declarations and implementations of classes are separated, so that one can fine-tune an implementation of a class without changing its declaration.

One advantage to project organization is that class declarations (which some authors call "specifications") are de-coupled from class implementations. This allows class implementations to be fine-tuned, or even reimplemented, without changing the public aspects (or, "public interface") of a class. Another advantage of project organization is that one can better accommodate the development of larger programs. For example, if one depends upon include directives only, one will eventually bump up against the maximum file size that the compiler can handle. Project organization allows the compiler to work on the source code in manageable chunks.

It is important to understand the difference between the compilation process and the linking process, especially insofar as member functions are concerned. Suppose a project contains the file cl.cxx that provides member function definitions for the class CL. During the compilation process, these member functions are translated into an intermediate object code that might contain some unresolved function calls. This means that the compiler does not know where the object code for the function being called is found, but it trusts that this issue will be resolved during the linking process. During the linking process, the linker attempts to resolve the unresolved function calls by looking for the function definitions in other files contained within the project. It is important to note that the object code that is eventually assembled by the linker only includes the object code for functions that are actually called. In an object-oriented system this means that a given class, such as CL, will generally contain quite a few functions that are not called in a given project. The compiled code for those functions (those that are not called) does not get incorporated into the final object code for the assembled project.

LABORATORY EXERCISE—IMPLEMENTING A SIMPLE class

This laboratory exercise involves implementing a simple class City, given part of its specification. You will be asked to:
1. Complete the specification by giving pre- and postconditions for each member function.
2. Implement the City class by providing the appropriate class declaration and member function definitions.
3. Write a simple test program, organized as a project, that demonstrates how your class implementation works.

Part 1 – The City Class

The first worksheet below contains a partial specification for the City class (partial because we have omitted the pre- and postconditions that you are to provide). The data members state_code and name should be declared to be of type string (this type was introduced at the end of Chapter 0).

Part 2 – Specify and Implement the City Class

1. Complete the specifications for the City class.
2. Implement the class by giving its declaration in a header file and its member function definitions in an implementation file.
3. Finally, write a simple test program that demonstrates that your functions work correctly. Organize your test program as a project.

Worksheet for Laboratory Exercise —
Specifying the `City class`

```
// Specifications for the class City
//
// Purpose of class:
//     A City object represents important information
//     about a city in the United States
//
// Private members:
// Data members:
//      string    name            name of city
//      string    state_code      two letter code for state
//      float     population      population in thousands
//
// Public members:


// Member functions:


// Constructors - destructor
//
// Constructor:  City()
// Purpose:      To initialize the receiver object
// Pre:

// Post:


//
// Destructor:   ~City()
// Purpose:      Destroys the receiver object
// Pre:

// Post:


//
// access:
//
// Function:  City::get_name()
// Purpose:   To return the name of the receiver city
// Pre:

// Post:
//
// Function:  City::get_state()
// Purpose:   To return the state code of the
//            receiver city
// Pre:

// Post:
//
```

Worksheet for Laboratory Exercise —
Specifying the `City` `class` (continued)

```
// Function:  City::get_population()
// Purpose:   To return the population of the
//            receiver city
// Pre:

// Post:
//
// modify:
//
// Function: City::set_name(aName)
// Purpose:  To set the receiver city's name to aName
// Pre:

// Post:
//
// Function: City::set_state(aCode)
// Purpose:  To set the receiver city's state code to
//           aCode
// Pre:

// Post:
//
// Function: City::set_population(aPop)
// Purpose:  To set the receiver city's population to aPop
// Pre:

// Post:
//
// display:
//
// Function: City::display()
// Purpose: To display the name, state code and population
//          of the receiver.
// Pre:

// Post:
//
// test:
//
// Function: City::has_more_people_than(anotherCity)
// Purpose:  Returns 1 (true) if receiver has greater
//           population than anotherCity and 0 (false)
//            otherwise
// Pre:

// Post:
```

Worksheet for Laboratory Exercise —
Testing the `City class`

```
/* --      Program name:  CityTest
   --      Programmer:
   --      Date:
   -- ** Overview
           .
           .
           .
                   */

#include < ... >

// GLOBAL CONSTANTS AND TYPEDEF'S

// GLOBAL FUNCTION PROTOTYPES


main()
{
   // FUNCTION PROTOTYPES


   // LOCAL DATA


   // STATEMENTS






}
// Function:
// Purpose:
// Pre:
// Post:
return-type function-name1(formal arguments)
{



}// end function-name1

   .
   .
   .
```

LABORATORY EXERCISE—THE `WeatherObs` CLASS

This laboratory exercise involves designing your own class based upon a verbal description of that class.

Part 1 — The `WeatherObs` Class

A `WeatherObs` (weather observation) object contains data for the weather at a particular reporting station at a particular time. A `WeatherObs` object contains the following data:
1. The name of the reporting station.
2. The sky condition (clear, cloudy, partly cloudy, fair, snow, rain, ice, fog, haze, thunder)
3. The temperature (in degrees Fahrenheit).
4. The wind direction (north, northeast, east, southeast, south, southwest, west, northwest, calm).
5. The wind speed (in miles per hour).
6. The total (melted) precipitation in previous 24 hours (in inches).

To simplify, we have omitted the date and time from this object and we shall assume that the client program "knows" the date and the time.

Part 2 — Design and Implement the `WeatherObs` Class

Design, implement and test this class. Organize your test program as a project. Provide member functions for accessing each individual data member, for reading in values for all data members all at once, and for modifying individual data members. Also, provide a member function for displaying all data members all at once. Your test program should test all member functions.

By "design" we mean to create a specification for the `WeatherObs` class using our design specification format. This includes providing appropriate pre- and postconditions.

Worksheet for Laboratory Exercise —
Specifying the `WeatherObs class`

```
// Specifications for the class WeatherObs
//
// Purpose of class:
//     A WeatherObs object represents ...
//
// Private members:
// Data members:
//
// Member functions:
// Constructors - destructor
//
// Constructor:  WeatherObs()
// Purpose:      To initialize the receiver object
// Pre:

// Post:

// Destructor:  ~WeatherObs()
// Purpose:      Destroys the receiver object
// Pre:

// Post:

// access
//
// Function:
// Purpose:
// Pre:

// Post:
//
// modify
//
// Function:
// Purpose:
//
// Pre:

// Post:
//
// display
//
// Function:
// Purpose:
//
// Pre:

// Post:
//
```

Worksheet for Laboratory Exercise —
Testing the WeatherObs class

```
/* --      Program name:  WeatherObsTest
   --       Programmer:
   --       Date:
   -- ** Overview
           .
           .
           .
              */

#include < ... >

// GLOBAL CONSTANTS AND TYPEDEF'S

// GLOBAL FUNCTION PROTOTYPES


main()
{
   // FUNCTION PROTOTYPES


   // LOCAL DATA


   // STATEMENTS







}
// Function:
// Purpose:
// Pre:
// Post:
return-type function-name1(formal arguments)
{




}// end function-name1

    .
    .
    .
```

USE OF THE `#ifndef` PREPROCESSOR DIRECTIVE

The `#ifndef` preprocessor directive is important for the construction of large projects. While this directive is not needed for the exercises in this chapter, it is important for all subsequent chapters in this book. Consequently, this is an opportune time to introduce this important directive.

The need for the `#ifndef` preprocessor directive arises because it is possible for a given header file to be included two or more times in a given source code file (either another header file or an implementation file). This will have the general consequence that multiple declarations will be given for a particular program entity (such as class). This kind of situation will arise, for example, if the file `x.cxx` includes the files `cl1.h` and `cl2.h` and if file `cl2.h` includes `cl1.h`. This pattern will result in the file `x.cxx` including `cl1.h` twice. Suppose `cl1.h` declares the class `CL1`. Then, it will appear to the compiler that the file `x.cxx` contains two declarations for the class `CL1` and this will result in a fatal error.

The `#ifndef` preprocessor directive is used to prevent a given section of code from getting compiled more than once. The `#ifndef` directive, in effect, sets a switch. No matter how many times a segment of code that is marked with the `#ifndef` directive (in the proper manner) has been included in a file, that segment of code will only get compiled once. The compiler will skip over the redundant copies of the properly marked code segments.

The following syntax specification shows how to use the `#ifndef` compiler directive in a header file so as to set up the "switch" mechanism alluded to in the previous paragraph:

Syntax: `#ifndef` compiler directive

```
// File:        filename.h
//
// Programmer:  J. Q. Student
// Date:        Feb 2, 1994
//

#ifndef FILENAME_H
#define FILENAME_H

.... code that will get compiled once and only once
.... goes here; e.g., a class declaration

#endif
```

Suppose a file includes the above file (`filename.h`) multiple times. Then, the compiler will encounter the `#ifndef` directive multiple times. The first encounter will cause the code that needs to get compiled to get compiled. But all subsequent encounters will cause the compiler to skip over the marked sections of code.

Here is a more detailed accounting of what happens: The `#ifndef` directive says, "If the symbol `FILENAME_H` is not defined, then compile everything between this `#ifndef` directive and the matching `#endif` directive. If the symbol `FILENAME_H` is defined, then ignore all of the code between this directive and the matching `#endif` directive." If the symbol `FILENAME_H` is not defined, the compiler encounters the `#define` directive, which tells it to define the symbol `FILENAME_H`. From this point on, `FILENAME_H` will be defined. Suppose this has happened and the compiler now encounters another section of marked code. Since `FILENAME_H` is now defined, the redundant code, redundant because of some pattern of inclusions, is not compiled again.

The usual convention is that a file whose name is `filename.h` will be associated with the symbol `FILENAME_H`, using all upper case letters and the underscore. For example, the `#ifndef` directive for a header file called `elements.h` will read:

```
#ifndef ELEMENTS_H
```

STRUCTURES

C++ programmers ought to know about structures and structure types, although they are not used much in this text with its emphasis on object-orientation. Structures are important in C programs and they are also useful in C++. C++ structures differ in important ways from C structures. C++ structures extend the original concept of a structure as found in C.

Structure types correspond to classes and structures to objects. A structure type in C++ is very similar to a class, except that the members of a structure are `public` by default, whereas the members of a class are `private` by default. It is not unusual for a structure type to include `public` data members only, and no member functions. The syntax for declaring such a type is shown in the following syntax specification:

Syntax: declaring a structure type

```
struct struct-type-name
{
    // DATA MEMBERS ...
    data member declarations

}; // end struct type-name
```

The data member declarations take the same form as the data member declarations for a class. However, the data members are `public` by default.

The following code declares an `Order` structure appropriate for the Generic College Coffee Shop (used in the Chapter 0 tutorial). The code then defines a structure called `ord`, which is an instance of this type:

```
struct Order
{
    // DATA MEMBERS ...
```

```
        string cust_name;
        int coffees, donuts, muffins;
        float total_bill;
};

Order ord;
```

The `ord` structure contains five data members and these are all `public`. Thus, any function that defines an `Order` structure can access and manipulate the members of an `Order` directly, using the dot operator, as in:

```
cin >> ord.coffees;
if (ord.donuts > ord.muffins) { .... }
```

The basic differences between traditional C structures and structures in C++ are the following:
1. In traditional C all members are `public`.
2. In traditional C all members are data members. Member functions are not allowed.

LABORATORY EXERCISE—WORKING WITH STRUCTURES

Go back to the program that you developed to implement and test the `City` class. Rewrite this program using structures instead of objects. Restrict yourself to a structure type that has no private members and no member functions. Compare the resulting code with what you obtained using classes and objects. What are the advantages / disadvantages of C-style structures versus C++ objects?

C++ Program Listing
`ObjSearcher`

```
/* -- Program name: Objsearcher


   -- Programmer:   Student programmer
   -- Date:         Sept. 21, 1992


   -- ** Overview
   -- This program allows the user to enter student data for
   -- all students in a class.  It then allows the user to
   -- access each student's final average.


   -- The program begins by presenting the user with
      instructions.


   -- It then asks the user to enter the number of students in
   -- the class (an integer).


   -- It then asks the user to enter the grade data for that
   -- many students.  For each student, the following data is
   -- entered:


   --   STUDENT NAME          (a string)
   --     FIRST HOURLY SCORE  (a float)
   --     SECOND HOURLY SCORE (a float)
   --     FINAL EXAM SCORE    (a float)


   -- The program uses this information to compute a final
   -- average for each student.


   -- Once all of the student data for the class has been
   -- entered, the student data is sorted alphabetically
   -- by student name.


   -- Finally, the program enters a "process requests" phase
   -- that allows the user to enter student names in a loop.
   -- For each student name entered, the program will either
```

```
        -- display that student's final average or, if no such
        -- student is contained in the name array, the program
        -- will display an appropriate error message.


        -- The user can terminate this process by entering an
        -- asterisk (*) in lieu of a student name.


        -- ** Warnings
        -- This program does virtually no integrity checks on the
        -- input data.  For example, exam scores are not checked
        -- for being in range (say 0 to 100).                    */


#include <iostream.h>
#include <string.h>
#include "section.h"


void main()
{
   // LOCAL DATA ...
   Section asection;


   // FUNCTION PROTOTYPES ...
   void give_instructions();
   void process_requests(Section&);


   // STATEMENTS ...
   give_instructions();
   asection.read_in();
   asection.compute_averages();
   asection.sort_by_name();
   process_requests(asection);
}


// Function:  give_instructions
// Purpose:   Gives the user instructions
// Pre:       output = empty
// Post:      output contains instructions for program use
void give_instructions()
{
   cout << "This program will ask you to enter student data.\n";
   cout << "It will then sort the student names and final\n";
   cout << "averages alphabetically by name.  Then, it will\n";
   cout << "allow you to request computed averages for \
           particular\n";
   cout << "students." << endl << endl << endl;
   cout << "Press enter to continue: ";
   cin.get();
   cin.ignore(LINESIZE, '\n');
```

```cpp
        cout << endl;
} // end give_instructions()



// Function: Process_requests()
// Purpose:  Processes user requests for student final averages.
// Pre:      input = (repetitions of aName) '*' and
//              output = oldStuff
// Post:      input = empty
//              output = oldstuff \n
//                    (repetitions of : student grade report for
//                  i-th aName)
void process_requests(Section& asection)
{
    // LOCAL DATA ...
    const int SENTINEL = '*';
    string  search_key;
    Student astudent;


    // statements
    cin.ignore(LINESIZE, '\n');
    cout << endl << "Begin searching phase ... " << endl;
    cout << "Please enter a student's name or *: ";
    read_string(search_key, MAXSTRING);
    while (search_key[0] != SENTINEL)
    {
       astudent = asection.search(search_key);
       if (!strcmp(astudent.get_name(), "not found"))
       cout << "No student in this class has that name." << endl;
       else
       astudent.display_average();
        cout << "Please enter a student's name or *: ";
        read_string(search_key, MAXSTRING);
    }
    // hang up program
    cout << "Press enter to exit: ";
    cin.get();
} // end process_requests
```

C++ Program Listing
`student.h`

```
// This is the header file for the Student class.
//
// Class description:
//    Objects in the student class represent one student
//    in the professor's class.
//
// Superclass:       None
//
// Data members:
// Private:
//    A student object contains the following private data:
//         string      student_name
//         float       first_hourly, second_hourly,
//                     final_exam, average   (final average)
//
//    Average is the weighted average of the exam scores.
//
// Member functions:
// Public:
//    Here is a summary of the Student class public member
//    functions:
//
//    constructor / destructor
//         Student()       initializes student_name to ""
//         ~Student()
//
//    access
//         string&   get_name()
//
//    modify
//         void      set_name(string)
//         void      read_in()
//             gets all data from user
//         void      compute_average(float, float, float)
//             sets average based on exam scores
//
//    display
//         void      display_average()
//


// GLOBAL CONSTANTS AND TYPEDEF'S ...
const int MAXSTRING = 20;  // maximum student name length
const int LINESIZE  = 80;  // maximum length of input line
typedef char string[MAXSTRING];
```

```cpp
// GLOBAL FUNCTION PROTOTYPE ...
void read_string(char*, int);


class Student
{
    private:
        // data members
        string student_name;
        float  first_hourly, second_hourly,
         final_exam, average;


    public:
        // member functions
        // constructor - destructor
        Student();
        ~Student();


        // access
        char* get_name();


        // modify
        void set_name(string);
        void read_in();
        void compute_average();


        // display
        void display_average();
}; // Student class
```

C++ Program Listing
`student.cxx`

```
// This file implements the Student class member functions.


#include <iostream.h>
#include <iomanip.h>
#include <string.h>
#include "student.h"


//
// constructor - destructor
//


// Constructor:  Student()
// Purpose:      To initialize the receiver object
// Pre:          None
// Post:         Initializes the receiver object with
//               student_name = ""
Student::Student()
{
   strcpy(student_name, "");
} // end Student::Student()


// Destructor:   ~Student()
// Purpose:      Destroys the receiver object
// Pre:          The receiver object is initialized
// Post:         The receiver object is destroyed
Student::~Student()
{
   ;  // no dynamic storage to be deallocated
} // end Student::~Student()


//
// access functions
//


// Function:  Student::get_name()
// Purpose:   To return the name of the receiver object
// Pre:       student_name = aName
// Post:      get_name = aName
//
```

```cpp
char* Student::get_name()
{
   return (student_name);
} // end Student::get_name()



//
// modify functions
//


// Function: Student::set_name()
// Purpose:  Sets the receiver object's name to aName
// Pre:      The receiver is intialized and aName = aString
// Post:     student_name = aString
void Student::set_name(string aName)
{
   strcpy(student_name, aName);
} // end Student::set_name()


// Function: Student::read_in()
// Purpose:  To prompt the user for and get the name and exam
//           scores for the receiver object.
// Pre:      The receiver object is initialized and
//           input = aName \n aScore1  \n aScore2  \n aScore3
//           \n restOfInput
// Post:     input = restOfInput and student_name = aName and
//           first_hourly = aScore1 and second_hourly = aScore2
//           and final_exam = aScore3
void Student::read_in()
{
   cout << "Please enter the student's name: ";
   read_string(student_name, MAXSTRING);
   cout << "Please enter an exam score when prompted:\n";
   cout << "First hourly score: ";
   cin  >> first_hourly;
   cout << "Second hourly score: ";
   cin  >> second_hourly;
   cout << "Final exam score: ";
   cin  >> final_exam;
} // end Student::read_in()


// Function:  Student::compute_average()
// Purpose:   To compute the receiver's average based
//            based upon the exam scores and exam weights
// Pre:       first_hourly, seond_hourly, and final_exam
//            are defined
// Post:      average = WEIGHT1 * first_hourly
//            + WEIGHT2 * second_hourly
//            + WEIGHTF * final_exam
void Student::compute_average()
{
   // LOCAL DATA ...
   const float WEIGHT1 = 0.25,
```

```
              WEIGHT2 = 0.25,
              WEIGHTF = 0.50;


   // STATEMENTS ...
   average = WEIGHT1 * first_hourly
     + WEIGHT2 * second_hourly
     + WEIGHTF * final_exam;
} // Student::compute_average()



//
// display function
//


// Function:  Student::display_average()
// Purpose:   To display the receiver's average at the
//            computer display
// Pre:       average = aFloat and output = oldStuff
// Post:      output = oldStuff This student's average is
//            aFloat \n
void Student::display_average()
{
   cout << "This student's average is " << setprecision(4)
     << average << endl;
}



//
// Non-member function
//


// Function:   read_string
// Purpose:    To read an input string from the keyboard.  This
//             function will truncate excess characters so that
//             the input stream position will be at the
//             beginning of the next line
// Define:     M = MAXSTRING
// Pre:        input = c1 c2 .... cN \n restOfInput, where
//             each cj is a character and N >= 0
// Post:       input = restOfInput and
//                 ((N > M ^ str = c1 c2 .... cM) or
//                  (N < M ^ str = c1 c2 .... cN))
//


void read_string(char* str, int len)
{
  cin.getline(str, len);
  if (cin.gcount() == len - 1)
  {
     cin.ignore(LINESIZE, '\n');
  }
} // end read_string
```

C++ Program Listing
`section.h`

```
// This is the header file for the Section class.
//
// Class description:
//    An object in this class represents one section of
//    a course.  A section may contain up to 50 (const
//    MAXCLASS) students.
//
// Superclass:   None
// Data members:
// Private:
//    A Section object contains the following private
//    data members:
//        Student    c[MAXCLASS]
//                   an array of Student objects
//        int        class_size
//
// Member functions:
// Public:
//    Here is a summary of the Section class public
//    member functions:
//
//    constructor / destructor
//        Section()
//        ~Section()
//
//    access
//        Student search(string)
//                   performs linear search on receiver for
//                   student with given name; returns Student
//                   object that is found
//
//    modify
//        void    read_in()
//                   reads in class data by "broadcasting"
//                   the Student::read_in() function to Student
//                   objects in receiver
//        void    add_student(Student)
//                   adds Student object to receiver
//        void    compute_averages()
//                   computes averages for individual Students
//                   in receiver by "broadcasting" the
//                   compute_average() function
//        void    sort_by_name()
//                   bubblesorts Student objects in receiver
//                   alphabetically by name
//
#include "student.h"
```

```
// GLOBAL CONSTANT DEFINITION ...
const int MAXCLASS = 50;


class Section
{
    private:
        // data members
        Student c[MAXCLASS];
        int class_size;


    public:
        // member functions
        // constructor - destructor
        Section();
        ~Section();


        // access
        Student search(string);


        // modify
        void read_in();
        void add_student(Student);
        void compute_averages();
        void sort_by_name();
};  // Section class
```

C++ Program Listing
`section.cxx`

```
// This file implements the Section class member functions.
//
#include <string.h>
#include <iostream.h>
#include <iomanip.h>
#include "section.h"


//
// constructor - destructor
//


// Constructor:  Section()
// Purpose:      To initialize the receiver.  This will
//               apply the Student() constructor to all
//               Student objects in the receiver.
// Pre:          None
// Post:         The receiver is initialized and
//               for all i in [1..MAXCLASS]
//                         : c[i-1] is initialized
//               and class_size = 0.
Section::Section()
{
   class_size = 0;
}   // end Section::Section()


// Destructor: ~Section()
// Purpose:      To destroy the receiver.  This will apply
//               the ~Student() destructor to all Student
//               objects in the receiver.
// Pre:          The receiver is initialized.
// Post:         The receiver is destroyed and
//                 for all i in [1..MAXCLASS]
//                           : c[i-1] is destroyed.
Section::~Section()
{
    ;   // no dynamic objects to deallocate
}   // end Section::~Section()


//
// access
//
```

```
// Function: search(string)
// Used:      To search through the receiver for a Student
//            whose name is search_key.  Either returns that
//            Student object or returns a Student object whose
//            name is "not_found".  Uses a linear search.
// Pre:       class_size >= 0 and search_key is defined and
//              c is sorted in ascending order by name
// Post:      (there exists i in [0..class_size-1] :
//                  c[i].get_name() = search_key
//                  and search = c[i]) or
//            (for all i in [0..class_size-1] :
//                  c[i].get_name() != search_key
//                  and search.get_name = "not_found")
Student Section::search(string search_key)
{
    // LOCAL VARIABLES ...
    int index = 0;
    Student astudent;
    int comparison;
    string cur_name;  // speeds things up a little
    enum {found, not_found_yet} status = not_found_yet;


    // STATEMENTS ...
    while ((status == not_found_yet) && (index < class_size))
    {
        strcpy(cur_name, c[index].get_name());
        comparison = strcmp(search_key, cur_name);
        if (!comparison)
        {
        // match
        status = found;
        }
        else if (comparison < 0)
        {
        // search fails
        index = class_size;
        }
        else
        {
        // try another (unless at end)
        index++;
        }
    } // end while


    if (status == not_found_yet)
    {
        // search failed
        astudent.set_name("not found");
        //
        // The Microsoft C/C++ compiler 7.00
        // fails to promote the char[] automatically
        // so you must resort to a string copy
        // string tmp;
        // strcpy(tmp,"not found");
        // astudent.set_name(tmp);
```

```
      }
      else
      {
         // search succeeded
         astudent = c[index];
      }
      return astudent;
} // end Section::search()



//
// modify
//


// Function:  Section::read_in()
// Purpose:   To read in all of the data for the receiver
//            section.
// Define:    inputPattern = aName FHScore SHScore FScore
// Define:    the notation c[i].Student::read_in()
//            means that the function read_in()
//            has been applied to the Student c[i].
//            This implies that the post condition for
//            Student::read_in() applies.
// Pre:       The receiver is initialized class_size = 0 and
//            input = N (N repetitions of: inputPattern)
//            and N <= MAXCLASS
// Post:      class_size = N and N <= MAXCLASS and
//                for all i in [1..class_size] :
//                    c[i-1].Student::read_in()
void Section::read_in()
{
   // LOCAL DATA ...
   Student astudent;
   int num;


   // STATEMENTS ...
   cout << "How many students are in the class? ";
   cin  >> num;
   for (int i = 0; i < num; i++)
   {
      cin.ignore(LINESIZE, '\n');// go to beginning of next line
      astudent.read_in();
      this -> add_student(astudent);  // increments class_size
   }
} // Section::read_in()


// Function:  Section::add_student(Student)
// Purpose:   To add astudent to the receiver section.
// Pre:       class_size = n and N < MAXCLASS
// Post:      c[N] = astudent and class_size = old(class_size) + 1
void Section::add_student(Student astudent)
{
   c[class_size++] = astudent;
}  // end Section::add_student
```

```
// function: Section::compute_averages()
// Purpose:  To update each Student object in the
//           receiver by computing its final average
// Define:   the notation c[i].Student::compute_average()
//           means that the function compute_average()
//           has been applied to the Student c[i].
//           This implies that the post condition for
//           Student::compute_average() applies.
// Pre:      for i in [0..class_size-1] :
//              (c[i].first_hourly, c[i].second_hourly,
//               c[i].final_exam, c[i].on_nerves are defined)
// Post      for i in [0..class_size-1] :
//              c[i].Student::compute_average()
void Section::compute_averages()
{
    for (int i = 0; i < class_size; i++)
    {
      c[i].compute_average();
    }
}  // end Section::compute_averages()



// Function: Section::sort_by_name()
// Purpose:  To sort the receiver collection of Student objects
//           in ascending order by name.  Uses bubblesort.
// Pre:      class_size >= 0 and for all i in [0..class_size-1] :
//              c[i].student_name is defined
// Post:     c is a permutation of old(c) and
//              for all i in [0..class_size-2] :
//                  c[i].student_name <= c[i+1].student_name
void Section::sort_by_name()
{
    // LOCAL DATA ...
    enum {false, true} done = false;
    Student tstudent;
    int limit = class_size - 1;


    // STATEMENTS ...
    // outer loop:
    for (int pass = 1; !done && (pass <= limit); pass++)
    {
      done = true;
      // inner loop:
      for (int i = 0; i < (class_size - pass); i++)
      {
      if (strcmp( c[i].get_name(), c[i+1].get_name()) > 0)
      {
        tstudent = c[i];
        c[i]   = c[i+1];
        c[i+1] = tstudent;
        done = false;
      }
      } // end inner loop
    } // end outer loop
}  // end sort_by_name()
```

CHAPTER 2

INHERITANCE, POLYMORPHISM AND GENERIC CLASSES

This chapter presents the C++ constructs needed to construct heterogeneous data structures. In addition, C++ file stream objects and their use are introduced.

FILE STREAM OBJECTS

This section discusses file stream objects. These allow the programmer to write data out to disk and to retrieve data from disk. File stream objects can be manipulated much like the input and output stream objects, cin and cout, discussed in Chapter 0. In particular, the insertion and extraction operators (<< and >>) are also defined for file streams and have the same semantics that they had when they were used with cin and cout.

In order to use file stream objects, you must include the fstream.h header file. Since this header file includes iostream.h, there is no need to include iostream.h in a file that already includes fstream.h. The fstream.h header file allows definition of ifstream (input file stream) and ofstream (output file stream) objects that bear some resemblance to the objects cin and cout that were used for keyboard input and video display output.

Conceptually, there are two basic kinds of files: text and binary. Text files are streams of characters. When you write numerical data out to a text file, it is converted from binary form (the way in which the data is represented within the computer's primary storage) to character form (i.e., the ASCII character code). For example, an integer variable whose value is 12345 might occupy two bytes of the computer's memory. When that value is written to a text file, it is converted to a character string (i.e., "12345") and that string is what actually gets written out to the file. Thus, a two byte integer might be written out as a string that contains up to six (6) characters (due to the minus sign).

When numerical data is read from a text file, it is converted from character form to binary form. When numerical data is written out to a binary file, it is not converted to character form. Instead, the contents of the computer's memory is copied directly to the storage medium. Similarly, when numerical data is read from a binary file, the bit pattern stored on the disk is copied directly into the computer's memory without any kind of data conversion occurring. A two byte integer is stored on disk as a two byte bit pattern, regardless of the value of that integer.

We shall focus exclusively upon text file operations in this chapter. Also bear in mind that this is not a complete discussion of files in C++. Our primary objective is to get you to the point where you can use text files without difficulty.

Input File Streams

If you want to read data from an external file, you will need to define an input file stream (`ifstream`) object. An `ifstream` object captures an abstraction that we shall call an "input file stream." Here are the basic operations that we shall discuss relative to `ifstream` objects:

1. defining an `ifstream` object,
2. opening an input file stream,
3. testing the status of an input file stream,
4. testing for the position in an input file stream,
5. reading data from an input file stream using the extraction operator,
6. reading strings from an input file stream using the `getline` function,
7. ignoring extraneous characters in an input line,
8. peeking at the current character in the input file stream without advancing the file pointer,
9. reading one character at a time from an input file stream, and
10. closing an input file stream.

Since `ifstream` is a class, one can define an `ifstream` object as follows:

Syntax: defining an **ifstream** object

```
ifstream ifs-object;
```

This establishes *ifs-object* as an `ifstream` object. This object is not yet associated with an external file. Associating an `ifstream` object with an external file is the purpose of the `open` function:

Syntax: opening an input file stream

```
ifs-object.open("file-name", ios::in)[1];
```

The `open` function is used to open a file. This means that an association is established between the object *ifs-object* and the operating system file whose name is *file-name*.

---

1. In Symantec C++, use:
```
ifs-object.open(file-name, ios::in | ios::nocreate);
```
This is necessary because in Symantec C++ the system will create a new file if a file with the indicated name does not already exist. The `ios::nocreate` switch will not allow the creation of a new file in this situation. Turbo C++ and GNU C++ will also work properly if the open function is applied with the `ios::nocreate` as shown.

Associated with an `ifstream` object is a bit pattern called the "stream state." Normally, all bits in the stream state are set to 0, but when unusual situations arise, particular bits are set to 1. C++ provides several `int`-valued functions that can be used to test the stream state. Some of those functions are given in Table 2–1 below.

TABLE 2–1 C++ FILE STREAM STATUS FUNCTIONS

Function	Meaning
`good()`	returns 1 if stream state is 0 (good state)
`eof()`	returns 1 if end-of-file bit (1 bit) is set
`fail()`	returns 1 if any of the following bits are set:
	fail bit (2), bad bit (4) or unrecoverable error bit (128)
`bad()`	returns 1 if either of the following is set:
	bad bit (4) or unrecoverable error bit (128)
`rdstate()`	returns current stream state

Our primary need for these functions is to check whether an input file actually exists on disk when we open it for input. The following code will write out an error message if the file "`perdat.txt`" does not exist:

```
ifstream in_file;
in_file.open("perdat.txt", ios::in);
if (in_file.fail())
{
  cout << "Could not open file. \n";
  cout << "Perhaps file does not exist. \n";
}
```

One can define and open an `ifstream` object in a single definition. For example, the following statement defines `in_file` as an `ifstream` object and associates that object with the external file whose name is `"perdat.txt"`:

```
ifstream in_file("perdat.txt", ios::in);
```

An input file stream consists of a sequence of bytes. At any point in time, there is a unique byte that determines the position in the file with respect to input. The next input operation will begin scanning from that position. We can test for this position in the file using the `tellg` function:

Syntax: the `tellg` function

```
ifs-object.tellg();
```

The `tellg` function returns a `long int` value which specifies the absolute position in the input file stream. "Absolute" means relative to the beginning of the file, which is given the value 0.

One can use the extraction operator to read data from a text file in much the same manner as one reads in data from the keyboard:

Syntax: file input using `>>`

ifs-object `>>` *variable1* `>>` *variable2* `>>` `....` `>>` *variableN*;

The above pattern suggests how one can read in the values for the variables *variable1*, *variable2*, ..., *variableN* from an input file stream. The considerations for input file streams are the same as for input from the keyboard. Most importantly, the extraction operator will skip over white space in trying to satisfy its argument.

The extraction operator cannot be used to read in a string that contains any white space characters. For that purpose, one should use the `getline` function:

Syntax: the `getline` function

ifs-object`.getline(`*string-var*`, `*string-len*`);`

This function reads up to *string-len* characters into *string-var*. The input process stops after the end of line marker (`'\n'`) is read in or when *string-len* characters have been extracted. In the latter case, unread characters will be left in the current input line. The new line character is not placed in *string-var*.

Sometimes (as noted above) extraneous characters are left in an input line after the use of the `getline` function. The `ignore` function can be used to skip over these extraneous characters. The syntax specification for the use of the `ignore` function is analogous to its use with the `cin` object.

Syntax: the `ignore` function

ifs-object`.ignore(`*char-count*`, `*term-char*`);`

This application of `ignore` will cause the system to skip over at most the next *char-count* characters in the input file stream until *term-char* is encountered. Normally, *term-char* is set to `'\n'`. If *term-char* is encountered, it is extracted.[2]

Sometimes it is useful to process an input file stream character by character (although this is not done in the examples in Chapter 2 of the text). This can be accomplished by using the `peek` and `get` functions:

Syntax: the `peek` and `get` functions

---

2. However, in GNU C++ *term–char* is left in the input file stream! This is an important and troublesome discrepancy.

```
ifs-object.peek();
```

```
ifs-object.get();
```

The peek function returns the next character in the input file stream or EOF (a special symbol that connotes the end-of-file character). It does not advance the stream position (i.e., the value returned by tellg). The get function returns the next character in the input file stream or EOF. It differs from peek in that it does advance the file position one byte.

One closes the file associated with an ifstream object using the close function.

Syntax: the close function

```
ifs-object.close();
```

Output File Streams

To write data out to an external file, you will need to define an output file stream (ofstream) object. The basic operations for ofstream objects are parallel to those for ifstream objects:
1. defining an ofstream object,
2. opening an output file stream,
3. testing the status of an output file stream,
4. testing for the position in an output file stream,
5. writing data to an output file stream using the insertion operator, and
6. writing one character at a time to an output file stream.

One closes an output file stream in the same manner in which one closes an input file stream, by means of the close function. One must include the fstream.h header file in any file that refers to one or more ofstream objects.

One can define an ofstream object as follows:

Syntax: defining an ofstream object

```
ofstream ofs-object;
```

This establishes ofs-object as an ofstream object. This object is not yet associated with an external file. Associating an ofstream object with an external file is the purpose of the open function:

Syntax: opening an output file stream

```
ofs-object.open("file-name", ios::out);
```

This establishes an association between the object *ofs-object* and the operating system file whose name is *file-name*.

The functions that were introduced earlier for testing the state of an input file stream can also be used to test the state of an output file stream.

The `tellp` function returns the position in an output file stream:

Syntax: the `tellp` function

```
ofs-object.tellp();
```

For example, `tellp` will return 0 if we are at the beginning of the file.

The insertion operator is overloaded so that it can be used with `ofstream` objects. The pattern for writing out data to an output file stream using the insertion operator is similar to that for `cout` objects:

Syntax: file output using `<<`

```
ofs-object << expression1 << expression2 << .... << expressionN;
```

The above pattern suggests how one can write out the values of a sequence of expressions using the insertion operator. The semantics of `<<` for output file streams is consistent with the semantics of `<<` in the `cout` `<<` pattern. This implies that the `endl`, `setw` and `setprecision` manipulators are applicable.

Sometimes it is convenient to write data out to a file character by character. This can be accomplished using the `put` function:

Syntax: the `put` function

```
ofs-object.put(out-char);
```

This writes out the character *out-char* to the output file stream associated with *ofs-object*. The character is written out to the current file position (as indicated by the result of the `tellp` function) and the file position is then advanced one byte.

LABORATORY EXERCISE—REMOVING DUPLICATES

In this exercise, you are asked to develop a C++ program that finds and displays all the unique numbers in a list of 1000 or fewer numbers. For instance, if we provide the following input:

```
3   7   2   5   3   3   7   1   0   9   5
```

the program should identify exactly those numbers that appear in the list, but only once. The output for this particular list should be:

```
3   7   2   5   1   0   9
```

This problem can be solved using an array provided that we can predict the maximum number of (unique) numbers that will occur as input. This proviso is needed because the declaration of an array in C++ requires its dimension to be a constant, such as 1000. (This assumes that we are not using dynamic memory allocation.)

Moreover, the very nature of the problem requires that the program keep track of all unique numbers that have been processed so far, even as it examines the next input number. That is, the problem cannot be solved *without* using an array (or some equivalent device for storing an entire list of numbers). For instance, consider the second occurrence of the number 7 in the above list. When the program examines it, the only way to "remember" that another 7 has already been encountered and displayed is to have saved it in an array and then to search that array when the second 7 is reached.

The input data for this problem will come from an external file. That file is called 'rand1000.dat' and is provided on the distribution disk. That file contains 1,000 random numbers in the range {0, ..., 32767}. The output data will be sent both to the computer display and to a new external file (a file whose name is not 'rand1000.dat').

Part 1 — Develop the Specifications

Write pre- and postconditions that describe the set of all possible inputs and corresponding outputs for the functions in this program.

Part 2 — Develop the Program

Write a complete C++ program that solves this problem.

Part 3 — Run the Program

Run the program using the above sample input, and be sure that it gives the correct output. Rerun the program with several other alternative inputs.

Questions

1. What if the size of the input file for this problem were unknown? That is, the file might contain 23 numbers or it might contain 23,000 numbers. What kinds of assumptions about the individual numbers in this file need to be made so that the problem can still be solved using an array?

2. Your program should contain a loop that compares each new input number with all previous input numbers that have already been determined to be unique and have been displayed. For the ith input number, how many times is that loop repeated? What assumptions about the nature of

the input must be made in order to answer this question? (Hint: What if all the previous input numbers are the same? What if they are all different?)

3. Assuming that all the input numbers are different and the input file contains exactly 1000 numbers, how many times is the loop of Question 2 repeated? What if the input file contains an unknown number, n, of mutually unique numbers?

Worksheet for Laboratory Exercise —
Removing Duplicates

```
/* -- Program name:
   -- Programmer:
   -- Date:
   -- ** Overview
          .
          .
          .
                */

#include < ... >

// GLOBAL CONSTANTS AND TYPEDEF'S

// GLOBAL FUNCTION PROTOTYPES

main()
{
    // FUNCTION PROTOTYPES


    // LOCAL DATA


    // STATEMENTS




}
// Function:
// Purpose:
// Pre:
// Post:
return-type function-name1(formal arguments)
{


}// end function-name1
    .
    .
    .
```

Notes for Answers to Questions
1.

2.

3.

MORE ABOUT CLASSES

This section introduces the following new topics:
1. inline functions,
2. virtual functions,
3. overloaded operators,
4. inheritance,
5. pointer and reference type casting, and
6. file streams as function arguments.

inline Functions

inline functions are a means of getting more efficient object code from C++ programs. They amount to a suggestion to the compiler that a function call be expanded "in line." This means that the code contained within the function definition will be substituted into the source code in lieu of the usual function call apparatus.

Within a class declaration, inline functions can be declared in one of two ways:
1. using the inline key word to declare a function as being inline explicitly
2. giving the complete function definition within the class declaration, without use of the word inline.

In the former case, the function declaration is separate from the function definition and the function definition takes the usual form.

The following class declaration, extracted from Chapter 2 of the text, illustrates both ways of declaring an inline function:

Extract: declaration of the class Element

```
// GLOBAL DECLARATION, DEFINITION ...
typedef char class_name[21];


enum boolean {FALSE,TRUE};


class Element {
   protected:
      // DATA MEMBER ...
      class_name my_class;


   public:
      // MEMBER FUNCTIONS ...
      // constructor - destructor
      inline Element();
      inline virtual ~Element();
```

```
        // access
        virtual char* get_class();


        // display
        virtual void display() { };
        // not implemented at this level


        // comparison operators
        virtual int operator ==(Element&);
        virtual int operator !=(Element&);
        virtual int operator >(Element&);
        virtual int operator <(Element&);
        virtual int operator <=(Element&);
        virtual int operator >=(Element&);


        // read in
        virtual void read_in() { };
        // not implemented at this level


        // file in - file out
        virtual void file_in(ifstream&) { };
        // not implemented at this level
        virtual void file_out(ofstream&) { };
        // not implemented at this level
};   // end class Element
```

The function `get_class` is declared inline using the `inline` key word. Thus, the definition for this function is given separately in an implementation file. The function `read_in` (for example) is implicitly declared inline, because the function body is given along with the function declaration. In this case, the function body does nothing interesting because it was not our intention to implement this function at this level in the class hierarchy.

The explicit `inline` declaration can also be used with stand-alone functions, that is, functions that are not a member of any class.

The key word *protected* in the declaration of the `my_class` data member means that `my_class` will be inherited by subclasses of `Element` that are declared using the `public` qualifier, which is the usual pattern, as will be shown below.

`virtual` Functions

The `Element` class declaration given above also includes declarations for some `virtual` functions. The idea of a `virtual` function is restricted to member functions (and operators, as we shall see).

A member function is declared `virtual` when its prototype is declared with the key word `virtual` in its class or in any of its base classes. For example, the fact that the function `read_in` declared above is `virtual`, means that all polymorphic redefinitions of `read_in` in classes that are derived from the class `Element` will automatically be considered `virtual`. (That is, these functions will inherit this characteristic). Although the key word `virtual` is optional in these derived classes, we prefer to use it redundantly for the sake of clarity.

Suppose the compiler encounters the pattern

```
object.func();
```

in a program where `object` belongs to the class `CL`. The compiler first checks to assure that `func` is a function that can be applied to an object that belongs to the class `CL`. This is a matter of checking whether `func` (with no arguments) is a member of `CL` or one of the base classes from which `CL` is derived. If it is established that `func` can be applied to an object that belongs to the class `CL`, then the compiler checks whether `func` is a `static` function (which is the default) or a `virtual` function. If `func` is `static`, then the compiler has all of the information that it needs to determine which function is being called. This is analogous to the situation with which you are already familiar. The generated code causes a jump into that function (e.g., `CL::func`). If the function is `virtual`, then the compiler does not assume that it has all of the information that it needs in order to make that determination. It assumes that this is a decision that will be deferred until run-time. Thus, the compiler generates code that will allow for the dynamic (i.e., run-time) binding of the function call to a particular function. This is called deferred binding.

While this may seem quite obscure at this time, it will become more clear as you read on in Chapter 2 of the main text. The key is that there are times when variable `object` in the above code is "polymorphic." That is, the compiler will not have enough information to determine what class `object` will belong to at run-time. `Object` might be bound to one of a collection of classes in a class hierarchy or a class lattice (the latter being the case if multiple inheritance is used). Thus, the identity of the function being called must be deferred until the class of `object` is known.

Overloaded Operators

The `Element` class overloads the comparison operators <, <=, <, >=, == and !=. Note the syntax used for the declaration and definition of an overloaded operator that is declared as a member of a class:

Syntax: declaring an overloaded operator as a `class` member

```
return-type operator op-symbol(arg-list);
```

Syntax: defining an overloaded operator declared as shown above

```
return-type class-name::operator op-symbol(arg-list)
{
```

```
      . . . . .
}
```

An overloaded operator is declared and defined much like a function. It has a return type and an argument list. The key word `operator` is used in the prototype and in the function header to indicate an overloaded operator.

Overloaded operators (when they are members of a class) can be declared `virtual`, as is the case with all of the overloaded operators in the `Element` class. Note that a binary operator should only have one argument, since the other operand will be the receiver object. For example, the prototype for `==` is reproduced below:

```
int Element::operator ==(Element&);
```

When we use the overloaded `==` operator, as in:

```
if (e1 == e2) { .... }
```

`e1` is the receiver object and `e2` is the argument. The definition of `==` will acknowledge the role of the receiver (`e1`) as the left operand (of the operator) and the role of the argument (`e2`) as the right operand (of the operator).

Inheritance

A class may be declared as a derived class of one or more base classes. For the time being, we shall limit our discussion to single inheritance (when a class is declared as having one base class). In single inheritance, the base class is called the *superclass* and the derived class is called the *subclass*.

The class `IntObj` is declared as a subclass of `Element` as shown in the extract below:

Extract: declaration of `IntObj`

```
class IntObj : public Element
{
   protected:
      // DATA MEMBER ...
      int value;


   public:
      // MEMBER FUNCTIONS ...
      // constructors - destructor
      inline IntObj(int);
      inline IntObj();          // default constructor
      inline virtual ~IntObj();


      // display
      virtual void display();
```

```
        // convert to and from standard int
        inline virtual int get_val();
        inline virtual void set_val(int);


        // comparison operators
        virtual int operator ==(Element&);
        virtual int operator !=(Element&);
        virtual int operator >(Element&);
        virtual int operator <(Element&);
        virtual int operator <=(Element&);
        virtual int operator >=(Element&);


        // file in / file out
        virtual void file_in(ifstream&);
        virtual void file_out(ofstream&);
};    // end class IntObj
```

Note the syntax that is used in declaring IntObj a subclass of Element. Since IntObj is declared as being a public subclass of Element, all of the protected and public aspects of Element are inherited. This includes all of the Element member functions and the protected my_class data member. If Element had included private members, they would not be inherited. Note that we redundantly declared the virtual functions inherited from Element as virtual, for the sake of clarity and emphasis.

Pointer and Reference Type Casting

An important technique in C++ is to take a pointer or a reference of one type and to *type cast* it into a pointer or a reference of another type. This is illustrated by the definitions of the overloaded comparison operators in the IntObj class. All of these definitions involve type casting a reference to an Element to a reference to an IntObj. For example, the following extract presents the definition of the operator IntObj::==:

Extract: definition of **IntObj::==**

```
// Operator:     IntObj::==(e)
// Purpose:      Returns true if receiver and *eptr are
//               value equal. ASSUMES *eptr IS AN IntObj.
// Pre:          e.get_class() = "IntObj" and
//               e.get_val() = firstInt
//               and value = secondInt
// Post:         ==() = (firstInt = secondInt)
int IntObj::operator ==(Element& e)
{
    return (value == ((IntObj&) e).get_val( ));
}   // end IntObj::operator ==
```

The argument e is declared as a reference to an Element. However, we need to compare the data member value against the value of e. One way to accomplish this is to apply the function `get_val` to `e`. However, the compiler will not allow this because `get_val` is not a member function of the class `Element` and the `get_val` of `IntObj` sees `e` as a reference to an `Element`. Thus, we must type cast `e` to a reference to an `IntObj`. The compiler views the following expression as a reference to an `IntObj`:

```
(IntObj&) e
```

Thus, we can apply the function `get_val` to this reference as follows:

```
((IntObj&) e).get_val()
```

Pointer type casting works in a similar manner.

File Streams as Function Arguments

The class `Element` introduces the functions `file_in` and `file_out` which are implemented throughout the hierarchy of classes that inherit from `Element`. This hierarchy includes `IntObj`, which redefines `file_in` and `file_out`. The idea of the `file_in` function is to read the value of the receiver object from an external file. This assumes that the data in the external file is of the proper format for the kind of object being read. The `file_out` function writes out the values of all data members to an external file. This includes the value of `my_class`, which records the class name of the receiver object. This strategy allows reconstruction of heterogeneous data structures from data stored on a disk. The details as to how this is accomplished are given in Chapter 2 of the text.

Note that the `ifstream` and `ofstream` objects that are declared as function arguments to `file_in` and `file_out` are declared as pass by reference arguments. This is required because `file_in` and `file_out` will be changing the state of their arguments and the calling function must be apprised of these changes.

The definitions for `IntObj::file_in` and `IntObj::file_out` are given in the extract below.

Extract: `IntObj::file_in` and `IntObj::file_out`

```
// Function:       IntObj::file_in(in_file)
// Purpose:        To read in a value for the receiver from a
//                 text file, in_file.  This function assumes
//                 that the line containing the class string has
//                 already been read in.
// Pre:            in_file = anInt restOfFile
// Post:           in_file = restOfFile and value = anInt
void IntObj::file_in(ifstream& in_file)
{
    in_file >> value;
    in_file.ignore(LINESIZE, '\n');
}  // end IntObj::file_in()
```

```
// Function:        IntObj::file_out(out_file)
// Purpose:         To write out a representation of the receiver
//                  to a text file, out_file.
// Pre:             out_file = oldStuff and my_class = "IntObj"
//                      and value = anInt
// Post:            (oldStuff != "" and out_file = oldStuff
//                      \n "IntObj" \n anInt) or
//                  (oldStuff = "" and out_file = oldStuff
//                      "IntObj" \n anInt)
void IntObj::file_out(ofstream& out_file)
{
    if (out_file.tellp())
    {
    // this is not first object in file
    // need to advance to new line
    out_file << endl;
    }
    out_file << my_class << endl;
    out_file << value;
}   // end IntObj::file_out()
```

The file_in function shows the use of the extraction operator and the ignore function with the ifstream object, in_file. This function assumes
that we already know that the value for an IntObj object is out there in the file
waiting for us to read it. The file_out function is usually used in a loop in
which many objects are being written to an external file in sequence. We dis-
tinguish between writing the first object and writing all of the subsequent objects. This is required so that the end of file test will work in the most
straightforward manner. Thus, we check the file position using the function
tellp. If tellp returns 0, then this is the first object in the file, and a new
line character is not written. If tellp returns any other value, then this is not
the first object in the file, and a new line character needs to be written to separate this object from the previous one.

LABORATORY EXERCISE—element CLASSES

This laboratory exercise involves modifying the City class (see Chapter 1 of
this manual) so that it is a subclass of the Element class. This will involve
overloading all of the comparison operators for the class City. It will also involve defining the functions file_in and file_out.

Part 1 — The Class City as an Element Subclass

Here are the function prototypes for the comparison operators:

```
int operator ==(Element& e);
        // returns true if receiver has the same
        // name, state and population as e.
int operator !=(Element& e);
        // returns true if the receiver differs
```

```
                  // in some regard from e.
int operator <(Element& e);
                  // returns true if the receiver's name
                  // comes alphabetically before e's name
int operator <=(Element& e);
                  // returns true if the receiver's name
                  // comes alphabetically before or is
                  // identical to e's name
int operator >(Element& e);
                  // returns true if the receiver's name
                  // comes alphabetically after e's name
int operator >=(Element& e);
                  // returns true if the receiver's name
                  // comes alphabetically after or is
                  // identical to e's name
```

Note that the descriptions of == and != are based upon value identity. Two `City` objects are equal if all of their data members have identical values. However, the relational operators (<, <=, >, >=) are defined based upon city name alone. This is designed to make these operators to be useful for sorting. We have ignored, and you may ignore, the complication that two cities with the same name might be in different states.

Here are the prototypes for `file_in` and `file_out`:

```
void file_in(ifstream& in_file);
                  // read in city name, state and population
                  // from three separate lines in the input file.
void file_out(ofstream& in_file);
                  // write out class name, city name, state and
                  // population to four separate lines in the
                  // output file.
```

The `City::file_out` function should use the strategy illustrated by `IntObj::file_out`. In particular, you must use the `tellp` function to look for the special case that an object being written out is the first object in the file.

Implement the `City` class as described above and develop a test program to check that all functions are working properly.

Worksheet for Laboratory Exercise —
Implementation of `city` as a Subclass of `Element`

```
/* -- Program name:
   -- Programmer:
   -- Date:             */
   // Implementation file for the City class.
#include < ... >
// constructor - destructor
// Constructor: City::City()
// Purpose:
// Pre:
// Post:
City::City()
{

}
//
// access
//
// Function:
// Purpose:
// Pre:
// Post:
return-type function-name1(formal arguments)
{


}// end function-name1

    .
    .

//
// comparison operators
//
    .

    .
//
// access
//
    .

    .
//
// modify
//
    .

    .
//
// file_in - file_out
//
```

Worksheet for Laboratory Exercise —
Testing the `city` Class

```
/* --       Program name:  CityTest
   --       Programmer:
   --       Date:
   -- ** Overview
             .
             .
             .
                   */

#include < ... >

// GLOBAL CONSTANTS AND TYPEDEF'S

// GLOBAL FUNCTION PROTOTYPES


main()
{
    // FUNCTION PROTOTYPES


    // LOCAL DATA


    // STATEMENTS






}
// Function:
// Purpose:
// Pre:
// Post:
return-type function-name1(formal arguments)
{



}// end function-name1

    .
    .
    .
```

Part 2 — Reading a File of Cities

Assume that a text file is set up with the following format:

```
<number of cities, N>
<data for city 1>
<data for city 2>
...
<data for city N>
```

That is, the first line of the text file indicates the number (N) of cities whose representations are contained in the file followed by N sets of data, one set for each city. Each set contains four lines which carry, respectively, the following data: the string 'City', the city's name, its state code, and its population. A sample file of cities is on the distribution disk with the name cities.dat.

Design and write a program that will read this data and display the names and populations of the cities that have populations that are above average (that is, above the average population for all the cities in the file). Do this by writing a program that uses the following definition:

```
City city_list[100];
```

Worksheet for Laboratory Exercise —
Reading a File of Cities

```
/* -- Program name:
   -- Programmer:
   -- Date:
   -- ** Overview
          .
          .
          .
                  */

#include < ... >

// GLOBAL CONSTANTS AND TYPEDEF'S

// GLOBAL FUNCTION PROTOTYPES

main()
{
   // FUNCTION PROTOTYPES


   // LOCAL DATA


   // STATEMENTS










}
// Function:
// Purpose:
// Pre:
// Post:
return-type function-name1(formal arguments)
{




}// end function-name1

   .
   .
   .
```

Part 3 — Creating a File of Cities

Design a function that will take an array of `City` objects and write them out as a text file. The function prototype for this stand-alone function will be:

```
void create_file(City city_list[], int n);
```

Here, `city_list` is the array and `n` represents the number of cities in the array. This function will:

1. Ask the user for the file name to use,
2. Open a file with the given name,
3. Write out the value of `n` as the first line of the file,
4. Apply `City::file_out` to all of the `City` objects in the array.
5. Close the file.

Write a program that will test this function. Then rerun the program you developed in part two using a text file created by this function.

Worksheet for Laboratory Exercise —
Creating a File of Cities

```
/* -- Program name:
   -- Programmer:
   -- Date:
   -- ** Overview
         .
         .
         .
                   */

#include < ... >

// GLOBAL CONSTANTS AND TYPEDEF'S

// GLOBAL FUNCTION PROTOTYPES

main()
{
   // FUNCTION PROTOTYPES


   // LOCAL DATA


   // STATEMENTS




}
// Function:
// Purpose:
// Pre:
// Post:
void create_file(City city_list[], int n);
{




}// end create_file

   .
   .
   .
```

POINTERS AND DYNAMIC OBJECTS

This section introduces pointers and dynamic objects. In particular, we need to learn about the following:
1. declaring pointer types,
2. defining pointer variables,
3. allocating dynamic objects using the `new` operator,
4. deallocating dynamic objects using the `delete` operator,
5. dereferencing a pointer variable,
6. use of the address operator, and
7. sending messages to objects by indirection.

Definition A pointer variable is a variable whose value is the address of another variable.

A pointer variable has a *base type* which constrains the pointer so that it is only allowed to contain the address of a variable whose type is that base type. For example, if a pointer variable has the base type `IntObj`, then that pointer variable is only allowed to point to objects that belong to the class `IntObj`. It is possible to do an end run around this constraint by pointer type casting (although one should do this judiciously!). Pointer variables are extremely important in the C++ language and in object-oriented programming.

Pointer Types

One can declare a pointer type as follows:

Syntax: declaring a pointer type

```
typedef base-type* type-name;
```

This defines *type-name* as a pointer type whose base type is *base-type*. This means that we can use the identifier *type-name* to define pointer variables.

Defining a Pointer Variable

One can define a pointer variable using one of the following patterns:

Syntax: defining pointer variables

```
pointer-type-name pointer-var;
        // pattern #1
type-name *pointer-var;
        // pattern #2
```

For example, the following definition defines `iptr` and `jptr` as pointer variables whose base type is `IntObj`. The variable `ibj` is just an ordinary `IntObj` object:

```
IntObj *iptr, *jptr, ibj;
```

Assuming that these are automatic variables (defined within a function body), they are undefined until the function is called.

Allocating Dynamic Objects

Pointer variables are used to point to other variables. For example, the variable `iptr` in the above definition is permitted to point to any `IntObj` object. Usually, such a variable will point to an `IntObj` object that is stored in dynamic memory, which is sometimes called the heap. An object that is stored in the heap is called a *dynamic object*. One creates a dynamic object using the `new` operator.

The following syntax specification shows how the `new` operator is used to create a dynamic object:

Syntax: the `new` operator

```
pointer-var = new constructor(arg-list);
```

For example, since the class `IntObj` has a constructor `IntObj(int)` that creates an `IntObj` that is initialized to a particular `int` value, the following statement will cause `iptr` to point to a new dynamic `IntObj` object whose value is 3:

```
iptr = new IntObj(3);
```

The semantics for the use of the `new` operator, as shown in the above syntax specification, is as follows:
1. Allocate space on the heap for one object whose class is that named by the constructor.
2. Apply the indicated constructor (the one that conforms to the given argument list) to the dynamic object.
3. Return the address of the `new` object as the operator result.
4. Store the address of the `new` object in the variable *pointer-var*.

This description assumes that the base type of *pointer-var* is a class. However, one can also use the `new` operator to allocate dynamic variables whose type is not a class. For example, the following code will create a dynamic `float` variable:

```
float *xptr;    // xptr is a pointer to a float
xptr = new float
```

Since the type `float` is not a class, no constructor is applied to the dynamic variable that is created. This is simply a dynamic variable whose type is `float`.

The `new` operator can be used to allocate arrays in dynamic memory. For example, the following application of `new` allocates space for ten `IntObj` objects in dynamic memory:

```
jptr = new IntObj[10];
```

In this case, `jptr` points to the base address of that array. One would use the pointer arithmetic techniques shown in the next section to manipulate that array. The above application of `new` would cause the default `IntObj` class constructor to be applied to each of the ten `IntObj` objects in the array.

Deallocating Dynamic Objects

C++ places the responsibility for dynamic memory management (i.e., heap memory management) upon the programmer. Thus, when you are finished with a dynamic object, you must explicitly free the memory that it occupies. This is done using the `delete` operator. The syntax specification for the use of the `delete` operator follows:

Syntax: the `delete` operator

```
delete pointer-var;
```

This causes the space allocated for the variable that *pointer-var* points to to be returned to free storage. This means that this space can be used for other dynamic variables.

The semantics for `delete`, as shown above, is as follows:
1. Apply the destructor for the base type of *pointer-var* to the object that *pointer-var* points to.
2. Deallocate the storage that was allocated for the dynamic object that *pointer-var* points to.

This description assumes that the base type of *pointer-var* is a class. Otherwise (for example, if the base class is simply `int` or `float` or some other type that is not a class), there is no destructor that must be applied to the dynamic variable.

The following code assumes that `iptr` points to a single dynamic `IntObj` object (and not to an array of such objects). This code causes the memory occupied by the dynamic object that `iptr` points to to be returned to free storage:

```
delete iptr;
```

If `jptr` points to an array of dynamically allocated `IntObj` objects (based upon the earlier assignment to `jptr` of a value returned by new), then we deallocate that array using the following call to delete:

```
delete []jptr;
```

Dereferencing Pointer Variables

If `pointer-var` contains the address of an object (or any dynamic variable), then we can refer to the object that `pointer-var` points to by means of the dereferencing operator. This is shown in the following syntax specification:

Syntax: the dereferencing operator

```
*pointer-var
```

If the base type of `pointer-var` is CL (a class), then the type of the dereferenced pointer (i.e., the type of the expression *pointer-var*) is CL. For example, `*iptr` is of type `IntObj` if `iptr` is defined as an `IntObj` pointer.

The Address Operator

Every variable has an address and we can access the address of a variable by means of the address operator. The syntax specification for the use of this operator is as follows:

Syntax: the address operator

```
&variable
```

If *variable* is a pointer variable, &*variable* is the address of the pointer variable and not the address that the pointer variable contains. If *variable* is not a pointer variable, then &*variable* is just the address of that variable. In other words, the semantics of the address operator is the same regardless of the kind of variable that it is being applied to.

Sending Messages by Indirection

The arrow operator is used to apply a function to an object that a pointer variable points to. This is called *sending a message to an object by indirection*. The syntax for doing this is as follows:

Syntax: the arrow operator

```
pointer-var -> function-name(arg-list)
```

Assuming that `pointer-var` is pointing to an object that `function-name` can be applied to, this causes the function to be applied to that object. The compiler will generate an error if the indicated function is not declared for the base type of *pointer-var*.   If *function-name* is a static function, the compiler implements this as a call to that function.   If *function-name* is a virtual function, the compiler generates code which will allow for the dynamic determination of which function is being called. The type of the above expression is the return type of *function-name*.

For example, display is a void function that is defined for the IntObj class. If iptr points to a dynamic IntObj object, the following statement will cause the display function to be applied to *iptr (i.e., the object that iptr points to):

```
iptr -> display();
```

LABORATORY EXERCISE—DYNAMIC OBJECTS

Design and write a program that will read a list of integers that are input from the keyboard. The program should then compute the average of those integers, and finally display all of the integers that are above average.

Part 1 — Using an Array of Dynamic **IntObj** Objects

You are constrained to use dynamic IntObj objects to accomplish this.   In particular, your main function should declare an array of IntObj pointers (called dint_list) as follows:

```
IntObj* dint_list[100];    // array of IntObj pointers
```

Note that dint_list[i] will be of type IntObj*. Thus, dint_list[i] will be a pointer to a dynamic IntObj object.

Part 2 — Design the Program

Design the program, using the elements.h, elements.cxx, standobj.h and standobj.cxx files that are available on your distribution diskette.

Part 3 — Test the Program

The program can be tested using small lists of integers from the keyboard.

Worksheet for Laboratory Exercise —
Dynamic Objects

```
/* -- Program name:
   -- Programmer:
   -- Date:
   -- ** Overview
          .
          .
          .
              */

#include < ... >

// GLOBAL CONSTANTS AND TYPEDEF'S

// GLOBAL FUNCTION PROTOTYPES


main()
{
   // FUNCTION PROTOTYPES


   // LOCAL DATA
IntObj* dint_list[100];   //array of IntObj pointers

   // STATEMENTS




}
// Function:
// Purpose:
// Pre:
// Post:
return-type function-name1(formal arguments)
{



}// end function-name1

    .
    .
    .
```

POINTERS AND ARRAYS

In this section, we discuss the use of pointers to manipulate arrays and the basics of pointer arithmetic in C++. In particular, the following topics will be covered:

1. array names as addresses,
2. incrementing and decrementing pointers,
3. pointer arithmetic as a means of manipulating pointer variables, and
4. pointer comparisons.

Array Names as Addresses

When the name of an array is used in an expression, the array name is interpreted as the base address of the array. In this case, we say that the array name is being used as an *r-value*. Another way of expressing this is that if the component type of the array x is t, then, when the symbol x is used in an expression, the compiler views the type of x as being $t*$ (i.e., a pointer to a t). For example, consider the following code:

```
float c[10], *fptr;
fptr = c;
```

The array name, c, in the assignment statement is being used as an r-value (i.e., in an expression, albeit a trivial one). Thus, the compiler views c as being of type `float*`, since the component type of the array c is float. Consequently, the assignment is legal and represents the copying of the base address of c into the pointer variable fptr.

The base address of c is just the address of c[0]. Consequently, *when c is used as an r-value*, the following identity holds:

```
c == &c[0]
```

Since the compiler views c as being of type `float*`, then we can dereference c, and the following identity holds:

```
*c == c[0]
```

The basic constraint is that we never use an array name as an *l-value*, that is, on the left hand side of the assignment sign or the equivalent. In other words, we are not allowed to change the address of an array. The following code yields a fatal compiler error:

```
c = fptr;
```

Here, an array name is being used as an l-value.

Incrementing and Decrementing Pointer Variables

Suppose `tptr` is a pointer variable whose base type is t. Suppose further that the number of bytes required to store a variable of type t is denoted by sizeof(t). In fact, sizeof is a function provided by C++ in stdlib.h. Now, suppose tptr has a legal value. Then, tptr++ and tptr-- are assigned the following meanings:

tptr++   means move tptr forward sizeof(t) bytes, and

tptr--   means move tptr backward sizeof(t) bytes.

If tptr had been assigned the address of x[0], where x is an array whose component type is t, then after the application of the increment operator, tptr would point to x[1]. Another application of the increment operator will bring tptr to point to x[2], and so forth. This suggests that we can traverse an array, such as x, using the following strategy:

1. Define tptr as a pointer with base type t and initialize tptr to the base address of x, using:

    tptr = x;

2. Repeatedly increment tptr using the increment operator until tptr points to an address that is past the end of the array.

We shall discuss how we can determine whether the pointer has gone past the end of the array later.

Pointer Arithmetic

We can also manipulate pointers using "pointer arithmetic." This means that the arithmetic operators + and − are overloaded so that they have a special meaning when they are used with pointers. Again assume that tptr is a pointer variable whose base type is t. Pointer arithmetic allows us to construct expressions, such as tptr + k and tptr − k, that have the following meanings:

tptr + k   means evaluate to *tptr + k * sizeof(t)*

tptr − k   means evaluate to *tptr − k * sizeof(t)*.

Thus, the following statements are equivalent:

tptr++;

tptr = tptr + 1;

Please note that the expressions

tptr = tptr + k;

and

*tptr = tptr + k * sizeof(t);*

are not interchangeable in a C++ program. We present the latter as the semantics of the former (and thus, have presented the latter in italics). If you actually include the statement

```
tptr = tptr + k * sizeof(t);
```

in a program, then the new value of `tptr` will be its former value plus k times the square of `sizeof(t)`!

Suppose x is an array whose component type is t. Then, the following fundamental identity holds:

```
x + i  == &x[i]
```

When `i == 0`, this just gives us the identity given earlier, namely:

```
x == &x[0]
```

We can deference an expression such as `x + i`, and this gives us an additional identity:

```
*(x + i) == x[i]
```


Comparing Pointers

The comparison operators can also be used with pointers. Thus, if `tptr` and `rptr` are pointer variables whose base type is t, then `tptr == rptr` is true if and only if the address that `tptr` contains is the same as the address that `rptr` contains. The expression `tptr < rptr` will be true if and only if the address that `tptr` contains is less than the address that `rptr` contains. Suppose the following identities hold:

```
tptr == &x[i]
rptr == &x[j]
```

In other words, `tptr` points to `x[i]` and `rptr` points to `x[j]`. Then, `tptr < rptr` will be true if and only if i < j.

Suppose x is an array with n components. Perhaps the dimension of x is larger than n, but x contains n components with valid data. These components are `x[0]`, `x[1]`, ..., `x[n-1]`. If we are using a pointer `tptr` to traverse this array from `x[0]` through `x[n-1]`, then we are done when the following condition holds:

```
tptr == &x[n]
```

When `tptr` satisfies this condition, `tptr` has gone past the end of the array. This condition can also be expressed as:

```
tptr == x + n
```

since x + n == &x[n], by our fundamental identity.

Consequently, the following code presents a typical pattern, using a for loop, for traversing an array x that contains n elements and whose component type is t:

```
t* tptr = x;    // initialize tptr to base address of x
for (; tptr < x + n;  tptr++)
{
    ... do what needs to be done
    ... with *tptr
}
```

LABORATORY EXERCISE—POINTERS AND ARRAYS

Redo the previous laboratory exercise, "Dynamic Objects," using pointers in lieu of indices to manipulate the array dint_list.

Since dint_list is an array of IntObj pointers, this will require the use of pointers to pointers. For example, suppose you define a variable tptr that will be used to traverse the array as follows:

```
IntObj **tptr;
```

The variable tptr is a pointer to a pointer, and can be used to point to components of the array dint_list since this is an array of IntObj pointers. Thus, if tptr is going to be used to traverse the array, the following statement would initialize tptr in the appropriate manner:

```
tptr = dint_list;
```

Since dint_list is an array whose component type is IntObj*, the compiler views the type of dint_list in the above expression as being IntObj** (i.e., a pointer to an IntObj pointer).

Worksheet for Laboratory Exercise —
Dynamic Objects

```
/* -- Program name:
   -- Programmer:
   -- Date:
   -- ** Overview
            .
            .
            .
                  */

#include < ... >

// GLOBAL CONSTANTS AND TYPEDEF'S

// GLOBAL FUNCTION PROTOTYPES


main()
{
   // FUNCTION PROTOTYPES


   // LOCAL DATA


   // STATEMENTS




}
// Function:
// Purpose:
// Pre:
// Post:
return-type function-name1(formal arguments)
{




}// end function-name1

   .
   .
   .
```

POLYMORPHIC OBJECTS AND TRUE POLYMORPHISM

The power of object-oriented programming derives, in large measure, from the property of polymorphism, which enables an object to choose, at run-time, the correct interpretation for a message that it has received. This requires the use of virtual functions and polymorphic objects.

A *polymorphic object* is one whose class is not completely determined at compile time. In some sense, one might view the type that the compiler assigns to the object as being somewhat provisional, or standing for a range of types that the object might assume dynamically during the execution of the program. The function `ElementSet::add` presented in Chapter 2 of the main text illustrates the idea of a polymorphic object. The following extracts present the declaration of the `ElementSet` class and the implementation of the `ElementSet::add` function:

Extract: declaration of the class `ElementSet`

```
class ElementSet
{
    protected:
        // DATA MEMBERS ...
        ElementPtr s[CAPACITY];
        int current;  // index of current ElementPtr
        int size;


    public:
        // MEMBER FUNCTIONS ...
        // constructor - destructor
        inline ElementSet();
        inline virtual ~ElementSet();


        // test
        int is_member_of(ElementPtr);
        int cardinality();
        inline int is_full();
        inline int is_empty();


        // access
        ElementPtr get_any();


        // modify
        virtual int add(ElementPtr);
        void clear();


        // display
        virtual void display();
};  // end class ElementSet
```

Extract: the function `ElementSet::add`

```
// Function:   ElementSet::add(eptr)
// Purpose: To add the element eptr points to the receiver
//      set.  This function returns 1 if add succeeds
//      and 0 if add fails.  Add will fail if receiver
//      set is already full or if *eptr is a duplicate
//      element.  This function will set current to 0
//      if current was never set.
// Pre:   size = N and *eptr is intialized
// Post:  (N = 0 and size = 1 and s[0] = eptr and
//         current = 0 and add = 1)
//           or
//        (N = CAPACITY and size = old(size) and add = 0)
//           or
//        (N > 0 and there exists i in [1..N] :
//         *s[i-1] = *eptr and size = old(size) and add = 0)
//           or
//        (N > 0 and for all i in [1..N] : *s[i-1] != *eptr
//            and size = old(size) + 1 and s[size] = eptr
//            and add = 1)
int ElementSet::add(ElementPtr eptr)
{
    // LOCAL DATA ...
    ElementPtr *ptr = s;


    // STATEMENTS ...
    // check if receiver is already full
    if (this -> is_full())
    {
        return 0;    // set already full
    }


    // not full; check if *eptr is already in set
    if (this -> is_member_of(eptr))
    {
        return 0;       // duplicate; already in set
    }


    // not full; not duplicate.
    // insert
    ptr = s + size;  // set pointer to end
    *ptr = eptr;
    size++;
    // set current if this is first element
    if (size == 1) current = 0;
    return 1;  // success flag
}   // end ElementSet::add()
```

The class `ElementSet` implements a heterogeneous set of elements. An element is any object that belongs to the class `Element` or any of its subclasses. The function `add` is used to add the object that `eptr` points to (where the type of eptr is Element* or ElementPtr) to the receiver ElementSet. The argument eptr is called a "polymorphic object" because it can point to any kind of element. That is, it can point to an IntObj or a FloatObj or a Person or a Student or any other kind of object that is part of the class hierarchy that descends from the class Element. The fact that eptr is polymorphic is the key to the heterogeneity of the ElementSet implementation.

True polymorphism arises when we apply a virtual function to a polymorphic object. In this case, the compiler does not know beforehand what kind of object will be receiving the message, since the object is polymorphic. The compiler generates code which allows for the run-time determination of the class to which the object belongs and the correct interpretation for the message that it has received. This is illustrated in the following extract that presents the function ElementSet::display:

Extract: the function `ElementSet::display`

```
// Function:  ElementSet::display()
// Purpose: To display each of the elements in the receiver set.
// Pre:    size = N
// Post:   for all in in [1..N] : s[i-1] -> display()
void ElementSet::display()
{
   // LOCAL DATA ...
   ElementPtr *ptr = s;


   // STATEMENTS ...
   for (; ptr < s + size; ptr++)
   {
      (*ptr) -> display();
   }
}  // end ElementSet::display()
```

The dereferenced pointer *ptr in the function ElementSet::display is polymorphic. This is because *ptr assumes the values of s[0], s[1], ... in turn, and s[i] pointers can point to different kinds of element objects. When the compiler encounters the statement

```
(*ptr) -> display();
```

it has no way of determining whether *ptr is pointing to an IntObj or a FloatObj or whatever. Since display is declared virtual, the compiler generates code that will allow for the run-time determination of whether the program should execute IntObj::display, FloatObj::display or some other version of the ubiquitous display function. Recall that we term the function display "ubiquitous" because it is implemented throughout the class hierarchy that descends from the class Element.

It is this apparent ability of a polymorphic object, such as *ptr in the above example, to dynamically select the correct interpretation for a message that it receives that is called *true polymorphism*.

Pointer type casting, introduced earlier, plays an important role in the use of heterogeneous data structures. For example, the function `Element-Set::get_any`, declared above, returns a value of the type `ElementPtr` (i.e., `Element*`). A client program that uses the `ElementSet` implementation may want to retrieve an object from an `ElementSet` (using `get_any`) and then may want to send that object a message which is not implemented at the `Element` class level in the class hierarchy. For example, consider the following code:

```
ElementPtr eptr;
ElementSet aset;
....
eptr = aset.get_any();
eptr -> func();
```

Assuming that `func` is not declared at the `Element` class level, the compiler will not accept the above code. It will generate a message that "`func` is not a member of the class `Element`." It behaves in this way since `eptr` is viewed as being a pointer to an `Element` and thus, only a public member function of the class `Element` is acceptable on the right hand side of the arrow operator.

In order to correct this problem, we must type cast `eptr` to a new pointer type which will be acceptable to the compiler. For example, suppose `eptr` points to an object of type `CL`, where `CL` is an element class (i.e., a subclass of `Element`). Suppose further that `CL::func` is the function that we want to apply to the object that `eptr` points to. The following application of `func` to the object that `eptr` points to is acceptable:

```
((CL*) eptr) -> func();
```

The compiler views the expression `((CL*) eptr)` as being of type `CL*`, and since `func` is declared for the `CL` class, the compiler sees the above code as calling for the application of `CL::func` to the object that `eptr` points to.

The function `display_three` in the `Setter` program given in the text illustrates the use of pointer type casting in a context such as the one described above. This function is presented in the extract given below. The argument `the_set` is a heterogeneous set that contains objects that belong to the classes `IntObj`, `FloatObj`, `CharObj` and `StringObj`. We retrieve objects from `the_set` using `get_any` with the intention of applying the function `get_val` to the objects that we retrieved. Since `get_val` is not implemented at the `Element` class level in our class hierarchy, we must type cast `eptr` to be of the appropriate type.

Extract: the function `display_three` from the `Setter` program

```
// Function:  display_three(the_set)
// Purpose:   To display the elements in the_set using the
//            functions get_any and get_val().  This requires
//            type casting.
// Pre:       the_set is initialized
// Post:      All elements in the_set are displayed at the screen
```

```
void display_three(ElementSet& the_set)
{
   // DATA MEMBERS ...
   int set_size = the_set.cardinality();
   ElementPtr eptr;


   // STATEMENTS ...
   cout << endl
     << "Here are the set elements shown using " << endl
     << "get_any() and the appropriate version " << endl
     << "of the get_val() function: " << endl;
   for (int i = 0; i < set_size; i++)
   {
      // capture pointer, since every use of get_any()
      // will change current object in set
      eptr = the_set.get_any();
      if (!strcmp(eptr -> get_class(), "FloatObj"))
      {
      cout << ((FloatObj*) eptr) -> get_val() << endl;
      }
      else if (!strcmp(eptr -> get_class(), "StringObj"))
      {
      cout << ((StringObj*) eptr) -> get_val() << endl;
      }
      else if (!strcmp(eptr -> get_class(), "CharObj"))
      {
      cout << ((CharObj*) eptr) -> get_val() << endl;
      }
      else // must be IntObj
      {
      cout << ((IntObj*) eptr) -> get_val() << endl;
      }
   }  // end for
   cout << "STRIKE ANY KEY" << endl;
   cin.get();
}  // end display_three()
```

LABORATORY EXERCISE—USING THE `ElementSet` CLASS

Later in this course, you will be implementing your own heterogeneous data structures. The emphasis now is on understanding the concepts that are needed to implement such data structures rather than using them at this time. Consequently, these laboratory exercises relate only to the use of the ElementSet class, as opposed to the implementation of some new heterogeneous data structure.

In order to use the ElementSet class in a program, you must:
1. Include the eleset.h header file in any program file that will refer to the ElementSet class.
2. Include the eleset.cxx (eleset.cpp) implementation file in your project. This provides the ElementSet member function definitions.

Part 1 — Creating a Set of IntObj objects

Write a program that will use an ElementSet to create a set of IntObj objects. Your program will ask the user to enter N integer values from the keyboard (where the value of N will be specified by the user). Those integer values will be used to create N dynamic IntObj objects and these will be added to an ElementSet. After the ElementSet has been created, you will apply the display message in order to see that the integers have been successfully added. Use the following definitions:

```
int ival;     // int value read in from user
IntObj iptr; // pointer to dynamic IntObj
ElementSet the_set;     // set of IntObj objects
```

Note that you need only one pointer variable, iptr. You do not need one such variable for each dynamic object that you will be creating. In a loop, you will repeatedly apply the new operator in order to create new IntObj objects. You will then add the dynamic objects to the_set. The relevant pattern then is:

```
iptr = new IntObj(ival);
the_set.add(iptr);
```

Worksheet for Laboratory Exercise —
Creating a Set of Intobj Objects

```
/* -- Program name:
   -- Programmer:
   -- Date:
   -- ** Overview
          .
          .
          .
                */

#include < ... >

// GLOBAL CONSTANTS AND TYPEDEF'S

// GLOBAL FUNCTION PROTOTYPES


main()
{
    // FUNCTION PROTOTYPES


    // LOCAL DATA


    // STATEMENTS
```

```
}
```

Part 2 — Manipulating a Set of `IntObj` objects

Write a program that will create an `ElementSet` (called `the_set`) whose
membership is restricted to `IntObj` objects (as was done in part 1). Once a set
of N `IntObj` objects has been created, your program will find the maximum
and minimum values in `the_set` and will compute the sum of all of the values
in `the_set`. These results will then be displayed at the computer screen. Accomplishing this will require repeated applications of the function `Element-
Set::get_any` and the use of pointer type casting. If there are N elements in
`the_set`, N successive applications of `get_any` will cycle through all N objects in `the_set`.

Worksheet for Laboratory Exercise —
Manipulating a Set of Intobj Objects

```
/* -- Program name:
   -- Programmer:
   -- Date:
   -- ** Overview
         .
         .
         .
               */

#include < ... >

// GLOBAL CONSTANTS AND TYPEDEF'S

// GLOBAL FUNCTION PROTOTYPES


main()
{
    // FUNCTION PROTOTYPES


    // LOCAL DATA


    // STATEMENTS












}
```

CREATING A SPECIALIZED COLLECTION CLASS

The `PersonSet` class presented in the main text is a specialization of the `ElementSet` class. The `PersonSet` class limits membership to `Person`, `Professor` and `Student` classes. The fact that we know that all objects in a `PersonSet` must belong to one of these three classes enables us to introduce and implement the `file_in` function, which is used to `file_in` a collection of person objects (i.e., `Person`, `Professor` and `Student` objects) from an external file.

LABORATORY EXERCISE—RESTRICTED COLLECTION CLASSES

A `CitySet` is a specialized `ElementSet` for which membership is restricted to `City` objects (as described in earlier laboratory exercises). Here is the declaration for the `CitySet` class:

```
class CitySet : public ElementSet
{
    public:
        // MEMBER FUNCTIONS ...
        // constructor - destructor
        CitySet();
        virtual ~CitySet();

        // modify
        virtual int add(ElementPtr);

        // file in - file out
        virtual int file_in(string);
        virtual int file_out(string);
};   // end class CitySet
```

Implement the new `CitySet` member functions:
1. the constructor, `CitySet`
2. the destructor, `~CitySet`
3. add
4. file_in
5. file_out

Write a program that will test your `CitySet` implementation.

Worksheet for Laboratory Exercise —
Restricted Collection Classes

```
/* -- Program name:
   -- Programmer:
   -- Date:
   -- ** Overview
            •
            •
            •
                    */

#include < ... >

// GLOBAL CONSTANTS AND TYPEDEF'S

// GLOBAL FUNCTION PROTOTYPES


main()
{
    // FUNCTION PROTOTYPES


    // LOCAL DATA


    // STATEMENTS
```

```
}
```

C++ Program Listing

elements.h

```
// This is the header file for the Element class
// that is an abstract class that serves as the
// root class for the hierarchy of element classes.


#ifndef ELEMENTS_H
#define ELEMENTS_H


#include <string.h>
#include <iostream.h>
#include <fstream.h>


// GLOBAL DECLARATION, DEFINITION ...
typedef char class_name[21];


enum boolean {FALSE,TRUE};


class Element {
    protected:
        // DATA MEMBER ...
        class_name my_class;


    public:
        // MEMBER FUNCTIONS ...
        // constructor - destructor
        inline Element();
        inline virtual ~Element();


        // access
        virtual char* get_class();


        // display
        virtual void display() { };
        // not implemented at this level


        // comparison operators
        virtual int operator ==(Element&);
```

```
        virtual int operator !=(Element&);
        virtual int operator >(Element&);
        virtual int operator <(Element&);
        virtual int operator <=(Element&);
        virtual int operator >=(Element&);


        // read in
        virtual void read_in() { };
         // not implemented at this level


        // file in - file out
        virtual void file_in(ifstream&) { };
         // not implemented at this level
        virtual void file_out(ofstream&) { };
         // not implemented at this level
};   // end class Element


// POINTER TYPE ...
typedef Element* ElementPtr;


#endif
```

C++ Program Listing

elements.cxx

```cpp
// This is the implementation file for the Element class.


#include "elements.h"


//
// constructor - destructor
//


// Constructor:    Element::Element()
// Purpose:        To initialize the receiver.
// Pre:            None
// Post:           my_class = "Element"
Element::Element()
{
    strcpy(my_class, "Element");
}   // end Element::Element()


// Destructor:     Element::~Element()
// Purpose:        To destroy the receiver
// Pre:            The receiver is initialized
// Post:           The receiver is destroyed
Element::~Element()
{
    ;
}   // end Element::~Element()


//
// access
//


// Function:       Element::get_class()
// Purpose:        Returns the class of the receiver
//                 This function is inherited by all
//                 derived classes.
// Pre:            my_class = aClassName
// Post:           get_class = aClassName
char* Element::get_class()
{
    return my_class;
}   // end Element::get_class()
```

```
//
// comparison operators
//


// Operator:        Element::==(e)
// Purpose:         This operator introduces the notion of
//                  value identity into our class hierarchy.
//                  At this level, the function always returns 1,
//                  since any two Element objects are equal.
// Pre:             *eptr belongs to the class Element.
// Post:            ==() = 1
int Element::operator ==(Element& e)
{
    return 1;
}  // end operator Element::==


// Operator:        Element::!=(e)
// Purpose:         This operator introduces the notion of
//                  value inequality into our class hierarchy.
//                  At this level, the function always returns 0,
//                  since any two Element objects are equal.
// Pre:             *eptr belongs to the class Element.
// Post:            !=() = 0
int Element::operator !=(Element& e)
{
    return 0;
}  // end operator Element::!=


// Operator:        Element::<(e)
// Purpose:         This operator introduces the notion of a
//                  linear ordering into our class hierarchy.
//                  At this level, this operator always
//                  returns 0 since any two Element objects are
//                  equal.
// Pre:             *eptr belongs to the class Element.
// Post:            <() = 0
int Element::operator <(Element& e)
{
    return 0;
}  // end operator Element::<


// Operator:        Element::>(e)
// Purpose:         This operator introduces the notion of a
//                  linear ordering into our class hierarchy.
//                  At this level, this operator always
//                  returns 0 since any two Element objects are
//                  equal.
// Pre:             *eptr belongs to the class Element.
// Post:            >() = 0
int Element::operator >(Element& e)
{
    return 0;
}  // end operator Element::>
```

```
// Operator:      Element::<=(e)
// Purpose:       This operator introduces the notion of
//                less than or equal to based upon value
//                identity into our class hierarchy.
//                At this level, the function always returns 1,
//                since any two Element objects are equal.
// Pre:           *eptr belongs to the class Element.
// Post:          <=() = 1
int Element::operator <=(Element& e)
{
    return 1;
}  // end operator Element::<=


// Operator:      Element::>=(e)
// Purpose:       This operator introduces the notion of
//                greater than or equal to based upon value
//                identity into our class hierarchy.
//                At this level, the function always returns 1,
//                since any two Element objects are equal.
// Pre:           *eptr belongs to the class Element.
// Post:          >=() = 1
int Element::operator >=(Element& e)
{
    return 1;
}  // end operator Element::>=
```

C++ Program Listing
standobj.h

```
// This is the header file for the standard object classes:
//    StringObj  FloatObj  IntObj  CharObj


#ifndef STDOBJ_H
#define STDOBJ_H


#include <string.h>
#include "strg.h"
#include "elements.h"


// ************************************************************


class IntObj : public Element
{
    protected:
        // DATA MEMBER ...
        int value;


    public:
        // MEMBER FUNCTIONS ...
        // constructors - destructor
        inline IntObj(int);
        inline IntObj();            // default constructor
        inline virtual ~IntObj();


        // display
        virtual void display();


        // convert to and from standard int
        inline virtual int get_val();
        inline virtual void set_val(int);


        // comparison operators
        virtual int operator ==(Element&);
        virtual int operator !=(Element&);
        virtual int operator >(Element&);
```

```cpp
        virtual int operator <(Element&);
        virtual int operator <=(Element&);
        virtual int operator >=(Element&);



        // file in / file out
        virtual void file_in(ifstream&);
        virtual void file_out(ofstream&);
};   // end class IntObj



// *****************************************************************



class FloatObj : public Element
{
    protected:
        // DATA MEMBER ...
        float value;


    public:
        // MEMBER FUNCTIONS ...
        // constructors - destructor
        inline FloatObj(float);
        inline FloatObj();           // default constructor
        inline virtual ~FloatObj();


        // display
        virtual void display();


        // convert to and from standard float
        inline virtual float get_val();
        inline virtual void set_val(float);


        // comparison operators
        virtual int operator ==(Element&);
        virtual int operator !=(Element&);
        virtual int operator >(Element&);
        virtual int operator <(Element&);
        virtual int operator <=(Element&);
        virtual int operator >=(Element&);


        // file in / file out
        virtual void file_in(ifstream&);
        virtual void file_out(ofstream&);
};   // end class FloatObj



// *********************************************************
```

```cpp
class StringObj : public Element
{
   protected:
      // DATA MEMBER ...
      string value;


   public:
      // MEMBER FUNCTIONS ...
      // constructors - destructor
      inline StringObj(string);
      inline StringObj();          // default constructor
      inline virtual ~StringObj();


      // display
      virtual void display();


      // convert to and from string
      inline virtual char* get_val();
      inline virtual void set_val(string);


      // comparison operators
      virtual int operator ==(Element&);
      virtual int operator !=(Element&);
      virtual int operator >(Element&);
      virtual int operator <(Element&);
      virtual int operator <=(Element&);
      virtual int operator >=(Element&);


      // file in / file out
      virtual void file_in(ifstream&);
      virtual void file_out(ofstream&);
};   // end class StringObj


// ******************************************************************


class CharObj : public Element
{
   protected:
      // DATA MEMBER ...
      char value;


   public:
      // MEMBER FUNCTIONS ...
      // constructors - destructor
      inline CharObj(char);
      inline CharObj();          // default constructor
      inline virtual ~CharObj();
```

```
                    // display
                    virtual void display();


                    // convert to and from standard char
                    inline virtual char get_val();
                    inline virtual void set_val(char);


                    // comparison operators
                    virtual int operator ==(Element&);
                    virtual int operator !=(Element&);
                    virtual int operator >(Element&);
                    virtual int operator <(Element&);
                    virtual int operator <=(Element&);
                    virtual int operator >=(Element&);


                    // file in / file out
                    virtual void file_in(ifstream&);
                    virtual void file_out(ofstream&);
};   // end class CharObj


        #endif
```

C++ Program Listing

standobj.cxx

```
// This is the implementation file for the standard object
// classes:       StringObj  FloatObj  IntObj  CharObj


#include "standobj.h"


//
// ******************** IntObj class *********************
//


//
// constructors - destructor
//


// Constructor:    IntObj::IntObj(an_int)
// Purpose:        Initializes the receiver and sets its
//                 value to an_int.
// Pre:            an_int = anInt
// Post:           my_class = "IntObj" and value = anInt
IntObj::IntObj(int an_int)
{
   strcpy(my_class, "IntObj");
   value = an_int;
}  // end IntObj::IntObj(int)


// Constructor:    IntObj::IntObj()
// Purpose:        Initializes the receiver without
//                 initializing its value.
// Pre:            None
// Post:           my_class = "IntObj"
IntObj::IntObj()
{
   strcpy(my_class, "IntObj");
}  // end IntObj::IntObj()


// Constructor:    IntObj::~IntObj()
// Purpose:        To destroy the receiver
// Pre:            The receiver is initialized
// Post:           The receiver is destroyed
IntObj::~IntObj()
```

```
{
   ;
}   // end IntObj::~IntObj()



//
// display
//


// Function:        IntObj::display()
// Purpose:         To display a representation of the receiver
//                  at the computer screen
// Pre:             value = anInt and output = oldStuff
// Post:            output = oldStuff anInt \n
void IntObj::display()
{
   cout << value << endl;
}   // end IntObj::display()



//
// convert to and from standard int
//


// Function:        IntObj::get_val()
// Purpose:         To return the value of the receiver as an
//                  integer
// Pre:             value = anInt
// Post:            get_val = anInt
int IntObj::get_val()
{
   return value;
}   // end IntObj::get_val()



// Function:        IntObj::set_val(an_int)
// Purpose:         To set the receiver's value to an_int
// Pre:             an_int = anInt
// Post:            value = anInt
void IntObj::set_val(int an_int)
{
   value = an_int;
}   // end IntObj::set_val()



//
// comparison operators
//


// Operator:        IntObj::==(e)
// Purpose:         Returns true if receiver and *eptr are
//                  value equal. ASSUMES *eptr IS AN IntObj.
```

```
// Pre:            e.get_class() = "IntObj" and
//                 e.get_val() = firstInt
//                 and value = secondInt
// Post:           ==() = (firstInt = secondInt)
int IntObj::operator ==(Element& e)
{
   return (value == ((IntObj&) e).get_val( ));
}  // end IntObj::operator ==


// Operator:       IntObj::!=(e)
// Purpose:        Returns true if receiver and *eptr are not
//                 value equal. ASSUMES *eptr IS AN IntObj.
// Pre:            e.get_class() = "IntObj" and
//                 e.get_val() = firstInt
//                 and value = secondInt
// Post:           !=() = (firstInt != secondInt)
int IntObj::operator !=(Element& e)
{
   return (value != ((IntObj&) e).get_val( ));
}  // end IntObj::operator !=


// Operator:       IntObj::<(e)
// Purpose:        Returns true if receiver is less than e.
//                 ASSUMES e IS AN IntObj.
// Pre:            e.get_class() = "IntObj" and
//                 e.get_val() = firstInt
//                 and value = secondInt
// Post:           <() = (firstInt < secondInt)
int IntObj::operator <(Element& e)
{
   return (value < ((IntObj&) e).get_val());
}  // end IntObj::operator <


// Operator:       IntObj::<=(e)
// Purpose:        Returns true if receiver is less than
//                 or equal to e.  ASSUMES e IS AN IntObj.
// Pre:            e.get_class() = "IntObj" and
//                 e.get_val() = firstInt
//                 and value = secondInt
// Post:           <=() = (firstInt <= secondInt)
int IntObj::operator <=(Element& e)
{
   return (value <= ((IntObj&) e).get_val());
}  // end IntObj::operator <=


// Operator:       IntObj::>(e)
// Purpose:        Returns true if receiver is greater than e.
//                 ASSUMES e IS AN IntObj.
// Pre:            e.get_class() = "IntObj" and
//                 e.get_val() = firstInt
//                 and value = secondInt
// Post:           >() = (firstInt > secondInt)
```

```
int IntObj::operator >(Element& e)
{
   return (value > ((IntObj&) e).get_val());
}   // end IntObj::operator >


// Operator:       IntObj::>=(e)
// Purpose:        Returns true if receiver is less than
//                 or equal to e.  ASSUMES e IS AN IntObj.
// Pre:            e.get_class() = "IntObj" and
//                 e.get_val() = firstInt
//                 and value = secondInt
// Post:           >=() = (firstInt >= secondInt)
int IntObj::operator >=(Element& e)
{
   return (value >= ((IntObj&) e).get_val());
}   // end IntObj::operator >=



//
// file in / file out
//



// Function:       IntObj::file_in(in_file)
// Purpose:        To read in a value for the receiver from a
//                 text file, in_file.  This function assumes
//                 that the line containing the class string has
//                 already been read in.
// Pre:            in_file = anInt restOfFile
// Post:           in_file = restOfFile and value = anInt
void IntObj::file_in(ifstream& in_file)
{
   in_file >> value;
   in_file.ignore(LINESIZE, '\n');
}   // end IntObj::file_in()



// Function:       IntObj::file_out(out_file)
// Purpose:        To write out a representation of the receiver
//                 to a text file, out_file.
// Pre:            out_file = oldStuff and my_class = "IntObj"
//                  and value = anInt
// Post:           (oldStuff != "" and out_file = oldStuff
//                   \n "IntObj" \n anInt) or
//                 (oldStuff = "" and out_file = oldStuff
//                   "IntObj" \n anInt)
void IntObj::file_out(ofstream& out_file)
{
   if (out_file.tellp())
   {
   // this is not first object in file
   // need to advance to new line
   out_file << endl;
   }
   out_file << my_class << endl;
```

```
      out_file << value;
}   // end IntObj::file_out()



//
// ************** FloatObj class **************
//



//
// constructors - destructor
//


FloatObj::FloatObj(float a_float)
{
   strcpy(my_class, "FloatObj");
   value = a_float;
}   // end FloatObj::FloatObj(float)


FloatObj::FloatObj()
{
   strcpy(my_class, "FloatObj");
}   // end FloatObj::FloatObj()


FloatObj::~FloatObj()
{
   ;
}   // end FloatObj::~FloatObj()



//
// display
//


void FloatObj::display()
{
   cout << value << endl;
}   // end FloatObj::display()



//
// convert to and from standard float
//


float FloatObj::get_val()
{
   return value;
}   // end FloatObj::get_val()
```

```
void FloatObj::set_val(float a_float)
{
   value = a_float;
}  // end FloatObj::set_val()



//
// comparison operators
//


// Operator:      FloatObj::==(e)
// Purpose:       Returns true if receiver and e are
//                value equal.  ASSUMES e IS A FloatObj
// Pre:           e.get_class() = "FloatObj" and
//                e.get_val() = firstFloat
//                and value = secondFloat
// Post:          ==() = (firstFloat = secondFloat)
int FloatObj::operator ==(Element& e)
{
   return (value == ((FloatObj&) e).get_val());
}  // end FloatObj::operator ==


// Operator:      FloatObj::!=(e)
// Purpose:       Returns true if receiver and e are not
//                value equal.  ASSUMES e IS A FloatObj
// Pre:           e.get_class() = "FloatObj" and
//                e.get_val() = firstFloat
//                and value = secondFloat
// Post:          !=() = (firstFloat != secondFloat)
int FloatObj::operator !=(Element& e)
{
   return (value != ((FloatObj&) e).get_val());
}  // end FloatObj::operator !=


// Operator:      FloatObj::<(e)
// Purpose:       Returns true if receiver is less than e.
//                ASSUMES e IS A FloatObj.
// Pre:           e.get_class() = "FloatObj" and
//                e.get_val() = firstFloat
//                and value = secondFloat
// Post:          <() = (firstFloat < secondFloat)
int FloatObj::operator <(Element& e)
{
     return (value < ((FloatObj&) e).get_val());
}  // end FloatObj::operator <


// Operator:      FloatObj::<=(e)
// Purpose:       Returns true if receiver is less than or value
//                equal to e.  ASSUMES e IS A FloatObj.
// Pre:           e.get_class() = "FloatObj" and
//                e.get_val() = firstFloat
//                and value = secondFloat
```

```
// Post:              <=() = (firstFloat <= secondFloat)
int FloatObj::operator <=(Element& e)
{
      return (value <= ((FloatObj&) e).get_val());
}  // end FloatObj::operator <=


// Operator:       FloatObj::>(e)
// Purpose:        Returns true if receiver is greater than e.
//                 ASSUMES e IS A FloatObj.
// Pre:            e.get_class() = "FloatObj" and
//                 e.get_val() = firstFloat
//                 and value = secondFloat
// Post:           >() = (firstFloat > secondFloat)
int FloatObj::operator >(Element& e)
{
      return (value > ((FloatObj&) e).get_val());
}  // end FloatObj::operator >


// Operator:       FloatObj::>=(e)
// Purpose:        Returns true if receiver is greater than or
//                 value equal to e.  ASSUMES e IS A FloatObj.
// Pre:            e.get_class() = "FloatObj" and
//                 e.get_val() = firstFloat
//                 and value = secondFloat
// Post:           >=() = (firstFloat >= secondFloat)
int FloatObj::operator >=(Element& e)
{
      return (value >= ((FloatObj&) e).get_val());
}  // end FloatObj::operator >=


//
// file in / file out
//


void FloatObj::file_in(ifstream& in_file)
{
   in_file >> value;
   in_file.ignore(LINESIZE, '\n');
}  // end FloatObj::file_in()


void FloatObj::file_out(ofstream& out_file)
{
    if (out_file.tellp())
    {
    // this is not first object in file
    // need to advance to new line
    out_file << endl;
    }
   out_file << my_class << endl;
   out_file << value;
}  // end FloatObj::file_out()
```

```cpp
//
// *************** StringObj class ***************
//


//
// constructors - destructor
//


StringObj::StringObj(string a_string)
{
   strcpy(my_class, "StringObj");
   strcpy(value, a_string);
}   // end StringObj::StringObj(string)


StringObj::StringObj()
{
   strcpy(my_class, "StringObj");
}   // end StringObj::StringObj()


StringObj::~StringObj()
{
   ;
}   // end StringObj::~StringObj()


//
// display
//


void StringObj::display()
{
   cout << value << endl;
}   // end StringObj::display()


//
// convert to and from standard string
//


char* StringObj::get_val()
{
   return value;
}   // end StringObj::get_val()


void StringObj::set_val(string a_string)
{
   strcpy(value, a_string);
}   // end StringObj::set_val()
```

```
//
// comparison operators
//


// Operator:       StringObj::==(e)
// Purpose:        Returns true if receiver and e are
//                 value equal.  ASSUMES e IS A StringObj
// Pre:            e.get_class() = "StringObj" and
//                 e.get_val() = firstString
//                 and value = secondString
// Post:           ==() = (firstString = secondString))
int StringObj::operator ==(Element& e)
{
   if (!strcmp(value, ((StringObj*) &e) -> get_val()))
      return 1;
   else
      return 0;
}  // end StringObj::operator ==


// Operator:       StringObj::!=(e)
// Purpose:        Returns true if receiver and e are not
//                 value equal.  ASSUMES e IS A StringObj
// Pre:            e.get_class() = "StringObj" and
//                 e.get_val() = firstString
//                 and value = secondString
// Post:           !=() = (firstString != secondString))
int StringObj::operator !=(Element& e)
{
   if (strcmp(value, ((StringObj&) e).get_val()))
      return 1;
   else
      return 0;
}  // end StringObj::operator !=


// Operator:       StringObj::<(e)
// Purpose:        Returns true if receiver is less than e.
//                 ASSUMES e IS A StringObj
// Pre:            e.get_class() = "StringObj" and
//                 e.get_val() = firstString
//                 and value = secondString
// Post:           <() = (firstString < secondString)
int StringObj::operator <(Element& e)
{
  if (strcmp(value, ((StringObj&) e).get_val()) < 0)
     return 1;
  else
     return 0;
}  // end StringObj::operator <


// Operator:       StringObj::<=(e)
// Purpose:        Returns true if receiver is less than or value
//                 equal to e. ASSUMES e IS A StringObj
```

```cpp
// Pre:            e.get_class() = "StringObj" and
//                 e.get_val() = firstString
//                 and value = secondString
// Post:           <=() = (firstString <= secondString)
int StringObj::operator <=(Element& e)
{
  if (strcmp(value, ((StringObj&) e).get_val()) <= 0)
     return 1;
  else
     return 0;
}  // end StringObj::operator <=


// Operator:       StringObj::>(e)
// Purpose:        Returns true if receiver is greater than e.
//                 ASSUMES e IS A StringObj
// Pre:            e.get_class() = "StringObj" and
//                 e.get_val() = firstString
//                 and value = secondString
// Post:           >() = (firstString > secondString)
int StringObj::operator >(Element& e)
{
  if (strcmp(value, ((StringObj&) e).get_val()) > 0)
     return 1;
  else
     return 0;
}  // end StringObj::operator >


// Operator:       StringObj::>=(e)
// Purpose:        Returns true if receiver is greater than or
//                 value equal to e. ASSUMES e IS A StringObj
// Pre:            e.get_class() = "StringObj" and
//                 e.get_val() = firstString
//                 and value = secondString
// Post:           >=() = (firstString >= secondString)
int StringObj::operator >=(Element& e)
{
  if (strcmp(value, ((StringObj&) e).get_val()) >= 0)
     return 1;
  else
     return 0;
}  // end StringObj::operator <=


//
// file in / file out
//


void StringObj::file_in(ifstream& in_file)
{
   in_file.getline(value, MAXSTRING);
   if (in_file.gcount() == MAXSTRING - 1)
   {
      in_file.ignore(LINESIZE, '\n');
```

```
    }
}  // end StringObj::file_in()


void StringObj::file_out(ofstream& out_file)
{
    if (out_file.tellp())
    {
     // this is not first object in file
     // need to advance to new line
     out_file << endl;
    }
    out_file << my_class << endl;
    out_file << value;
}  // end StringObj::file_out()



//
// ************** CharObj class **************
//


//
// constructors - destructor
//


CharObj::CharObj(char a_char)
{
    strcpy(my_class, "CharObj");
    value = a_char;
}  // end CharObj::CharObj(char)


CharObj::CharObj()
{
    strcpy(my_class, "CharObj");
}  // end CharObj::CharObj()


CharObj::~CharObj()
{
    ;
}  // end CharObj::~CharObj()



//
// display
//


void CharObj::display()
{
    cout << value << endl;
}  // end CharObj::display()
```

```cpp
//
// convert to and from standard char
//


char CharObj::get_val()
{
   return value;
}  // end CharObj::get_val()


void CharObj::set_val(char a_char)
{
   value = a_char;
}  // end CharObj::set_val()


// Operator:      CharObj::==(e)
// Purpose:       Returns true if receiver and e are
//                value equal.  ASSUMES e IS A CharObj.
// Pre:           e.get_class() = "CharObj" and
//                e.get_val() = firstChar
//                and value = secondChar
// Post:          ==() = (firstChar = secondChar)
int CharObj::operator ==(Element& e)
{
   return (value == ((CharObj&) e).get_val());
}  // end CharObj::operator ==


// Operator:      CharObj::!=(e)
// Purpose:       Returns true if receiver and e are
//                value equal.  ASSUMES e IS A CharObj.
// Pre:           e.get_class() = "CharObj" and
//                e.get_val() = firstChar
//                and value = secondChar
// Post:          !=() = (firstChar != secondChar)
int CharObj::operator !=(Element& e)
{
   return (value != ((CharObj&) e).get_val());
}  // end CharObj::operator !=


// Operator:      CharObj::<(e)
// Purpose:       Returns true if receiver is less than e.
//                ASSUMES *eptr IS A CharObj.
// Pre:           e.get_class() = "CharObj" and
//                e.get_val() = firstChar
//                and value = secondChar
// Post:          <() = (firstChar < secondChar)
int CharObj::operator <(Element& e)
{
   return (value < ((CharObj&) e).get_val());
}  // end CharObj::operator <


// Operator:      CharObj::<=(e)
// Purpose:       Returns true if receiver is less than or value
```

```
//                    equal to e.   ASSUMES *eptr IS A CharObj.
// Pre:              e.get_class() = "CharObj" and
//                   e.get_val() = firstChar
//                   and value = secondChar
// Post:             <=() = (firstChar <= secondChar)
int CharObj::operator <=(Element& e)
{
   return (value <= ((CharObj&) e).get_val());
}  // end CharObj::operator <=


// Operator:        CharObj::>(e)
// Purpose:         Returns true if receiver is greater than e.
//                  ASSUMES *eptr IS A CharObj.
// Pre:             e.get_class() = "CharObj" and
//                  e.get_val() = firstChar
//                  and value = secondChar
// Post:            >() = (firstChar > secondChar)
int CharObj::operator >(Element& e)
{
   return (value > ((CharObj&) e).get_val());
}  // end CharObj::operator >


// Operator:        CharObj::>=(e)
// Purpose:         Returns true if receiver is greater than or
//                  value equal to e.  ASSUMES *eptr IS A CharObj.
// Pre:             e.get_class() = "CharObj" and
//                  e.get_val() = firstChar
//                  and value = secondChar
// Post:            >=() = (firstChar >= secondChar)
int CharObj::operator >=(Element& e)
{
   return (value >= ((CharObj&) e).get_val());
}  // end CharObj::operator >=


//
// file in / file out
//


void CharObj::file_in(ifstream& in_file)
{
   in_file >> value;
   in_file.ignore(LINESIZE, '\n');
}  // end CharObj::file_in()


void CharObj::file_out(ofstream& out_file)
{
    if (out_file.tellp())
    {
    // this is not first object in file
    // need to advance to new line
    out_file << endl;
```

```
    }
  out_file << my_class << endl;
  out_file << value << endl;
}  // end CharObj::file_out()
```

CHAPTER **3**

COMPLEXITY, SEARCHING, AND SORTING

This chapter contains laboratory exercises that explore the efficiency of algorithms. Several different sorting and searching routines are provided with this manual; you will examine their efficiency empirically. The resulting empirical efficiency measures can then be compared with the theoretical complexity measures that were derived in the text. The concluding sections ask you to write some routines and measure their efficiency, both theoretically and empirically.

TOOLS FOR TIMING PROGRAMS

Every computer has an internal clock and a way for programs to read the time on the clock. However, this feature is not a standard part of C++, so each different compiler implements it differently. The C and C++ libraries include the function `times` which will, among other things, return times for the currently executing process and all of its terminated child processes. The argument for the `times` function is a pointer designating the place to store the time recorded at the call.

In order to use `times` to gather empirical timings, you need to add the following steps, shown in Figure 3–1, to your program:

```
#include <sys/tyoes.h>
#include <sys/times.h>
     •
     •
     •
clock_t times();
struct tms starttime, endtime;
int user_time;
     •
     •
     •
//  Get the start time
times (&starttime);

//  The part of the program to be timed goes here.

//  Get the end time
```

211

```
times (&endtime);
    •
    •
    •
//   Compute the elapsed time
user_time = endtime.tms_utime - starttime.tms_utime;

//   Print out the elapsed time.
cout<<"CPU time used executing " << algorithm_name
    << " was, in 1/60 seconds:  "<< user_time;
    •
    •
    •
```

FIGURE 3–1   C++ setup for timing particular algorithms.

Note that here `algorithm_name` is a string used to identify the particular algorithm being timed and `user_time` is an `int` used to hold the execution time, in 1/60 of a second units, to execute the algorithm enclosed between the two calls to `times`. Use this general format for all of the timing exercises in this and the chapters which follow.

LABORATORY EXERCISE—LINEAR VS. BINARY SEARCH

This laboratory exercise requires empirical evaluation of the efficiency of two different search algorithms, linear search and binary search, using a rather large list of random numbers that your program will generate. The purpose of this lab is to corroborate the theoretical complexities of these two search algorithms, and to become familiar with the tools for timing algorithms.

Part 1 — Develop the Program

Design a program that generates a large list of random numbers and searches the list for a number known *not* to be in the file, using the linear search function from Chapter 2 of the text. Your program should display the elapsed time, in 1/60 of a second units, that it takes for the search to be completed. This process is a test of the *worst case complexity* of the linear search.

Copy the functions `randget` and `LinSearch` from the system course directory (or your diskette) into your working directory for this course. The function `randget` is used to generate a set of random numbers and place them in a specified array. The calling sequence is:

```
randget (a, n);
```

where   a is an `IntArr`, as defined below, and
              n is an `int` representing the number of random integers to be
              generated, $0 \le n \le$ MAXARRSIZE.

In order for this to correctly compile and execute, you will need to add some `includes` and declarations as shown in Figure 3–2 in your header file for this lab program.

```
#include <iostream.h>
#include <fstream.h>
#include <stdlib.h>      //for rand()
#include <time.h>        //for clock()
#include "strg.h"

const MAXARRSIZE = 10001;
typedef int IntArr[MAXARRSIZE];
```

FIGURE 3–2   C++ `includes` and declarations for the lab program.

You will need to adjust the number of random numbers used with regard to the speed of the processor you are using. A list size of 1,000 or 2,000 would be appropriate for a smaller PC or Macintosh, while 8,000 to 10,000 may be better for a workstation. Now use the functions `LinSearch` to search the array for a number known not to be in the array. The calling sequence for `LinSearch` is:

```
LinSearch(a, n, x)
```

where   a is the name of the array of numbers to be searched,
             n is the size of the array, a, and
             x is the number to be searched for.

Part 2 — Augment the Program

Now add to the program a capability to read an *ordered* array of numbers, search the array for a number known to be larger than any number in the array, and display the elapsed time for this search, using the binary search procedure from the text.

Copy the functions `SectionSort` and `BinarySearch` from the system course directory into your working directory for this problem. Use `SelectionSort` to order the previously generated set of random numbers. The calling sequence for `SelectionSort` is:

```
SelectionSort (a, n);
```

where   a[0..n] is the array of numbers to be sorted, and
             n represents the size of the array (n+1).

Now use the function `BinarySearch` to search for a number known not to be in the array of random numbers. The calling sequence for `BinarySearch` is:

```
BinarySearch (a, n, x);
```

where   a[0..n] is the array of numbers to be sorted,
           n represents the size of the array (n+1), and
           x is the number to be searched for.
Again, use the timing tools to determine, empirically, the timing for the worst case of a binary search.

Part 3 — Run the Program and Record the Timing Results

The program should be designed to perform the linear and binary searches several times, each time varying the size of the array searched (use at least 5 appropriate array sizes, that is, array sizes that give meaningful timings).

Part 4 — Graph the Results of the Runs

Plot the running times that your program displays, using a graph whose horizontal axis is the size of the array searched and vertical axis the elapsed time.

Questions

1. Does the empirical complexity of the linear search seem to follow a straight line on your graph—that is, does it seem to be O(n), where n is the size of the array searched?
2. Does the empirical complexity of the binary search seem to follow a logarithmic line on your graph—that is, does it seem to be O($\log_2 n$)?
3. Note the pre- and postconditions for the search algorithms. Are the linear and binary search algorithms correct? That is, do they find an element in the array if and only if it is really there? How does this sense of correctness reflect itself in the pre- and postconditions?

Worksheet for Laboratory Exercise —
Linear vs. Binary Search

```
/* -- Program name:
   -- Programmer:
   -- Date:
   -- ** Overview
          .
          .
          .
               */

#include <iostream.h>
#include <fstream.h>
#include <stdlib.h>     //for rand()
#include <time.h>       //for clock()
#include <sys/types.h>
#include <sys/times.h>
#include "strg.h"

// GLOBAL CONSTANTS AND TYPEDEF'S

// GLOBAL FUNCTION PROTOTYPES


main()
{
   // pre:

   // FUNCTION PROTOTYPES

   // LOCAL DATA

   // STATEMENTS




   //                                               post:
}
```

Notes for Answers to Questions

1.

2.

3.

(TEAM) LABORATORY EXERCISE—EMPIRICAL EVALUATION OF SORTING

Using the six sorting algorithms presented in this chapter, the team should conduct an empirical analysis of their performance, using an internal timer and arrays of random numbers generated as described in Part 1 of the Laboratory Exercise—Linear vs. Binary Search above. Use at least 7 different array sizes selected with respect to the internal speed of your computer to give meaningful readings. The analysis should collect execution times for each of the algorithms and each of the given array sizes. Each member of the team in this project should gather and plot the resulting execution times for two or three of the six algorithms. The team should then compare each of its six plots with the average case theoretical complexities for each of the six algorithms, as given in the text. For convenience, the six sorting algorithms are provided in the system course directory (or your diskette).

Part 1 — Get the Team Organized

In team projects, the first step is to specifically identify the tasks that each member will carry out. For this particular project, this step is fairly straightforward. For a two-member team, each member should run three of the six sorts; for a three-member team, each member should run two sorts. This can be done either by designing a single program, to be shared by all members of the team, or separate programs. The latter alternative, of course, creates some duplication of effort, but may be necessary because of members' work schedules. In any event, task identification is essential before proceeding further with this lab.

Part 2 — Design and Test the Program

After the tasks have been assigned, the team should agree on an overall design, and then individual team members should design and implement their own parts of the program. Testing should then be done in accordance with agreed-upon array sizes, output format, and completion time responsibilities.

Part 3 — Run the Program and Record the Timings

After the team designs a single program, one team member should run the program and record the results. This is fairly tedious business, and it's not necessary for all members to sit around watching sorts run. If different programs are testing different sorting algorithms, then each team member is responsible for gathering the timing data for his/her own program.

Part 4 — Plot the Results

If one person on the team ran the program and recorded the timings, then plotting the results should be done by the other(s). When different programs are used for different sorts, all team members plot their own timing data (after the team agrees on a common format for the plot). If you have access to graphical software on your computer, use it to facilitate your graph-plotting and curve-fitting work for this lab.

Questions

1. Carefully discuss the empirical complexities of the six sorts, in comparison with their respective theoretical complexities. That is, does the empirical complexity of the insertion sort seem to follow a quadratic equation (i.e., $O(n^2)$) on your graph? Does the empirical complexity of the heap sort seem to follow an $n\log_2 n$ equation? And so on. This discussion should include and make reference to the six plots that you developed in Part 4 of this exercise.

2. Are the sorting algorithms correct? Do they really rearrange the list's elements into ascending sequence? How can your program be altered so that it quickly makes an empirical check on the correctness of these algorithms?

Worksheet for Laboratory Exercise —
Empirical Evaluation of Sorting

```
/* -- Program name:
   -- Programmer:
   -- Date:
   -- ** Overview
          .
          .              .                    */

#include <iostream.h>
#include <fstream.h>
#include <stdlib.h>     //for rand()
#include <time.h>       //for clock()
#include <sys/types.h>
#include <sys/times.h>
#include "strg.h"

// GLOBAL CONSTANTS AND TYPEDEF'S

// GLOBAL FUNCTION PROTOTYPES

main()
{
   // pre:

   // FUNCTION PROTOTYPES

   // LOCAL DATA

   // STATEMENTS




   // post:

}
```

Notes for Answers to Questions

1.

2.

LABORATORY EXERCISE—MATRIX MULTIPLICATION

In this lab, you will be asked to write your own algorithm, analyze it both theoretically and empirically, and evaluate the results. The algorithm you will be writing is matrix multiplication.

A matrix is a rectangular array. In this lab, the word matrix will refer to two-dimensional arrays of real numbers. Matrix multiplication is a generalization of the familiar notion of the "dot product" from elementary calculus. That is, suppose we have two vectors (one-dimensional arrays):

$$p = (p_1, p_2, ..., p_n)$$
$$\text{and} \quad q = (q_1, q_2, ..., q_n).$$

Then the dot product $p \cdot q$ is defined as

$$p \cdot q = p_1 q_1 + p_2 q_2 + ... + p_n q_n$$
$$= \sum_{i=1}^{n} p_i q_i$$

Now suppose we have two matrices A and B, where A is an m x k matrix and B is a k x n matrix:

$$A = \begin{bmatrix} a_{11} & \cdots & a_{1k} \\ \vdots & \vdots & \vdots \\ a_{m1} & \cdots & a_{mk} \end{bmatrix} \text{ and } B = \begin{bmatrix} b_{11} & \cdots & b_{1n} \\ \vdots & \vdots & \vdots \\ b_{k1} & \cdots & b_{kn} \end{bmatrix}$$

Note that the number k of columns in A must match the number of rows in B. We then denote the product of A and B by AB, and define it to be the m x n matrix whose ijth entry is the dot product of the ith row of A and the jth column of B. That is, if the matrix C denotes the product AB, then

$$c_{ij} = \sum_{m=1}^{n} a_{im} b_{mj}.$$

For instance, suppose

$$A = \begin{bmatrix} 2 & 1 \\ -1 & 2 \end{bmatrix} \text{ and } B = \begin{bmatrix} -1 & 0 \\ 3 & 1 \end{bmatrix}$$

Then

$$AB = \begin{bmatrix} 1 & 1 \\ 7 & 2 \end{bmatrix}$$

Part 1 — Design the Algorithm

This problem is a good example of a situation in which the method of top–down design is not especially helpful. This is because the algorithm itself is rather short; thus very little decomposition of the problem is necessary. Rather, the main task is understanding the concept of matrix multiplication well enough to express it algorithmically. We strongly suggest that after you have written a first draft of your algorithm, you desk check it on the above example. Be sure to write correct specifications.

Part 2 — Compute Its Theoretical Complexity

Using the techniques presented in the text, calculate the theoretical complexity of your algorithm when applied to square matrices. This will enable you to express the complexity in terms of a single variable, n.

Part 3 — Code and Test Your Program

After coding the program, go over it systematically and convince yourself that any input which satisfies the preconditions must also satisfy the postconditions. Note that in a problem like this, formal verification is especially helpful. While testing is very effective for finding coding errors, a thorough understanding is required for correcting conceptual errors.

Part 4 — Collect and Analyze Data on Its Complexity

Test your algorithm for different size square matrices and estimate its empirical complexity. If you have access to graphical software on your computer, use it to facilitate your graph-plotting and curve-fitting work for this lab.

Questions

1. Collect timing data for each of several different square matrices.
2. Fit a curve to these data points.
3. Are your theoretical and empirical results consistent?   Explain.

Worksheet for Laboratory Exercise —
Matrix Multiplication

```
/* -- Program name:
   -- Programmer:
   -- Date:
   -- ** Overview
         .
         .             .                      */

#include <iostream.h>
#include <fstream.h>
#include <sys/types.h>
#include <sys/times.h>
#include "strg.h"

// GLOBAL CONSTANTS AND TYPEDEF'S

// GLOBAL FUNCTION PROTOTYPES


main()
{
   // pre:

   // FUNCTION PROTOTYPES

   // LOCAL DATA

   // STATEMENTS






   // post:

}
```

Notes for Answers to Questions

1.

2.

3.

GAUSSIAN ELIMINATION

Mathematical models often involve simultaneous linear equations. Such models arise in any situation in which there is more than one variable present and the dynamics of the underlying situation are "linear." That is, variables can be multiplied by constants and added but never multiplied by themselves or by other variables. For instance, these models occur frequently in economics, where they often have equations of the form

$$c_1 x_1 + c_2 x_2 + \ldots + c_n x_n = b$$

in which the c_i are constant prices and the x_i are variable quantities. Additional linear equations arise from placing "constraints," or restrictions, on the quantities available.

Because simultaneous linear equations arise so often, they have been widely studied. Perhaps the best known systematic method for solving them is an algorithm called Gaussian elimination, developed by Carl Friedrich Gauss (1777–1855). In this section, our main objective is to present this algorithm informally.

The Basic Idea

Suppose we have a pair of simultaneous equations such as:

x + y = 2
2x − y = 3

The method for solving these equations typically taught in high school goes like this:

Multiply the first equation by –2, giving:

$$-2x - 2y = -4$$

Add this to the second equation. Our pair of equations is then:

$$x + y = 2$$
$$-3y = -1$$

Now solve the second equation for y giving $y = \frac{1}{3}$.

Substitute this into the first equation giving:

$$x + \left(\frac{1}{3}\right) = 2$$

Hence we conclude that $x = \frac{5}{3}$.

The Use of Matrices

Gaussian elimination is a direct generalization of the technique just applied. Note that a system of simultaneous equations can be represented by matrices. For instance, the above system can be written:

$$\begin{bmatrix} 1 & 1 \\ 2 & -1 \end{bmatrix} \begin{bmatrix} x \\ y \end{bmatrix} = \begin{bmatrix} 2 \\ 3 \end{bmatrix}.$$

(If you are unfamiliar with the multiplication of $\begin{bmatrix} 1 & 1 \\ 2 & -1 \end{bmatrix}$ by $\begin{bmatrix} x \\ y \end{bmatrix}$, see the beginning of the Laboratory Exercise—Matrix Multiplication just above.)

Suppose we have n equations in n unknowns. Gaussian elimination is based on the augmented coefficient matrix, which is the $n \times n$ coefficient matrix with an $n+1$th column added. The additional column is the vector containing the right hand sides of the system of equations. Thus, the augmented coefficient matrix for the above system is:

$$\begin{bmatrix} 1 & 1 & 2 \\ 2 & -1 & 3 \end{bmatrix}$$

Now apply the same sequence of steps that we applied to the system of equations above to the augmented coefficient matrix. We start with

$$\begin{bmatrix} 1 & 1 & 2 \\ 2 & -1 & 3 \end{bmatrix}.$$

Multiplying the first row by –2 gives:

$$[\, -2 \quad -2 \quad -4 \,]$$

Adding this result to the second row, the matrix becomes:

$$\begin{bmatrix} 1 & 1 & 2 \\ 0 & -3 & -1 \end{bmatrix}$$

Dividing the second row by –3, we get:

$$\begin{bmatrix} 1 & 1 & 2 \\ 0 & 1 & 1/3 \end{bmatrix}.$$

Hence, $y = \frac{1}{3}$. Rewriting the first row as an equation and substituting for y (called back substitution), we obtain:

$$x + \left(\frac{1}{3}\right) = 2$$

yielding $x = \frac{5}{3}$.

Example: We can use this method to solve the system of equations:

$$x + y - z = 2$$
$$2x - y - 3z = 3$$
$$-x + 3y + 2z = 0$$

First, form the augmented coefficient matrix:

$$\begin{bmatrix} 1 & 1 & -1 & 2 \\ 2 & -1 & -3 & 3 \\ -1 & 3 & 2 & 0 \end{bmatrix}$$

Transform the matrix as follows.

$$\begin{bmatrix} 1 & 1 & -1 & 2 \\ 0 & -3 & -1 & -1 \\ -1 & 3 & 2 & 0 \end{bmatrix} \qquad \text{(Row 2 = -2 x Row 1 + Row 2)}$$

$$\begin{bmatrix} 1 & 1 & -1 & 2 \\ 0 & -3 & -1 & -1 \\ 0 & 4 & 1 & 2 \end{bmatrix} \qquad \text{(Row 3 = Row 3 + Row 1)}$$

$$\begin{bmatrix} 1 & 1 & -1 & 2 \\ 0 & 1 & 1/3 & 1/3 \\ 0 & 4 & 1 & 2 \end{bmatrix} \qquad \text{(Row 2 = Row 2 x -1/3)}$$

$$\begin{bmatrix} 1 & 1 & -1 & 2 \\ 0 & 1 & 1/3 & 1/3 \\ 0 & 0 & -1/3 & 2/3 \end{bmatrix} \qquad \text{(Row 3 = -4 x Row 2 + Row 3)}$$

$$\begin{bmatrix} 1 & 1 & -1 & 2 \\ 0 & 1 & 1/3 & 1/3 \\ 0 & 0 & 1 & -2 \end{bmatrix} \qquad \text{(Row 3 = -3 x Row 3)}$$

At this point we can immediately see that $z = -2$. Rewriting the second row as an equation and substituting for z, we get:

$$y + \left(\tfrac{1}{3}\right)*(-2) = \tfrac{1}{3}$$

Hence, $y = 1$. Finally, rewriting the first row as an equa

$$x + y - z = 2$$

Substituting for y and z, we have

$$x + 1 + 2 = 2$$

which gives $x = -1$.

Elementary Row Operations

There are three types of operations which can be used in the process of solving simultaneous equations by Gaussian elimination. We used two of them in the previous example. They are called *elementary row operations* or ERO's for short and may be applied to any augmented coefficient matrix. They have the effect of transforming a system of equations into an equivalent system — another system which has the same solution set. They are:

1. Any two rows may be interchanged.
2. Any row may be multiplied by a constant.
3. A constant multiple of any row may be added to another row.

The objective in applying the ERO's to an augmented coefficient matrix is to produce a matrix which is upper triangular (i.e., has all zeroes below the main diagonal) and the diagonal entries starting from the upper left are a series of 1's possibly followed by some 0's.

How Many Solutions Does a System Have?

Some systems of simultaneous linear equations have no solutions, some have only one, and some have infinitely many. To see why, consider the following geometric interpretation of systems of simultaneous linear equations. Examine again the first system we looked at:

$$x + y = 2$$
$$2x - y = 3$$

Graphically, they form a pair of straight lines and their point of intersection is on both lines. Thus, it has coordinates which satisfy both equations. Hence, the coordinates of this intersection point are the solution of the system of equations. If, however, the lines are parallel, they will never intersect. Thus the system of equations:

$$x + y = 2$$
$$x + y = 3$$

has no solution. If the two equations represent the same line, there will be infinitely many points satisfying both equations. For instance, the equations:

$$x + y = 2$$
$$3x = 6 - 3y$$

are a system with infinitely many solutions. Furthermore, if only one equation containing two unknowns was specified, it will have an infinite number of solutions.

The same principles hold for systems with three or more variables. A linear equation with three variables forms a plane; a linear equation with more than three variables is said to form a hyperplane. Suppose four linear equations each involve four variables. Then each will form a hyperplane. These hyperplanes could be parallel or they could intersect. Thus, just as with two or three equations, the system of four equations in four unknowns could have a unique solution, no solution, or infinitely many solutions.

Gaussian elimination can tell us whether or not a system of linear equations has a unique solution. For instance, recall again the first set of equations we examined:

$$x + y = 2$$
$$2x - y = 3$$

When we applied Gaussian elimination to the augmented coefficient matrix, the final form of our matrix after application of the ERO's was:

$$\begin{bmatrix} 1 & 1 & 2 \\ 0 & 1 & 1/3 \end{bmatrix}$$

In the second example, we solved the system:

$$x + y - z = 2$$
$$2x - y - 2z = 1$$
$$-x + 2y + z = 1$$

The final form of that augmented coefficient matrix after application of the ERO's was:

$$\begin{bmatrix} 1 & 1 & -1 & 2 \\ 0 & 1 & 1/3 & 1/3 \\ 0 & 0 & 1 & -2 \end{bmatrix}$$

Note that in both cases, the coefficient portion of the augmented coefficient matrix is upper triangular with all 1's on the diagonal. Now apply Gaussian elimination to the system:

$x + y = 2$
$x + y = 3$

The augmented coefficient matrix is:

$$\begin{bmatrix} 1 & 1 & 2 \\ 1 & 1 & 3 \end{bmatrix}$$

Applying the third ERO, this becomes:

$$\begin{bmatrix} 1 & 1 & 2 \\ 0 & 0 & 1 \end{bmatrix}$$

The coefficient portion is upper triangular, but the diagonal entries include a zero. Note that the last row says that $0x + 0y = 1$; i.e., $0 = 1$. Since this is impossible, this system has no solution. Systems whose equations reduce to a contradiction are said to be *inconsistent*.

Consider again the system:

$x + y = 2$
$3x = 6 - 3y$

Rewriting this with the variables on the left and constant on the right, we get:

$x + y = 2$
$3x + 3y = 6$

This yields the augmented coefficient matrix:

$$\begin{bmatrix} 1 & 1 & 2 \\ 3 & 3 & 6 \end{bmatrix}$$

Applying the third ERO to this, we get

$$\begin{bmatrix} 1 & 1 & 2 \\ 0 & 0 & 0 \end{bmatrix}$$

The last row tells us that $0x + 0y = 0$. Unlike the previous example, this is not inconsistent, but it does not tell us anything either. A system of equations which has a row-reduced augmented coefficient matrix containing a row of all zeroes is called redundant. If such a system has n equations in n unknowns (and no other rows are inconsistent), it has an infinite number of solutions.

This completes our introduction to the concept of Gaussian elimination. In the following laboratory exercise, you have an opportunity to implement this algorithm.

LABORATORY EXERCISE—GAUSSIAN ELIMINATION

In this lab, you will be asked to write your own algorithm, analyze it theoretically and empirically, and compare the results. The algorithm you will be writing is Gaussian elimination.

Part 1 — Design the Algorithm

Like the previous lab, this problem is another example of a situation in which the method of top-down design is not especially helpful. An input module, a processing module, and an output module are all that are needed. The main task is understanding the concept of Gaussian elimination well enough to express it algorithmically. Begin by writing careful specifications for the processing module; in order not to get bogged down in details, assume the algorithm will only be given systems of n equations in n unknowns which have unique solutions. We strongly suggest that after you have written a first draft of your algorithm, you desk check it on the examples discussed in the previous section.

Part 2 — Compute Its Theoretical Complexity

Using the techniques presented in the text, calculate the theoretical complexity of your algorithm when applied to systems of n equations in n unknowns. This will enable you to express the complexity in terms of a single variable, n.

Part 3 — Code and Test Your Program

After coding the program, go over it systematically and convince yourself that any input which satisfies the preconditions must also satisfy the postconditions. Note that in a problem like this, formal verification is especially helpful. While testing is very effective at finding coding errors, to correct conceptual errors a thorough understanding is required.

Part 4 — Collect and Analyze Data on Its Complexity

Test your algorithm for various systems of equations and estimate its empirical complexity. If you have access to graphical software on your computer, use it to facilitate your graph-plotting and curve-fitting work for this lab.

Questions

1. Are your theoretical and empirical results consistent? Show clearly the reasons for your answer.

2. An alternative method for solving systems of simultaneous equations is *Gauss-Jordan elimination*. It begins the same as Gaussian elimination, but omits the back-substitution steps. Rather it continues row reduction until the n x n coefficient portion of the matrix has all 1's on the diagonal and all zeroes elsewhere. At this point, the $n+1$th column will contain the solution. Compare the theoretical complexity of back-substitution to the corresponding portion of the Gauss-Jordan algorithm.

3. Once you have completed the four parts of this lab, modify your algorithm to handle systems of n equations in n unknowns which have no solutions or infinitely many solutions. Be sure to begin by revising your specifications.

4. You may have noticed that ERO 1 was not needed in your program or in answering any of the questions so far. But, in fact, it plays a very important role in Gaussian elimination. The way it is used is as follows. Before beginning to manipulate the augmented coefficient matrix, the first column is searched for the largest element. The row containing it is then swapped with the first row. (By ERO 1, this does not change the solution). Processing then proceeds as before on that column. Then in the second column, the largest element *on or below* the diagonal is selected. Its row is swapped with the second row before processing that column.

   Continuing in this fashion, this selection and swap process precedes the processing of each column. The purpose of these selections and swaps is to reduce round-off error. That is, since real numbers are only approximately represented in a computer, every real number contains a potential round-off error. For instance, suppose the coefficient matrix is $A = (a_{ij})$. Suppose $a_{11} = .01$ and $a_{12} = 1$. Without applying ERO 1, manipulating A would result in every element of row 1 being multiplied by 100. Thus the round-off error in every element would be multiplied by 100 also. However, if rows 1 and 2 are swapped, no increase in round-off errors occurs.

   Modify your program to include the improvement described here, but keep your old version. When you are done, run both versions on the system:

   $$\varepsilon x + y = 1$$
   $$x + y = 2$$

   where ε is the smallest non-zero, positive real number that can be represented on your computer. Plug both sets of results back into your original equations. Which is more accurate?

Worksheet for Laboratory Exercise — Gaussian Elimination

```
/* -- Program name:
   -- Programmer:
   -- Date:
   -- ** Overview
         .
         .            .                    */

#include <iostream.h>
#include <fstream.h>
#include <sys/types.h>
#include <sys/times.h>
#include "strg.h"

// GLOBAL CONSTANTS AND TYPEDEF'S

// GLOBAL FUNCTION PROTOTYPES


main()
{
   // pre:

   // FUNCTION PROTOTYPES

   // LOCAL DATA

   // STATEMENTS








   // post:

}
```

Notes for Answers to Questions

1.

2.

3.

4.

STACKS, QUEUES, AND LINKED STRUCTURES

This chapter provides discussions and laboratory exercises that help you master the applications of stacks and queues, as well as the use of pointers and linked structures in problem solving.

Pointers and dynamic storage allocation were introduced in Chapter 2 of this lab manual. In order to implement flexible solutions for problems, we need to understand how pointers can be used in C++ to build linked structures. With this understanding, we can build linked implementations of lists, stacks, queues, and other data structures that are discussed later in the text. Linked structures are sometimes preferable to arrays for implementing these classes.

LABORATORY EXERCISE—POLISH EXPRESSION EVALUATION

This exercise asks you to create an augmented version, to be called RPNcalc, of the SimpleRPNcalc program in the text that will have more functionality for evaluating Polish expressions. The following new functions should be added:

x CHS	To change the sign of x
x SQRT	To compute the square root of x
x SQR	To compute x^2
PRINT	To display the contents of the entire stack
EMPTY	To clear the stack of all operands
x INV	To compute $1/x$

These additions will make the program more like an actual electronic calculator in its functionality than the original program. For example, the following input

```
2 2 + SQRT CHS PRINT
```

will display the resulting Stack contents (-2). Intermediate Stack contents should not be displayed, as was done by the original SimpleRPNcalc program, except when the PRINT command is scanned within the expression.

Part 1 — Design the Specifications

Write pre- and postconditions that will define the exact input and output for this expanded program. These specifications need not be exact expressions in the predicate calculus. Try to state the input and output requirements as precisely as possible in English.

Part 2 — Develop the Program

Design this program as an expanded version of the `SimpleRPNcalc` program that appears in the text. To facilitate this task, a copy of that program is provided on the system course directory (or the distribution disk) in the file `simplerp.cxx`.

Part 3 — Exercise the Program

Run your program with several different Polish expressions and other strings that are not valid Polish expressions.

Questions

1. What does your program do with each of the following expressions?
   a. `3 7 4 - - PRINT`
   b. `3 7 - 4 -`
   c. `2 2 + SQRT CHS PRINT`
   d. `3 - 7 4 - PRINT`
   e. `3 7 4 - - - PRINT`
   f. `3 7 hello! 4 - - - PRINT`
2. Discuss how your program would be extended so that it properly handles invalid input, such as that given in Question 1*d*, 1*e*, and 1*f*.

Worksheet for Laboratory Exercise —
Evaluating Polish Expressions

```
/* -- Program name: RPNcalc
   -- Programmer:
   -- Date:
   -- ** Overview


                                                        */

#include <iostream.h>
#include <string.h>
#include "stack.h"
#include "morpheme.h"
   // GLOBAL CONSTANTS AND TYPEDEF'S

   // GLOBAL FUNCTION PROTOTYPES


main()
{
   // pre:
   // FUNCTION PROTOTYPES


   // LOCAL DATA


   // STATEMENTS












// post:
}
```

Notes for Answers to Questions

1.

2.

(TEAM) LABORATORY EXERCISE—CONVERSION FROM INFIX TO POLISH

This exercise requires that you design and implement a complete program that converts any number of infix arithmetic expressions to their equivalent Polish representations and displays each of the results in turn. For instance, if the program's input is

```
x + y*(z - 4)
```

then its displayed output should be:

```
x y z 4 - * +
```

The algorithm that does the conversion should be implemented as a separate function, following the steps outlined below. These steps use an auxiliary stack, `Operators`, that contains arithmetic operators, as well as an input expression, `Input`, that contains a series of tokens that are separated by blank spaces.

1. Scan the input expression from left to right and, for each token in it, perform one of Steps 1*a* through 1*d*.

   a. If the token is an operand, display it.
   b. If the token is a left parenthesis, push it onto the stack.
   c. If the token is a right parenthesis, pop and display elements from the `Operators` stack until a left parenthesis is reached. Pop, but do not display, that left parenthesis.
   d. If the token is an arithmetic operator, compare its priority with that of the topmost token on the stack. If it has higher priority than the top token, or if the stack is empty, then push this token onto the stack. Otherwise, pop and display the top token and repeat this step.

2. After the input expression has been completely scanned, pop and display the remaining operators on the stack (if there are any).

For the purpose of this exercise, you should assume the normal priorities among the arithmetic operators (^ is highest, * and / are next highest, + and – are lowest), with the additional caveat that the left parenthesis, (, has lower priority than any of the operators.

Part 1 — Define the Scope of the Program

The overall functioning of the program should be determined in a team discussion. This discussion should include the following considerations:

1. The program should be user-friendly; prompting the user for the next expression after it has converted the previous one to Polish form and displayed it.

2. The program should be able to detect an illegal expression, noting errors
    to the user and providing graceful ways for recovering and retyping the
    expression correctly. Note that the algorithm given above makes no
    provision for erroneous expressions; you must augment it to flag ex-
    pressions like the following as errors:

```
(a + b)(c + d)          a (+ b)
2 + 3 -                 - x
(a + b                  a + 2 * hello! c
```

3. The program should utilize existing classes and methods—especially
    `Stack`, `InputString`, and `Morpheme`—to the greatest extent possible.

Part 2 — Design the Program's Objects, Methods, and Specifications

Design appropriate objects and methods to realize the major entities and func-
tional aspects of the program, and then write pre- and postconditions for each
method.

Part 3 — Implement and Test the Program

Implement the program in C++, and then test it against all of the sample input
given above. Design additional input that exercises the program's ability to detect errors, and then run the program against that input as well.

Questions

1. Which step in the algorithm above will need to be modified to detect the
    presence of an unmatched left parenthesis in an input expression, and
    how should it be modified?
2. Which step in the algorithm above should be modified to detect the
    presence of an unmatched right parenthesis, and how should it be modi-
    fied?
3. What other kinds of errors can occur for this problem, and how can the
    algorithm be modified to detect them?

Worksheet for Laboratory Exercise —
Conversion from Infix to Polish

```
/* -- Program name: InfixToPolish
   -- Programmer:
   -- Date:
   -- ** Overview

                                                        */


#include <iostream.h>
#include <string.h>
#include "stack.h"
#include "morpheme.h"
#include "insupstring.h"
   // GLOBAL CONSTANTS AND TYPEDEF'S

   // GLOBAL FUNCTION PROTOTYPES


main()
{
   // pre:
   // FUNCTION PROTOTYPES


   // LOCAL DATA


   // STATEMENTS








// post:
}
```

Notes for Answers to Questions

1.

2.

3.

LABORATORY EXERCISE—COMPARISON OF RANDOM NUMBER GENERATORS

This lab asks you to exercise two different random number generators and evaluate the randomness of their output, using the C++ driver program given in Figure 4-26 from the text. The two generators to be exercised are from Chapter 4 of the text, the first is the function named `random` (see Figure 4-25) and the second is given as Exercise 4-14 at the end of Chapter 4. Your program should generate a list of 100 random numbers and compute the shortest cycle length and the distribution of the numbers over 100 equal intervals in each of the following ranges: {0, . . ., 99} and {0, . . ., 65535}, using each of these competing functions. Use the method and software described in the Section, Laboratory Exercise—Linear vs. Binary Search of Chapter 3 of this *Laboratory Manual*.

Part 1 — Adapt the RandomDriver Program

Make a copy of the file `randrive.cxx` from the system course directory (or the distribution disk) and adapt it to this particular task.

Part 2 — Run the Program

For each of the two random number generators, and for each of the two generation requirements, run the program and obtain the shortest cycle length and distribution over 100 intervals.

Questions

1. Which of the two random number generators is better in terms of its shortest cycle length? Explain.
2. Which of the two is better in terms of the distribution of its 100 numbers over the 100 equal intervals? Explain.
3. Are there any differences in the relative performance of these two generators when we vary the range of numbers generated from {0, . . ., 99} to {0, . . ., 65535}? Explain.

Worksheet for Laboratory Exercise —
Comparison of Random Number Generators

```
/* -- Program name: RandomDriver
   -- Programmer:
   -- Date:
   -- ** Overview


                                                                    */

#include <iostream.h>
#include <fstream.h>
#include <stdlib.h>
#include <time.h>
#include <string.h>
   // GLOBAL CONSTANTS AND TYPEDEF'S

   // GLOBAL FUNCTION PROTOTYPES


main()
{
   // pre:
   // FUNCTION PROTOTYPES


   // LOCAL DATA


   // STATEMENTS







// post:
}
```

Notes for Answers to Questions

1.

2.

3.

BUILDING LINKED STRUCTURES: A TUTORIAL

It is often preferable to defer the memory allocation for data structures until after the program or function has begun its execution, so that the program can dynamically adjust the amount of storage it uses to the size of the input. Without such a facility, we are forced to overestimate the amount of storage required in order to prepare for the worst case—that is, the largest amount of input that could possibly occur.

Basic Ideas: Pointers and Data

To accommodate this need, C++ provides facilities by which a program or function may *dynamically* activate an object. These facilities are provided by two language elements: the pointer type, and the `new` and `delete` procedures. We have already seen the use of the pointer in earlier chapters, where we used it to create dynamic objects. Here, we shall use the pointer to directly reference a block of storage. There are two parts to this process.

1. A *pointer* is a variable whose value is the address of a particular kind of memory block (which contains, in turn, a scalar, array, class, or `struct` value in memory). A pointer can be declared in the following way:

```
type * pointername;
```

Here, `type` names the type of object to which the variable `pointername` points. In reality, a pointer is nothing more than an address, and a pointer variable is thus an unsigned integer variable used to indirectly *address* the value of another variable in memory. For example,

```
int * p, * q, * r;
```

declares `p`, `q`, and `r` to be a pointers to integer-valued memory blocks.

2. The `new` and `delete` functions allocate and deallocate, respectively, a memory block when they are invoked in a program. For example, the following declaration allocates a new integer-valued storage area referenced by the pointer p.

```
int * p = new int;
```

The result is schematically shown in Figure 4–1, except that the value 49 shown there would not be present.

A pointer variable may either have no value, have the value `NULL` (which means that it points nowhere), or have a value which references a memory block for its associated type. The distinction between the `NULL` value and a non-`NULL` reference is depicted in graphical form by a tree-shaped symbol, as shown in Figure 4–2.

References to dynamically-allocated storage blocks may occur in C++ programs in any way that a conventional variable may occur. That is, such a reference may appear within an arithmetic expression, on the left of an assignment statement, as an argument in a function call, and so on. For example, the statement `*p = 49;` assigns the value 49 to the `integer` memory block currently addressed by p, as shown in Figure 4–1.

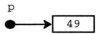

FIGURE 4–1   **Result of the assignment `*p = 49;`.**

A pointer variable may also be assigned either the value of another pointer variable or `NULL`, using an assignment statement. For instance, if p is initially as shown in Figure 4–1, the following pair of statements

```
q = p;
p = NULL;
```

leaves p and q as shown in Figure 4–2.

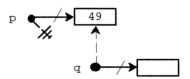

FIGURE 4–2   **Result of executing `q = p;  p = NULL;`.**

Figure 4–2 also illustrates the notational convention of showing a *change* to a pointer value by way of a *dashed* line for the new value and a diagonal line through the former pointer value.

When a dynamically-allocated memory block is of no further use to the program, it may be released by the program and returned to the system by the `delete` statement. The statement `delete p;`, for instance, releases the memory block currently addressed by p (along with any value that may be stored there) and may make undefined the value of the pointer p itself. No further access to that particular memory block or its value should be attempted after such a statement has been executed. No further use of the reference `*p` can be made until after p itself has been assigned a new value (either by an assignment statement or by another `p = new int;` statement).

Pointers and Linked Structures

A linked structure is characterized by a series of "nodes" that are connected to each other (chained together) by pointers. The simplest linked structure is the "single linked chain," which is pictured in Figure 4–3. Each node in the chain contains two parts, a data element e and a pointer link that connects the node to the next node in the chain.

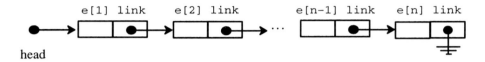

FIGURE 4–3   A single linked chain.

As a matter of convention, there is a special pointer called head that references the first node in the chain, and the last node in the chain has a NULL link to indicate that no more nodes follow it.

A node can be declared either as a class or as a record structure (called a struct). Below is a class declaration for the node described above (assuming its elements are integers):

```
class node
{
  public:                   // This is a single node in the
    node () {};              //    chain, which has an integer
    int e;                   //    value and a pointer to the
    node * link;             //    next link in the list.
};
```

The pointer to the first link in the chain, head, can be declared as follows:

```
node * head;
```

Recall that, in general, a C++ pointer is declared in the following way:

```
type * pointername;
```

Here, type denotes the type of value that the pointer will reference whenever it is activated.

When the program is run, a pointer can either be NULL, which means that it points nowhere, or point to a single block of storage for its declared type. Recall that the NULL value for a pointer is 0, and a pointer can be assigned that value just as if it were an integer, e.g.,

```
head = 0;
```

suggests the picture shown in Figure 4–4.

head

FIGURE 4–4 The NULL pointer value for head.

Individual nodes are dynamically created (that's called "allocated") and re-turned to the system (that's called "deallocated") by the program as they are needed. That is, linked structures are not fixed in size in the same way that vectors are. To create a new node with a pointer, say q, pointing to it, we use the node's constructor with the word new before it:

```
node * q = new node ();
assert (q!=0);
```

This suggests the picture shown in Figure 4–5:

Note the use of the assert statement to ensure that the block of storage has been allocated successfully (an e value of 0 means "failure"). Note also that neither an e value nor a nonnull link is assigned as a result of allocating this node, only the storage block is created and q is set to point to it.

To reference one of the fields within a node (i.e., its e value or its link), we use a two–character arrow with the pointer that references the node on the left and the field name on the right. For instance, to reference the e field of the above node, we would write:

```
q -> e
```

To assign the integer 3 to that value, we would write:

```
q -> e = 3 ;
```

leaving the picture shown in Figure 4–6:

:

A pointer can also be assigned the value of another pointer, in order to make it point to the same node. For instance, if we want to make the pointer head

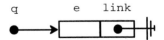

q   e   link

FIGURE 4–5 A new node referenced by pointer q.

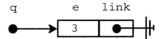

FIGURE 4–6   A new node referenced by pointer q.

point to the above–pictured node, which is currently pointed to by q, we would simply say:

```
head = q ;
```

Finally, to free a block of storage and return it to the system, we would write:

```
delete q ;
```

This also resets the value of pointer q to 0, or NULL.

Building a Single Linked Chain

With these ideas, we can think about constructing a simple linked chain in C++ in the following way:

1. An empty list will be signified by the state head == 0.
2. A list can be traversed (i.e., its individual nodes can be referenced one–by–one, beginning with the first) using a simple loop with a pointer used to 'index' the individual nodes. Here's a loop that visits each node in the list and simply displays its e value:

```
for (node * p = head; p != 0; p = p->link)
   cout << p->e << '\t';
```

Note here that p is initialized to reference the first node, p's e value is displayed upon each iteration, and p is "incremented" by assigning it to the value of p->link. The loop terminates when p becomes 0, which is the value of link for the last node in the chain.

Insertions at the beginning of a linked chain are easily made. Below is some code that accomplishes a single insertion as follows:

1. Creates a new node pointed to by q,
2. Reads an integer and assigns it to the e value field of that node, and
3. Inserts that node into the beginning of the list pointed to by head.

```
q = new node ();          // create new node
assert (q!=0);            // make sure storage is available
cin >> q->e;              // read and assign a new e value
q->link = head ;          // insert this node
head = q;                 // at the beginning of the list
```

We can picture what's happening here as shown in Fugure 4–7 (assuming the new e value read is 3):

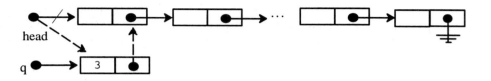

FIGURE 4–7 **Insertion at the head of a single linked chain.**

A deletion from the beginning of a list is also quite simple, once the notation is mastered:

```
assert (head!=0);      // be sure that there's a node to be deleted
q = head;              // save a temporary pointer to it
head = head -> link;   // establish 2nd element as 1st
delete q;              // remove original first element
```

Note that the storage freed by the deleted node is returned to the system.

More interesting situations for insertion and deletion are illustrated in the program below. Here, insertions into the middle of the list are needed, and a list search is also used to locate the position where an insertion should be made.

```
// This program is an exercise in using pointers to manage a
// simple linked chain.  It takes any number of integers
// as input, builds a list of them in sorted order, and then
// displays the resulting sorted list.
#include <iostream.h>
#include <assert.h>
void main ()
{
class node
{
  public:              // This is a single link in the
    node () {};        //    list, which has an integer
    int e;             //    e value and a pointer to the
    node * link;       //    next link in the list.
};

node * head = 0 ;      // pointer to the first link in
node * p ;             //    the list, and auxiliary pointers.
node * q ;
int inputValue ;       // a single input value to be inserted
                       //    into the list

cout << "Enter a series of integers followed by ctrl-d \n";
// read a series of integers, and insert each one in place
while (cin >> inputValue)
{
```

```
// make a new link for the integer just read
q = new node() ;
assert (q!=0);

// search for the place of insertion
p = head;
int inserted = 0;      // boolean to tell if insertion made
while ( p != 0 && !inserted)
{
   if (inputValue >= p->e)
      if (p->link == 0)     // insertion at end of the list
      {
         q->e = inputValue;
         q->link = 0;
         p->link = q;
         inserted = 1;
      }
      else
         p = p -> link;   // continue searching; move p along
   else
   {
      q->e = p->e;         // insertion before p in the list
      p->e = inputValue;
      q->link = p->link;
      p->link = q;
      inserted = 1;
   }
}
// end of search for a place to insert

   if (!inserted)          // insertion at beginning of list
   {
     q->e = inputValue;
     q->link = head;
     head = q;
   }
}  // end of loop for processing input
// Now display the final ordered list by traversing it from
// the beginning
for (p = head; p !=0; p = p->link)
   cout << p -> e << '\t';
}
```

(TEAM) LABORATORY EXERCISE—PRINT QUEUE SIMULATION

This laboratory exercise contains many ideas that appear in the bankline simulation problem discussed in Chapter 4 of the text. Students should review that problem and its solution before beginning this lab.. Like that problem, you are asked to devleop a simulation program, using a queue and a random number generator. Unlike that problem, you are asked to simulate the actions of a queue directly, by maintaining a simple linked chain, rather than use the pre-implemented queue class.

You may wish to implement the `enter`, `remove`, `front`, and `rear` functions that are defined for the queue class (see the `queue.h` listing in Appendix I) in solving this problem. You may also wish to use the `element` class rather than the simple `int` type to describe a single entry in the queue. However, the purpose of this lab is mainly to gain practice with the creation and maintenance of dynamic storage as a medium for data structures, so the entire queue class implementation should not be used.

Part 1 — The Problem

In managing a lab full of computers networked to a printer, the computer center director wants to know about how well the printer serves the needs of students who use the network. The director has a limited budget for purchasing new equipment and an old, slow printer on the network is stlll serviceable. The question being raised is, how many new, fast printers should be added to the network to satisfy student demand.

To simulate the expected situation, an educated guess is made about how often a student's print job will enter at the back of the line, or queue, of print jobs waiting to be printed, along with how many minutes it takes the old, slow printer to serve an individual print job (on the average). The simulation is then run over a fixed period of time (say, 500 minutes), with p (a number between 0 and 1) being the chance, or probability, that a print job will enter the queue in any given minute of that period and "nprinters" denoting the number of printers (including the old, slow one) on the network. One printer (the old, slow one) is known to complete a print job in 5 minutes, while a new (fast) printer can complete a print job in 2 minutes, on the average. At the end of a simulation run, the following statistics should be reported to the director:

```
period of time                          500
p                                        0.8
nprinters                                  4
number of print jobs served             396
average waiting time (minutes)          7.8
average queue length (print jobs)         6
maximum queue length (print jobs)        11
```

The numbers on the right show the effect of setting parameters p and nprinters on the average waiting time per print job (7.0 minutes), the average print queue length (6 print jobs), and the maximum queue length (11 print jobs) in a 500-minute simulation run.

Now suppose we want to find out what would happen if we were to reduce the number of printers (to save costs), or increase printing activity (by decreasing the value of p to, say, 0.85). That is, if we rerun this simulation with different parameters, what would be the effect of the change on the average and maximum queue length and number of print jobs served? This sort of repeated experiment is a useful measure for computer center directors who want to maximize customer service while minimizing hardware costs.

Part 2 — Designing the Simulation

In this problem, the queue is a simple linked chain that represents the waiting line of print jobs. Each node in the chain identifies an individual print job by the unique integer time value at which it entered the queue (assuming that no more than one print job enters the queue in any particular minute). Entry into the queue is prompted by the generation of a random number that is greater than the product p * 65536. For instance, if p = 0.8 and the random number generated at time interval 3 is greater than 0.8*65536, then a print job is added to the rear of the queue, as shown below (assuming none entered the queue at time 0 or 2 and one entered at time 1):

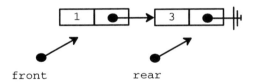

FIGURE 4–8   **Print queue simulation after jobs have entered at times 1 and 3.**

The overall logic of the program is made easy by the idea of a linked chain represesntation of the queue. Unlike an array, a linked chain allows unlimited quieue growth, which is critical in simulations such as this one where the maximum size of the queue cannot be easily predicted. Here's a sketch of the program itself:

1. Input the values of `time`, `p`, and `nprinters` from the user

2. Repeat the following steps for each minute of time:

    2.1. Determine whether or not a print job enters the queue by computing a random number and (possibly) adding it to the queue.

    2.2. If the queue is not empty, see if the slow printer is available. If not, look for another available printer. If either the slow printer or another (fast printer) available, the print job at the front of the queue leaves the queue and that printer becomes unavailable for the next 5 (or 2) minutes.

    2.3. Update the average and maximum queue length.

  3. Compute and display the results.

Note that an array of printers is also needed to keep track of the status (occupied or available) of each one. A simple way to do this is to initialize all printers[i] to 0 and then set each printer[i] = t + 5 whenever a printer becomes occupied at time t. Thus, as the time t advances, the test to determine whether or not printer[i] is available can be made by simply saying

```
if ( printer[i] <= t ) ...
```

Part 3 — Complete the Program

Complete and run this program, using a linked chain for the queue class and the above sketch of the solution.

Questions

1. By running your simulation, determine how many printers (at a minimum) are needed to keep the maximum line length down to 1 (i.e., provide "perfect" customer service) under the above assumptions.
2. By running your simulation several times again, determine how slow the printing activity in the lab must become (i.e., reducing the value of p) before the computer center director can get by with a minimum number (1) of printers (the old, slow one) to keep the waiting line down to 1 print job.
3. (Extra credit) What additional parameter could be added to allow this model to simulate "improved efficiency" in the lab. That is, reducing average line length can be accomplished not only by adding more printers but also by buying faster printers. Suggest ways to alter your program so that this new parameter can be taken into consideration.

Worksheet for Laboratory Exercise —
Print Queue Simulation

```
/* -- Program name: RandomDriver
   -- Programmer:
   -- Date:
   -- ** Overview

                                                  */

#include <iostream.h>
#include <fstream.h>
#include <stdlib.h>

    // GLOBAL CONSTANTS AND TYPEDEF'S

    // GLOBAL FUNCTION PROTOTYPES

main()
{
    // pre:
    // FUNCTION PROTOTYPES


    // LOCAL DATA


    // STATEMENTS








// post:
}
```

Notes for Answers to Questions

1.

2.

3.

APPENDIX **A**

C++ Program Listing
sequence.h

```
// Class description: The class Sequence provides the
//   methods that are shared by lists, stacks, and queues.
//   In our specifications a Sequence is represented as
//   Seq = (e[1] e[2] .... e[n])
//   where each e[i] denotes an object. The empty sequence
//   is denoted by Seq = ().


#ifndef SEQUENCE_H
#define SEQUENCE_H


#include <iostream.h>
#include <fstream.h>
#include "elements.h"


const int MAXELEMENTS = 500;


class Sequence
{
    protected:
        // DATA MEMBERS ...
        ElementPtr e[MAXELEMENTS];
        // array of pointers to elements
        int size;
        // number of elements


    public:
    // MEMBER FUNCTIONS ...
    // constructor - destructor
    inline Sequence();
    inline virtual ~Sequence();


    // test
    int is_full();
    int is_empty();


    // access
    int get_size();
    virtual void empty();
```

```
    // display
    virtual void display();
};  // end class Sequence


#endif
```

C++ Program Listing

sequence.cxx

```
// ********************** implementation of ******************
// ********************** Sequence methods ******************


#include "sequence.h"


//
// constructor - destructor
//


// Sequence::Sequence();
// Used: To initialize receiver sequence.
// Pre:  None
// Post: Receiver is intialized and size = 0 and Seq = ()
Sequence::Sequence()
{
    size = 0;
} // end Sequence::Sequence()


// Sequence::~Sequence();
// Used: To destroy the receiver sequence.
// Pre:  Receiver has been initialized.
// Post: Receiver is destroyed.
Sequence::~Sequence()
{
    empty();
}  // end Sequence::~Sequence()


//
// test
//


// Sequence::is_full();
// Used: To determine if the receiver sequence is full.
// Pre:  Receiver is initialized.
// Post: result = (size == MAXELEMENTS)
int Sequence::is_full()
{
    if (size == MAXELEMENTS)
        return 1;
```

```
      else
         return 0;
   }  // end Sequence::is_full()


// Sequence::is_empty();
// Used: To determine if the receiver sequence is empty.
// Pre:  Receiver is initialized.
// Post: result = (size == 0)
int Sequence::is_empty()
{
   if (!size)
      return 1;
   else
      return 0;
}  // end Sequence::is_empty()



//
// access
//


// Sequence::get_size();
// Used: To determine the size of the receiver sequence.
// Pre:  Receiver is initialized.
// Post: result = size
int Sequence::get_size()
{
   return size;
}  // end Sequence::get_size()


// Sequene::empty()
// Used: Resets the receiver to an empty sequence.
// Pre:  Receiver is initialized.
// Post: size = 0, Seq = () and each object in
//    the Seq is destroyed.
void Sequence::empty()
{
   for (int i = 0; i < size; i++)
   {
      delete e[i];
   }
   size = 0;
}  // end Sequence::empty()



//
// display
//


// Sequence::display();
// Used:   Displays each object in receiver sequence.
// Pre:    Seq = (e[1] e[2] ... e[n]) and size = n
```

```
//          and display() is defined for each object in Seq.
// Post: For all I in [1..n] : the object e[i]
//          is displayed on the screen.
void Sequence::display()
{
   cout << endl;
   for(int i = 0; i < size; i++)
   {
     e[i] -> display();
   }
}   // end Sequence::display()
```

C++ Program Listing
`list.h`

```
// Class description: The class List implements a list
//    of objects. The list class allows objects to be
//    inserted into and deleted from any position.
//    In our specifications a List is represented as
//    L = (e[1] e[2] .... e[n])
//  where each e[i] denotes an object.  The empty list is
//    denoted by L = ().


// ****** Specifications for class List ******************


#ifndef LIST_H
// Class description: The class List implements a list
//    of objects. The list class allows objects to be
//    inserted into and deleted from any position.
//    In our specifications a List is represented as
//    L = (e[1] e[2] .... e[n])
//    where each e[i] denotes an object.  The empty list is
//    denoted by L = ().


// ******** Specifications for the List class ******************


#define LIST_H


#include <stddef.h> // required by Microsoft
                    // compiler 7.0 for NULL
#include "sequence.h"


class List : public Sequence
{
    public:
        // MEMBER FUNCTIONS ...
        // constructor - destructor
        List(){ };
            // this is an inline definition.
            // Sequence constructor is called.
        ~List() { };
            // this is an inline definition
            // Sequence destructor is called.
```

```
            // access
            ElementPtr retrieve(int);


            // modify
            int store(ElementPtr, int);
            int insert(ElementPtr, int);
            int remove(int);
            int swap(int, int);
};   // end class List


#endif
```

C++ Program Listing
list.cxx

```
//***************** implementation of ********************
//***************** list methods ************************


#include "list.h"


//
// constructor - destructor
//


// Constructor: List::List();
// Used: To initialize a receiver list.
// Pre:  None
// Post: Receiver is initialized and size = 0 and L = ().


// Destructor: List::~List();
// Used: To destroy the receiver list.
// Pre:  Receiver has been initialized.
// Post: Receiver is destroyed.


//
// access
//


// Function: List::retrieve(int i);
// Used: To retrieve a pointer to the i-th element in list L.
// Pre:  L = (e[1] e[2] ... e[n]) and 1<=i<=n
// Post: (i is out of range and result = NULL) or
//        (result = e[i])
ElementPtr List::retrieve(int i)
{
   if ((i < 1) || (i > size))
      return NULL;
   else
      return e[i - 1];
}  // end List::retrieve()


//
// modify
//
```

```
// Function: List::store(ElementPtr eptr, int i);
// Used: Stores eptr in place of i-th element in list L.
// Pre:  L = (e[1] e[2] ... e[n]) and size = n
// Post: (i is out of range and result = 0) or
//          (L = (e[1] ... e[i-1] Eptr e[i+1] ... e[n]) and
//          result = 1)
int List::store(ElementPtr eptr, int i)
{
   if ((i < 1) || (i > size))
      return 0;
   else
   {
      e[i - 1] = eptr;
      return 1;
   }
}  // end List::store()


// Function: List::insert(ElementPtr eptr, int i);
// Used: Inserts eptr in the i-th position in list L.
// Pre:  L = (e[1] e[2] ... e[n]), size = n and 1<=i<=n+1
// Post: (i is out of range and result = 0) or
//          L = (e[1] ... e[i-1] eptr e[i+1] ... e[n]) and
//          (size = n + 1) and (result = 1)
int List::insert(ElementPtr eptr, int i)
{
   if (this -> is_full() || i < 1 || i > (size+1))
      return 0;
   else
   {
      // move elements e[i] ... e[size] down one
      for (ElementPtr* j = e + size; j >= e+i; j--)
    *j = *(j - 1);
      e[i - 1] = eptr;
      size++;
      return 1;
   }
}  // end List::insert()


// Function: List::remove(int i);
// Used: Deletes the i-th element in the list L.
// Pre:  L = (e[1] e[2] ... e[n]) and size = n
// Post: (i is out of range and result = 0) or
//          (L = (e[1] ... e[i-1] e[i+1] ... e[n]) and
//          size = n - 1 and result = 1)
int List::remove(int i)
{
   if ( (i < 1) || (i > size) )
      return 0;
   else
   {
   // Move elements e[i+1] ... e[size] up one
      delete e[i-1];
      for (ElementPtr* j = e + i ; j < (e + size); j++)
    *(j-1) = *j;
      size--;
```

```
         return 1;
      }
} // end List::remove()


// Function: List::swap(int i, int j);
// Used: Swaps i-th and j-th elements in a list L.
// Pre:  L = (e[1] ... e[i] ... e[j] ... e[n])
//       and 1<=i<=n and 1<=j<=n
// Post: i or j is out of range and result = 0
//       or L = (e[1] ... e[j] ... e[i] ... e[n])
int List::swap(int i, int j)
{
   if ( (i > 0) && (i <= size) && (j > 0) && (j <= size) )
   {
      ElementPtr temp = e[i - 1];
      e[i - 1] = e[j - 1];
      e[j - 1] = temp;
      return 1;
   }
   else
      return 0;
} // end List::swap
```

C++ Program Listing

morpheme.h

```
// FILENAME:  MORPHEME.H

// Morphemes are used in combinataion with Input_strings to
// provide generalized user input and parsing.  A Morpheme is
// a string of 16 or fewer readable characters from the
// ASCII set.

// *********** Specifications for class Morpheme ***********

#ifndef Morpheme_h
#define Morpheme_h

#include "elements.h"
#include <fstream.h>


// prototypes
boolean is_white_space (char c);
boolean is_delimiter (char c);

const MAXMORPHEME = 16;   // Maximum characters in a Morpheme.

class Morpheme: public Element
{
   private:
     char value[MAXMORPHEME+1];

   public:


     Morpheme();
     virtual ~Morpheme();


     void virtual display();


     // access
     void get(char* prompt);
     virtual char* get_val();
     virtual void set_val(char* astring);
     Morpheme set_val(float arg);
     float to_float();
     boolean is_word();
     boolean is_float();
     virtual int operator == (Element& e);
```

```
      virtual void file_in(ifstream& afile);
      virtual void file_out(ofstream& afile);
}; //Morpheme

typedef Morpheme* MorphemePtr;


#endif

// ******  Formal specifications for the Morpheme class.   ******

// Morpheme();
// Used: To set up receiver with its virtual methods.
// Pre:  None
// Post: Receiver is initialized and my_class = "Morpheme"

// virtual ~Morpheme();
// Used: To render receiver useless.
// Pre:  Receiver is initialized.
// Post: Receiver is no longer usable.

//access/test
// void virtual display();
// Used: To display a Morpheme.
// Pre:
// Post: receiver.value is displayed to the screen.

// virtual char* get_val();
// Used: To retrieve the value of a morpheme.
// Pre:
// Post: Returns the string value of the receiver.

// virtual char* get_class();
// Used: To test class membership of the receiver.
// Pre:  Receiver is intialized.
// Post: result = receiver's class

// boolean is_float();
// Used: To determine if m takes the form of a real
//       (float) number.
// Pre:
// Post: Returns TRUE iff m takes the form of a real
//       (float) number.

// boolean is_word();
// Used: To distinguish punctuation from other morphemes.
// Pre:
// Post: Returns TRUE iff receiver.value has no punctuation
//       or white spaces.

// file in / file out
// virtual void file_out(ofstream& afile);
// Used: To write a representation of the receiver to afile.
// Pre:  afile is opened for text output and afile = oldStuff
// Post: afile = oldStuff receiver.value

// virtual void file_in(ifstream& afile);
```

```
// Used: To read a representation of the receiver from a file.
// Pre:  afile is opened for text input and = stuff restofstuff
// Post: afile = restofstuff and receiver.value = stuff


//
// modify
//

// void get(char* prompt);
// Used: To input a Morpheme from the keyboard.
// Pre:  Prompt is a string used to prompt the user for input.
// Post: Returns a Morpheme read from the keyboard.

// virtual void set_val(char* astring);
// Used: To change the string value of a morpheme.
// Pre:
// Post: Receiver's value = astring

// float to_float();
// Used: To convert a Morpheme to a float.
// Pre:
// Post: Returns the float value of m or 0 if
//       NOT MorphIsReal(m). This can lead to an overflow error
//       if m is too big. Since different platforms have
//       different maximum floating point values, the overflow
//       checking is left to the client programmer.

// Morpheme set_val(float);
// Used: To store a float variable in a Morpheme.
// Pre:
// Post: Returns the Morpheme representation of the argument up
//       to MAXMORPHEME length.  The value will be rounded so
//       that it will fit in the Morpheme's value data member.

// virtual int operator == (Element& e);
// Used: To test for equality of two morpheme values.
// Pre:
// Post: (result = 1 and this.value == e.value) or
//       (result = 0 and this.value != e.value)
```

C++ Program Listing

`morpheme.cxx`

```cpp
//
//**************************************************************
//   *********** Implementation of class Morpheme **********


#include "morpheme.h"
#include <ctype.h>
#include <string.h>
#include <stdlib.h>
#include <stdio.h>

//
// constructor - destructor
//


Morpheme::Morpheme()
// Initializes the Morpheme variables.
{
    strcpy(my_class,"Morpheme");
    strcpy(value,"");
}


Morpheme::~Morpheme() { }


//
// display
//


void Morpheme::display()
// Output a Morpheme.
{
    cout.width(MAXMORPHEME);
    cout.flags(ios::left);
    cout << value;
}


//
// access
//
```

```cpp
void Morpheme::get(char* prompt)
// Initializes a Morpheme's value.
{
  // input must be buffered into a larger-than-necessary
  // temporary variable so that if its too large it doesn't
  // overwrite anything important
  char temp_value[255];
  temp_value[0] = 0;
  cout << prompt;
  cin.getline(temp_value,255);
  strncpy(value, temp_value, MAXMORPHEME);
}


char* Morpheme::get_val()
// Retrieve the value of a Morpheme.
{
  return value;
}


void Morpheme::set_val (char* astring)
// Changes a Morpheme's value.
{
    strncpy(value, astring, MAXMORPHEME+1);
}


Morpheme Morpheme::set_val(float arg)
// This function takes a float as an argument and converts it to
// a char string representation not longer than MAXMORPHEME, and
// sets the receiver's value to that string.  It also returns
// the dereferenced this pointer.
{
    char str[MAXMORPHEME*2];
      // need a sufficently large buffer
    sprintf(str, "%*.*g",MAXMORPHEME,MAXMORPHEME-1, arg);
    if (strlen(str) > MAXMORPHEME)
    {
      //  The string is too long, so we have to chop it down
      //  First find the position of the 'e', if it's present
      char exp_str[10] = "e";
      int exp_pos = strcspn(str,exp_str);
      if (exp_pos)
      {
        // 'e' is present:  first set exp_str
        // to just the expontnt portion
        strcpy(exp_str,str+exp_pos);
        // now put this in str so that it fits MAXMORPHEME
        strcpy(str+(MAXMORPHEME-strlen(exp_str)), exp_str);
      }
      else
      {
        // no 'e' is present.  Just chop off the string
        // so it fits.
        str[MAXMORPHEME+1] = 0;  // Put a null at the end
      }
```

```
      }
      // store the float-string in the value data member
      strcpy(value,str);
      return *this;
}


float Morpheme::to_float()
// This function takes a variable of type Morpheme and returns
// its real (float) number value. If the Morpheme cannot be
// converted to type float, then to_float returns 0. Note:
// Maximum floating point value is computer dependent.
// Therefore, error handling for floating point overflow is a
// chore left to the programmer.
{
  return atof(value);
}


//
// test
//


boolean Morpheme::is_word()
// A word is a Morpheme without punctuation characters.
{
    int i = 0;

    while (!is_white_space(value[i]) && !is_delimiter(value[i])
          && (i < strlen(value)))
      i++;

    if (i == strlen(value))  // no spaces and no delimiters
      return TRUE;
    else
      return FALSE;
}


boolean Morpheme::is_float()
// A real number (float) has an optional sign, a string of
// digits, an optional decimal point followed by more digits,
// and an optional integer exponent (using the
// scientific notation e or E).
{
    char *endptr;


    strtod(value, &endptr);
    if (endptr[0]==0)
      return TRUE;
    else
      return FALSE;
}
```

```
//
// comparison operator
//


int Morpheme::operator ==(Element& e)
{
   if (!strcmp(value, ((Morpheme&) e).get_val()))
      return 1;
   else
      return 0;
}  // end Morpheme::operator ==



//
// file in / file out
//


void Morpheme::file_in(ifstream &afile)
// File in a Morpheme's value from afile
{
    afile >> value;
}



void Morpheme::file_out(ofstream &afile)
// File out a Morpheme's value to afile
{
    afile << " " << value;
}



boolean is_white_space (char c)
// A whitespace is a character that separates words, numbers,
// etc... In this implementation, a whitespace is either a blank
// or any character that is less than or equal to a blank (i.e.,
// any nonprintable character).
{
    if (( c <= ' ') || (c == 127))   // 127 = the del character
      return TRUE;
    else
      return FALSE;
}



boolean is_delimiter (char c)
// A delimiter is any character that is not a letter (A-Z, a-z)
// or a digit (0-9) or a whitespace character
{
    if (!is_white_space(c) && !isdigit(c) &&  !isalpha(c) )
      return TRUE;
    else
      return FALSE;
}
```

C++ Program Listing
`inputstr.h`

```
// FILENAME:  INPUTSTR.H

// Input_string, combined with Morphemes, provide generalized
// user-input and parsing.  An Input_string is a string of 255
// or fewer characters from the ASCII set.

// ********** Specifications for class Input_string **********

#ifndef inputstr_h
#define inputstr_h

#include "elements.h"
#include "morpheme.h"

class Input_string: public Element
{
    private:
    // DATA MEMBERS ...
    boolean error;
    char value[256];

    public:

    Input_string();
    virtual ~Input_string();


    char* get_val();
    void set_val(char* str);


    void reformat (int &level);
    MorphemePtr retrieve(int i);
    int morpheme_count();


    virtual void file_in(ifstream& afile);
}; //input_string

#endif

// ********  Formal specification for Input_string  ********

//constructor/destructor
// Input_string();
// Used: To set up receiver with its virtual methods.
```

```
// Pre: None
// Post: Receiver is initialized and MyClass = 'InputString'

// virtual ~Input_string();
// Used: To render receiver useless.
// Pre:  Receiver is initialized.
// Post: Receiver is no longer usable.

//
//modify
//

// void set_val(char* str);
// Used: to set the value of the receiver.
// Pre:  str = astring
// Post: data member value = str

// char* get_val();
// Used: to access the value of the Input_string object.
// Pre:
// Post:  data member value is returned

// void reformat (int &level);
// Used: To format an input string into its constituent
//       morphemes.
// Pre:  receiver is a string of morphemes possibly bounded on
//       each side by input delimiters such as parentheses,
//       square brackets, or braces. Level is the starting
//       delimiter level (i.e. LeftDelim - RightDelim). When
//       reading in a list of strings for input, the first call
//       to ReadFormat should have level = 0.
// Post: Puts spaces around punctuation characters (except '.')
//       so they can be parsed as morphemes.

//
//test
//

// virtual char* get_class();
// Used: To test class membership of the receiver.
// Pre:  Receiver is intialized.
// Post: result = receiver's class

//
//access/display
//

// int morpheme_count();
// Used: To count the number of morphemes in a formatted string.
// Pre:  s has been formatted with ReadFormat.
// Post: Returns the number of morphemes in s.

// MorphemePtr retrieve(int i);
// Used: To retrieve the ith Morpheme from a formatted input
//       string s.
// Pre: s has been formatted by ReFormat and
//       1 <= i <= MorphCount(s).
```

```
// Post: result = the ith Morpheme in s.

// virtual void file_in(ifstream& afile);
// Used: To input an input line from data read in from afile.
// Pre:  Receiver is initialized and
//       afile = somevalue \n restOfFile
// Post: Receiver.value = somevalue and AFile = restOfFile
```

C++ Program Code
inputstr.cxx

```
// FILENAME: INPUTSTR.CXX

//
//****************************************************************
//*********** Implementation of class Input_string ***********

#include "inputstr.h"
#include <string.h>

boolean is_left_delim(char c);
boolean is_right_delim(char c);

Input_string::Input_string()
// Initializes the Input_string variables.
{
    strcpy(my_class, "Input_string");
    strcpy(value, "");
    error = FALSE;
}

Input_string::~Input_string() { }


char* Input_string::get_val()
{
    return value;
}


void Input_string::set_val(char* str)
{
    strncpy(value,str,255);
    value[255] = 0;  // Just in case the string is too long
}


void Input_string::reformat(int &level)
// Pre:  value = any string with different levels of
//       parenthesization.
// Post: Inserts spaces around all punctuation characters in
//       value, except for embedded or leading periods, at
//       the given level.
{
    char tmpstr[256], temp2[256];
    tmpstr[0] = 0;
    int i = 0; // Point to the beginning of the string.
```

```
    // Skip leading spaces.
    while ((is_white_space(value[i])) && (i < strlen(value)))
      i++;

    // Copy over to tempstr, putting spaces
    // around punctuation marks.
    strcat(tmpstr, " ");
    strcat(tmpstr, strncpy(temp2,value+i,strlen(value)
      - i + 1));
    strcat(tmpstr, " ");

    value[0] = 0;
    i = 1;
    while (i < (strlen(tmpstr)-1))
    {
      if (is_left_delim(tmpstr[i]))
        level++;
      else
        if (is_right_delim(tmpstr[i]))
          level--;

      // Put spaces around delimiters, except for
      // embedded or leading periods
      if (is_delimiter(tmpstr[i]) && (tmpstr[i] != '.'))
      {
        strcat(value, " ");
        strncat(value, tmpstr+i, 1);
        strcat(value, " ");
      }
      else
        if ((tmpstr[i] == '.') &&
          is_white_space(tmpstr[i + 1]))
        {
          strcat(value, " ");
          strncat(value, tmpstr + i, 1);
        }
        else
        {
          strncat(value, tmpstr+i, 1);
        }
      i ++;
    }
}


Morpheme* Input_string::retrieve (int i)
// This function returns the ith Morpheme in a formatted string.
{
    Morpheme* result;
    int start, len;
    // Initialize the search.
    int morph_number = 1;  // We start parsing at the first
                           // Morpheme in the string.
    int j = 0;   // We use "j" as the index of the string.

    // Skip leading whitespaces.
```

```
            while ( is_white_space(value[j]) && (j < strlen(value)))
               j++;

            // Skip over first i-1 Morphemes.
            while ((morph_number < i) && (j < strlen(value)))
            {
               // Count it.
                morph_number++;

               // Skip over it.
               do
               {
                  j++;
               } while (!(is_white_space(value[j]) ||
                       (j >= strlen(value))));

               // Skip morphspaces after token.
               while (is_white_space(value[j]) && (j < strlen(value)))
                  j++;
            }

            // Record the starting position.
            start = j;

            // Find the true strlen of the string. If the string is too
            // long for a morpheme, then truncate it to MaxMorph
            // characters and set the error value.
            len = 0;
            do
            {
               j++;
            } while (!(is_white_space(value[j]) ||
                    (j >= strlen(value))));

            len = j - start;

            if (len > MAXMORPHEME)
            {
               len = MAXMORPHEME;
               error = TRUE;
            }

            // Make a new morpheme and copy the result to it.
            result = new Morpheme;
            char morphstr[MAXMORPHEME+1];
            strncpy(morphstr, value + start, len);
            morphstr[len] = 0;
            result->Morpheme::set_val(morphstr);
            return result;
         }


int Input_string::morpheme_count()
// Counts the number of morphemes in a formatted string s.
{
      // Initialize the count.
      int n = 0; // Number of morphemes
```

```
    int i = 0; // String index

    // Skip leading whitespaces.
    while ( is_white_space(value[i]) && (i < strlen(value)) )
      i ++;

    while (i < strlen(value))
    {
        do
        {
          i++;
        }
        while ((i < strlen(value)) &&
              !is_white_space(value[i]) );

      // Skip spaces after token.
      while ( (i < strlen(value)) && is_white_space(value[i]) )
          i++;

      // Count the token.
        n++;

      }
    return n;
}


void Input_string::file_in(ifstream &afile)
{
    afile.getline(value,255);
} // Input_string::file_in


boolean is_left_delim(char c)
{
    if ((c == '{') || (c == '(') || (c == '['))
      return TRUE;
    else
      return FALSE;
}

boolean is_right_delim(char c)
{
    if ((c == '}') || (c == ')') || (c == ']'))
      return TRUE;
    else
      return FALSE;
}
```

C++ Program Listing
`queue.h`

```
// FILENAME: QUEUE.H

    // Class description: The class Queue implements a
    //    FIFO (first in - first out) sequential data
    //    structure. The queue class allows objects to
    //    enter at one end (the rear) and leave from the
    //    other (the front). In our specifications a Queue is
    //    denoted by:  Q = (e[f] e[next] .... e[r])
    //    where e[f] is the object at the front of the queue,
    //    e[next] is the next object and e[r] is the object at
    //    the rear of the queue.  The empty queue is denoted by
    //    Q = ().

// ******** Specification for the Queue class.   ********

#ifndef QUEUE_H
#define QUEUE_H

#include <stddef.h> // for NULL
#include "sequence.h"


class Queue : public Sequence
{
    protected:
    int f, r;

    public:
    //constructor - destructor
    Queue();
    virtual ~Queue();

    // modify
    int enter(ElementPtr);
    ElementPtr remove();
    virtual void empty();
    void rotate();

    // access
    ElementPtr front();
    ElementPtr rear();

    // display
    virtual  void display();
};   //end class Queue
```

```
#endif

// Formal specifications for the Queue class

//
//constructor / destructor
//

// Queue();
// Used: To initialize the receiver queue.
// Pre:  None
// Post: The receiver queue is intialized and
//   size = 0 and f = 1 and r = 0 and Q = ()

// ~Queue();
// Used: To destroy the receiver queue.
// Pre:   Receiver queue is initialized.
// Post: The receiver queue is destroyed.

//
// access / modify
//

// int enter(ElementPtr eptr);
// Used: To add a new object to the rear of the receiver queue.
// Pre:  Q = (e[f] ... e[r]) and size = n
// Post: (size = MAXELEMENTS and result = 0) or
//        (size < MAXELEMENTS and Q = (e[f] ... e[r] eptr
//        and size = n + 1 and result = 1 and
//        r = (old r) + 1 % MAXELEMENTS)

// ElementPtr remove();
// Used: To remove an object from the front of the queue.
// Pre:  Q = (e[f] e[next] ... e[r]) and size = n
// Post: (size = 0 and result  = 0)
//        (or n > 0 and Q = (e[next] ... e[r]) and size = n-1 and
//        result = 1 ) and receiver = e[f] and
//        f = (old f) + 1 % MAXELENTS)


// void empty();
// Used: To empty the receiver queue.
// Pre:  Q = (e[f] ... e[r]) and size = n
// Post  Q = () and size = 0 and each Element in Q is destroyed

// void rotate();
// Used: To move the object at the front of the queue
//       to the rear.
// Pre:  Q = (e[f] e[f+1] ... e[r]) and size = n
// Post: Q = (e[f+1] ... e[r] e[f]) or n = 0

// ElementPtr front();
// Used: To access the object at the front of the queue.
// Pre:  Q = (e[f] ... e[r]) and size = n
// Post: (size = 0 and result = NULL) or
//        (or size > 0 and result = e[f])
```

```
// ElementPtr rear();
// Used: To access the object at the rear of the queue.
// Pre:  Q = (e[f] ... e[r]) and size = n
// Post: (size = 0 and result = NULL)
//       (or size > 0 and result = e[r])

// void display();
// Used: To display the contents of the queue object.
// Pre:  Q = (e[f] ... e[r]) and size = n
// Post: output = Q
// Note: User MUST implement display for each type.
```

C++ Program Listing

queue.cxx

```
// FILENAME:  QUEUE.CXX
#include "queue.h"

//****************** implementation of ********************
//****************** Queue methods ***********************
const int MAX_QUEUE = MAXELEMENTS-1;

Queue::Queue()
{
   f = 0;
   r = -1;
} // end Queue::Queue()

Queue::~Queue()
{
   // LOCAL DATA ...
   ElementPtr *t;

   // STATEMENTS ...
   empty();
} // end Queue::~Queue()


int Queue::enter(ElementPtr eptr)
{
   if (this -> is_full())
      return 0;
   else
   {
      r = (r + 1) % MAXELEMENTS;
      e[r] = eptr;
      size++;
      return 1;
   }
} // end Queue::enter()

ElementPtr Queue::remove()
{
  if (this -> is_empty())
    return NULL;
  else
  {
    int tempint = f;
    f = (f + 1) % MAXELEMENTS;
    size--;
    return e[tempint];
  }
```

```
}   // end Queue::remove()

void Queue::empty()
{
  // LOCAL DATA ...
  ElementPtr *t;

  // STATEMENTS ...
  if (size)
  {
    // at least one element on queue
    if (f <= r)
    {
      for (t = e + f; t <= e + r; t++)
      {
      delete *t;
      }
    }
    else // f > r; queue wrapped around
    {
      for (t = e + f; t <= e + MAX_QUEUE; t++)
      {
      delete *t;
      }
      for (t = e; t <= e + r; t++)
      {
      delete *t;
      }
    } // if at least one element
  }
  f = 0;
  r = -1;
  size = 0;
} //end Queue::empty()


void Queue::rotate()
{
  if (!(this -> is_empty()))
  {
      enter(e[f]);
      remove();
  }
}   //end Queue::rotate()

ElementPtr Queue::front()
{
    if (this -> is_empty())
       return NULL;
    else
       return  e[f];
}   //end Queue::front()

ElementPtr Queue::rear()
{
    if (this -> is_empty())
       return NULL;
```

```
        else
            return e[r];
}   //end Queue::rear()

void Queue::display()
{
    // LOCAL DATA ...
    ElementPtr *t;

    // STATEMENTS ...
    if (size)
    {
        // at least one element on queue
        if (f <= r)
        {
        for (t = e + f; t <= e + r; t++)
        {
            (*t) -> display();
        }
        }
        else // f > r; queue wrapped around
        {
        for (t = e + f; t <= e + MAX_QUEUE; t++)
        {
            (*t) -> display();
        }
        for (t = e; t <= e + r; t++)
        {
            (*t) -> display();
        }
        } // if at least one element
    }
}   // end Queue::display()
```

C++ Program Listing

stack.h

```
// FILENAME STACK.H

// Class description: The class Stack is a sequence in
//    which objects can only be inserted or retrieved from
//    one end of the stack (called its top).
//    In our specifications a Stack will be denoted by
//        S = (e[1] e[2] .... e[n])
//    where each e[i] denotes an object. The empty
//    stack is denoted by S = ().


// ******* Specification for the Stack class.   ********

#ifndef Stack_h
#define Stack_h


#include <stddef.h>
    // required for Microsoft compiler 7.0 for NULL
#include "sequence.h"

class Stack : public Sequence
{
   public:
      // constructor / destructor
      Stack() { };
      ~Stack() { };

      // modifying
      int push(ElementPtr);
      ElementPtr pop();

      // access
      ElementPtr top();

      // display
      virtual void display();
};   // end class Stack

#endif

// ********  Formal specifications for the Stack class  ********

//
//constructor / destructor
//
```

```
// Stack();
// Used: To initialize the receiver stack.
// Pre:  None
// Post: Receiver stack is initialized and size = 0 and S = ()

// virtual ~Stack();
// Used: To destroy the receiver stack.
// Pre:  Receiver is initialized.
// Post: Receiver stack is destroyed.


//
// accessing / modifying
//

// int push(ElementPtr eptr);
// Used: To add a new element onto the top of the stack.
// Pre:  S = (e[1] e[2] ... e[n]) and size = n
// Post: n < MAXELEMENTS and size = n+1 and
//       S = (e[1] e[2] ... e[n] eptr) and result = 1
//       or n = MAXELEMENTS and result = 0

// ElementPtr pop();
// Used: To remove the top element from the stack.
// Pre:  S = (e[1] e[2] ... e[n]) and size = n
// Post: (n = 0 and result = 0) or
//       (n > 0 and S = (e[1] e[2] ... e[n-1]) and size = n-1
//       and result = ElementPtr)

// virtual ElementPtr top();
// Used: To access the element at the top of the stack.
// Pre:  S = (e[1] e[2] ... e[n]) and size = n
// Post: (n = 0 and result = NULL) or
//       (n > 0 and result = e[N])

// virtual void display();
// Used: To display the contents of the stack object.
// Pre:  S = (e[1] e[2] ... e[n]) and size = n
// Post: output = S
// Note: User MUST implement display for each type.
```

C++ Program Listing
stack.cxx

```
// FILENAME: STACK.CXX

#include "stack.h"

//****************** implementation of *******************
//****************** stack methods ***********************

int Stack::push(ElementPtr eptr)
{
  if (this -> is_full())
    return 0;
  else
  {
    e[size++] = eptr;
    return 1;
  }
}  // Stack::push()

ElementPtr Stack::pop()
{
  if (this -> is_empty())
    return NULL;
  else
  {
    return e[--size];
  }
}  //Stack::pop

ElementPtr Stack::top()
{
   if (this -> is_empty())
      return NULL;
   else
      return  e[size-1];
}  //Stack::top



void Stack::display()
{
  for (ElementPtr *eptr = e + size - 1; eptr >= e; eptr--)
  {
    (*eptr) -> display();
    cout << endl;
  }
}  // end Stack::display
```

CHAPTER 5

TREES AND GRAPHS

These laboratory exercises are designed to give you experience with the use of the `Tree` and `BinaryTree` classes and their methods in computing applications.

LABORATORY EXERCISE—BINARY SEARCH TREES

One of the most useful specializations of trees is *binary search trees*—binary trees that are designed to store data for rapid access. In this exercise, you will be asked to implement the four operations that are typically associated with data management—add, modify, delete, and search—using a binary search tree. You should utilize the `BinaryTree` methods specified in the text. The header file and implementations are in the files tree.h and tree.cxx in the system course directory (or on the distribution disk). In addition, you may also use the `binary_search` and `build` methods that appear in the text. You will need to create a loader which will create a `List L` by reading data from a text file; the binary search tree will be built from `L`. You will also need to write the `modify` and `delete` routines and an output routine which will write the data contained in the final (modified) tree back to the source file in the same format it had originally.

Your major difficulty will be with the `delete` routine. Note that you cannot simply use the generic `remove` member function since it not only removes an element, but all the nodes under it. For instance, suppose our data consists of strings of up to 16 characters and our `List L` is:

```
(Joe   Sandy   Anne   Patty   Regina   Anton   Don)
```

Then `build` will construct the tree in Figure 5–1.

Suppose we want to `delete Regina`. In this case, the action required is simple; find `Regina`, then use the generic tree `remove` method to delete the node. But suppose instead that we wanted to `delete Joe`. If we use the generic method, we will lose the entire tree. Thus, we have to find another element which can serve as the root of the tree and replace `Joe` by that element.

There are two ways to find an element to replace `Joe` at the point of deletion. One would be to step from `Joe` to its right child, then search left as far as

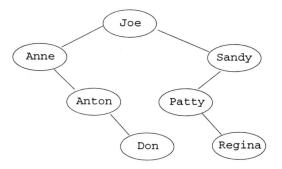

FIGURE 5–1 Binary search tree built from the `List` (Joe Sandy Anne Patty Regina Anton Don).

possible without stepping to a right child again. In this case, we halt at `Patty`, so that `Patty` is a possible replacement for `Joe`.

Another way would be to step left from `Joe`, then search right as far as possible without stepping left again. In this example, `Don` becomes a possible replacement for `Joe`. Suppose we use this strategy, finding `Don` as the new root. Then we should modify the contents of node `Joe` so that it contains `Don`, simultaneously deleting `Don` to complete the deletion of the single node, `Joe`. If, on the other hand, we had first stepped right from `Joe`, we would have replaced `Joe` by `Patty` and deleted `Patty` instead. Note that this alternative would be necessary if `Joe` had an empty left subtree.

Part 1 — Design a New Method — `delete`

Using the strategy discussed above, design a new method `delete` that will delete a single node from a `BinarySearchTree`. This design should include pre- and postconditions, and `BinarySearchTree` should be viewed as an extension of the class `BinaryTree`, along with the methods `binary_search` and `build` discussed in the text. Since all of the `Tree` and `BinaryTree` methods are available to you, you should familiarize yourself with them before you attempt to decompose your problem. Also, you should write your specifications in such a way that they are consistent with the `binary_search` and `build` routines given in the text.

Part 2 — Design a New Method — `modify`

Design and implement a member function, `modify` that will "replace" the the value of an entry in the `BinarySearchTree`, such as changing "`Sandy`" to "`Meg`." Note that this type of change is not as simple as it might at first seem, since it will, in general, lead to an alteration of the structure of the `Binary-SearchTree`. Therefore, a `modify` can be viewed as a `delete` followed by insert.

Part 3 — Design, Implement, and Test Your Complete Program

Implement these new methods and integrate it with the `BinarySearchTrees` extension of the class `BinaryTree`, as suggested in the worksheet below. Then complete the program so that it will build a `BinarySearchTree` from an input `List`, search for an individual element in the tree, and `delete` that element no matter where it is in the tree. Test the entire program on several different input `Lists`, including the one discussed at the beginning of this exercise.

Questions

1. Comment on your `delete` member function. Did you use recursion to implement it? If so, contrast your solution with that which might have been written without recursion.
2. Suppose the condition that all data items are distinct were removed. How would your new method have to be modified to accommodate this change?
3. Comment on the usefulness of your program as a technique for managing data. What do you see as its strengths and weaknesses?

Worksheet for Laboratory Exercise—
Binary Search Trees

```
/* -- Program name: Binary Search Trees
   -- Programmer:
   -- Date:
   -- ** Overview



                                                                      */

#include <iostream.h>
#include <fstream.h>
#include "elements.h"
#include "inputstr.h"
#include "morpheme.h"
#include "strg.h"
#include "list.h"
#include "tree.h"
   // GLOBAL CONSTANTS AND TYPEDEF'S

   // GLOBAL FUNCTION PROTOTYPES


main()
{
   // pre:
   // FUNCTION PROTOTYPES

   // LOCAL DATA


   // STATEMENTS










// post:
}
```

Notes for Answers to Questions

1.

2.

3.

REGULAR EXPRESSIONS

A useful tool in computing is one which allows us to describe an *entire class* of strings to search for in a larger text. For instance, suppose we want to find the first occurrence of *any one* of the strings the, a, or an in a large text. One type of expression that designates a whole group of strings that share certain properties is called a *regular expression*. For example, the following regular expression denotes "any one of the three strings the, a, or an."

the|a|an

The vertical bar | designates the logical **or** when used in a regular expression.

TABLE 5–1   MEANINGS OF THE REGULAR EXPRESSION OPERATORS

Operator	Meaning
c	The character c in the ASCII set. For example, the regular expression the denotes exactly the characters t, h, and e in that order.
.	Any character in the ASCII set. That is, the dot serves as a "wild card" character within a longer string. For example, the regular expression t.e denotes any 3-character sequence that begins with t and ends with e.
[]	A set of alternative characters. For example, the regular expression [Tt]he denotes either of the strings The or the.
c1 - c2	Any character in the range c1 through c2, according to the ordering of ASCII characters. For example, [A-Za-z] denotes any single letter of the alphabet, whether it is capitalized or not.
e1 | e2	A choice (alternative) between the strings given by expression e1 and those given by e2. For example, the|a|an denotes any one of the strings the, a, or an.
()	Overrides the normal precedence of concatenation over alternation (|). For example, the expression John Doe|Brown denotes either of the strings John Doe or Brown, whereas the expression John (Doe|Brown) denotes either of the strings John Doe or John Brown.
*	Zero or more occurrences of the expression that precedes it. For example, abba(dabba)* denotes any string that begins with abba and has 0 or more occurrences of dabba at its right end.
+	One or more occurrences of the expression that precedes it. For example, abba(dabba)+ denotes any string that begins with abba and has 1 or more occurrences of dabba at its right end.
?	Optional (0 or 1) occurrence of the expression that precedes it. For example, abba(dabba)? denotes either of the strings abba or abbadabba.

Regular expressions allow us to conveniently express many different classifications of strings. The operators in Table 5–1 have special meanings when they appear within a regular expression. An additional feature of regular expressions allows any one of the operators to denote itself (literally), rather than carry the meaning described there. For this to occur, the operator must be preceded by the escape character \ (backslash). For example, the regular expression ... represents *any* 3-character sequence, while the regular expression ..\. represents any 2-character sequence followed by a period.

These conventions provide a rich basis for describing sets of strings, in the same way that ordinary arithmetic expressions provide for describing sequences of mathematical calculations. In fact, regular expressions are used in many areas of computer science that deal formally with transformations on strings of characters. In programming language design, for instance, we need to describe precisely that class of strings that constitutes valid tokens within a program; identifiers, constants, and so forth. For this purpose, regular expressions are most useful.

Consider, for example, the notion of *identifier* in C++, which can be defined rather precisely as "any sequence of letters and digits, the first of which must be a letter." We are familiar with this notion, since we use it every time we need to invent a new variable or function name in a program. The following are valid C++ identifiers:

```
size i j real begin if end
```

The following regular expression defines precisely the same class of strings.

```
[A-Za-z][A-Za-z0-9]*
```

That is, an identifier is a lower- or upper-case letter followed by zero or more occurrences of a letter or a digit.

As another example, consider the description of *real number* that we use intuitively when we write numbers like the following.

```
3.14     0      -777.5     0.0001     12
```

That is, a real number is any sequence of decimal digits, optionally preceded by a sign and optionally followed by a decimal point and another sequence of decimal digits. A regular expression can be used to characterize this as follows:

```
[+|-]?[0-9]+(.[0-9]+)?
```

These two examples show the expressive power and simplicity of regular expressions, compared with English, for describing classes of strings that occur in the syntax of programming languages.

For this reason, regular expressions are widely used in text editors and other text processing applications. The UNIX operating system, for instance, contains a powerful function called grep (for *g*lobal *r*egular *e*xpression *p*rinter). grep is a useful programming tool for locating strings that match various complex patterns within a text.

(TEAM) LABORATORY EXERCISE—PRECEDENCE PARSING REGULAR EXPRESSIONS

In the style of the arithmetic expression parser in Chapter 4, you are asked in this project to design and implement a *regular expression* parser instead. Assume that regular expressions are defined as in the preceding section, but with the following restrictions.

1. Concatenation is explicitly marked in the expression by the operator ^, which has higher precedence than |.
2. The operators ?, +, ., –, and [] are disallowed.
3. The Individual tokens of regular expressions can be any morphemes, and are separated by spaces.
4. The priorities of the remaining operators are such that the star (*) has highest priority, followed by concatenation (^) at the next-highest level, and finally alternation (|) at the lowest level.

That is, regular expressions look similar to arithmetic expressions, where concatenation and alternation are similar to multiplication and division, and parentheses are used in the same way to override precedence. The postfix star operator * for regular expressions has no analog in arithmetic expressions.

Part 1 — Adjust the Expression Parser Algorithm to Handle Regular Expressions

Redesign the algorithm for parsing arithmetic expressions so that it parses these restricted regular expressions instead. In particular, your redesign should address the stack and tree list actions that should be done when the star (*) operator is encountered in the input string. Make appropriate changes to the ExpressionParser program that will implement this redesign.

Part 2 — Test the Adjusted Expression Parser Program

Run your revised ExpressionParser program with several different regular expressions as input. Include the following test cases, and be sure that your program derives parse trees like the ones shown on the right.

Regular expression

```
alpha ^ beta | gamma
alpha ^ beta *
a | b | c | d | e
(a ^ b) *
```

Parse Tree

```
(| (^ alpha beta) gamma)
(^ alpha (* beta))
(| (| (| (| a b) c) d) e)
(* (^ a b))
```

Questions

1. Comment on the amount of reprogramming that was required by this change. That is, to what extent could the basic strategy of the prece-

dence parsing algorithm be preserved, and to what extent did additional code need to be added?

2. What would be needed if you had to implement the additional regular expression operators that were omitted from this exercise? What additional properties would need to be defined or clarified? What additional programming considerations would need to be made beyond those that are already in the arithmetic expression parsing program?

Worksheet for Laboratory Exercise—
Precedence Parsing Regular Expressions

```
/* -- Program name: Regular Expression Parser
   -- Programmer:
   -- Date:
   -- ** Overview



                                                    */


#include <iostream.h>
#include <fstream.h>
#include "elements.h"
#include "inputstr.h"
#include "morpheme.h"
#include "strg.h"
#include "list.h"
#include "tree.h"
   // GLOBAL CONSTANTS AND TYPEDEF'S

   // GLOBAL FUNCTION PROTOTYPES


main()
{
   // pre:
   // FUNCTION PROTOTYPES

   // LOCAL DATA


   // STATEMENTS








// post:
}
```

Notes for Answers to Questions

1.

2.

LABORATORY EXERCISE—PRECEDENCE PARSING USING BINARY TREES

The purpose of this lab is to redesign and reimplement the precedence parsing program discussed in Chapter 5 of the text so that it uses the `BinaryTree` class rather than the general `Tree` class. This activity stems from the observation that infix arithmetic expressions never have more than two operands per operator, so that the binary tree is the most appropriate to represent their structure. The goal of the program is thus the same as that of the orignnal one: to take any infix arithmetic expression and develop a binary tree representation for it. For instance, if the input were:

```
a + 2 * ( b + 3 ) - c ^ 2          (^ means exponentiation)
```

the output would be the following parse tree:

```
( - ( + a ( * 2 ( + b 3 ) ) ) ( ^ c 2 ) )
```

Note that this parse takes into account the priority of ^ (exponentiation) over * and /, which in turn have higher priority than + and −. Two or more operators of the same priority at the same level of parenthesization within the expression are evaluated from left to right. Parentheses are used to override these rules in the usual way, so that parenthesized subexpressions appear lower in the tree.

A subsequent postorder scan of this parse tree gives a postfix representation of the original expression, as we have already seen. This algorithm represents, therefore, something like the task of a compiler when it translates an arithmetic expression into machine code, while the postfix expression evaluator that we studied earlier is analogous to the task of machine language execution.

Part 1 — Review of the Algorithm

The precedence parsing algorithm scans the input expression from left to right, one token at a time. It has two internal stacks, one called 'operators' that contains arithmetic operators encountered during the scan, and the other called 'operands' that contains binary trees representing partially constructed subexpressions that are built during the input scan. At the end of the process, the operands stack should contain a single binary tree, which is the outcome of the parse. That tree should be displayed as the output of the program.

Two utility functions are needed to assist with this algorithm. These are called `priority` and `CombineTrees`. They have the same tasks as described in Chapter 5 of the text, except that `BinaryTree` is the class of object being rransformed rather than `Tree`.

An algorithm for precedence parsing can be described in the following steps:

```
// 1.  repeat step 2 for each token in the input

// 2.  if the token is an operator, perform step 2.1.
        if the token is an operand, perform step 2.2.
        if the token is a left parenthesis "(", push it onto the
```

```
                  operands stack.
                  if the token is a right parenthesis, ")", perform step
                  2.3.

        // 2.1.    while the operators stack is not empty and the
        //         priority of the top operator on the stack >= the
        //         priority of the token
                  {
                      op = pop the top operator from the operators stack;
                      binaryTree Y = operands.pop();
                      binaryTree X = operands.pop();
                      X.combineTrees (op, Y);
                  }
                  push the token onto the operators stack

        //2.2.     form a new binary tree whose root is the token
                  push this tree onto the operands stack

        //2.3.     while the operators stack does not have "(" on top
                  {
                      op = pop the top operator from the operators stack;
                      binaryTree Y = operands.pop();
                      binaryTree X = operands.pop();
                      X.combineTrees (op, Y);
                  }
                  pop the "(" from the top of the operators stack

    // 3.    (end of input)
            while the operators stack is not empty
            {
                op = pop the top operator from the operators stack;
                binaryTree Y = operands.pop();
                binaryTree X = operands.pop();
                X.combineTrees (op, Y);
            }

    // 4.    display the top (remaining) tree on the operands stack
```

Part 2 — Implement and Run this Program

Implement this program and run it with each of the following arithmetic expressions. Check that the parse tree your program produces is correct.

a. a + 2 * (b + 3) – c ^ 2
b. alpha + beta * gamma
c. a + (b + c) * d
d. 3
e. (a + b) * (c + d * e)

Questions

1. Write the prefix, infix, and postfix representations for each of the expressions above.

2. What would happen to your precedence parser if the input expression were incorrect in each of the following ways>

    a. Two operands appear without an intervening operator, such as in the following:
    ```
    a + 2 b
    ```

    b. Two operators appear without an intervening operand, such as in the following:
    ```
    a + * b
    ```

    c. Parentheses are not properly matched, as in either of the following:
    ```
    a + ( b * c
    a + b * c )
    ```

    In each case, describe the consequences for the operands and operators stack, as well as the particular step in the algorithm where it would fail (if any!).

3. (extra credit) Suggest ways in which the algorithm for precedence parsing could be made more robust, in the sense that it would anticipate and give an appropriate error message when one of the above types of "syntax errors" is detected.

Worksheet for Laboratory Exercise—
Precedence Parsing Using Binary Trees

```
/* -- Program name: Regular Expression Parser
   -- Programmer:
   -- Date:
   -- ** Overview


                                                        */

#include <iostream.h>
#include <fstream.h>
#include "elements.h"
#include "inputstr.h"
#include "morpheme.h"
#include "strg.h"
#include "list.h"
#include "bintree.h"
   // GLOBAL CONSTANTS AND TYPEDEF'S

   // GLOBAL FUNCTION PROTOTYPES

main()
{
   // pre:
   // FUNCTION PROTOTYPES

   // LOCAL DATA


   // STATEMENTS






// post:
}
```

Notes for Answers to Questions

1.

2.

3.

C++ Program Listing

tree.h

```
// FILENAME:  TREE.H

// This unit contains the source code for the Tree class.
#ifndef Tree_h
#define Tree_h

#include "elements.h"
#include "inputstr.h"
#include "morpheme.h"


// GLOBAL DATA
enum step_type {to_root, to_parent, to_left_sib, to_right_sib,
 to_l_child, to_r_child};
enum traverse_type {breadth_first, depth_first, pre_order,
 in_order, post_order};


class Tree
{
protected:
  struct Tree_node
  {
     ElementPtr e;            // value stored in the node.
     int level;               // Level of Generation. Root = 0.
    Tree_node* parent;        // Pointer to parent (nil if Root)
    Tree_node* right_sib;     // Pointer to Right Sibling (nil if
                              // none)
    Tree_node* left_child;    // Pointer to Left Child (nil if
                              //   none)
    Tree_node* right_child;   // Pointer to Right Child (nil if
                              //   none)


     Tree_node(ElementPtr eptr)
     {
     e = eptr;
     parent = right_sib = left_child = right_child = NULL;
     }
  };


    typedef Tree_node* tree_link;
    enum tree_delete {yes_delete, no_delete};


    int size;            // Number of nodes in the tree.
    int height;          // Longest path from the root to a leaf
```

```
    int columns;        // columns for display; 0 means linear,
                        // >0 means tabular.
    int width;          // Width of each column
    Tree_node* current;// Pointer to the current node.
    Tree_node* root;    // Pointer to the root node.
    int error;
    int Tree::max_depth (Tree* t);
    tree_delete should_delete;      // Used in destructor
public:
    // costructor/destructor
    Tree();
    virtual ~Tree();


    // access
    int get_size() { return size; }
    void set_size(int s) { size = s; }
    Tree_node* get_current() { return current; }
    void set_current(Tree_node* t) { current = t; }
    int get_error() { return error; }
    void set_error(int e) { error = e; }
    int get_height() { return height; }
    tree_link get_root() { return root; }
    int get_columns() { return columns; }
    void set_columns(int c) { columns = c; }
    void set_delete(tree_delete d) {should_delete = d;}


    // modify
    void get (char* prompt);
    virtual void parse(Input_string &inputstrb,
                    boolean &setfirst);
    int is_leaf();
    ElementPtr store(ElementPtr m);
    virtual void insert(ElementPtr eptr);
    ElementPtr retrieve();
    void step (step_type to_where);
    virtual void traverse(traverse_type how);
    virtual void remove(tree_link delete_me);
    // Used: To remove all the nodes under (and including) the
    //  current tree node.
    // Pre:  current != nil
    void empty();
    virtual void graft (Tree* b);
    virtual int search (ElementPtr elem);


    // display
    virtual void display();


    // file_in/out
    virtual void file_in(char* savename);
    virtual int file_out(char* savename);
};
```

```
typedef Tree* TreePtr;

#endif

// ********** Formal Specifications for Tree_node ************

// Tree_node();
// Used: To allocate memory for a tree node and
//       initialize its pointers.
// Pre:
// Post: Allocates memory for node and initializes all
//       pointers and variables.



// *********** Formal Specifications for Tree ************

// int max_depth(Tree* t);
// Used: To recalculate the height of a tree after
//       pruning.  This is invisible to the user; it is
//       called automatically from Delete.
// Pre:
// Post: result = the maximum depth of all elements
//       in the receiver.



// Tree();
// Used: To initialize a tree.  Must be called before
//       any other tree function.
// Pre:
// Post: Root is allocated, pointers are set to nil,
//       and variables are initialized.

// virtual ~Tree();
// Used: To discontinue a tree.
// Pre:  Tree exists.
// Post: Tree is emptied, storage is freed.



// int get_size() { return size; }
// Used: To access the private data member size.
// Pre:
// Post: result = size

// Tree_node* get_current() { return current; }
// Used: To access the private data member current.
// Pre:
// Post: result = current

// void set_current(Tree_node* t) { current = t; }
// Used: To set the private data member current.
// Pre:
// Post: current = t

// int get_error() { return error; }
// Used: To access the private data member error.
```

```
// Pre:
// Post: result = error

// void set_error(int e) { error = e; }
// Used: To set the private data member error.
// Pre:
// Post: error = e

// int get_height() { return height; }
// Used: To access the private data member height.
// Pre:
// Post: result = height

// tree_link get_root() { return root; }
// Used: To access the private data member root.
// Pre:
// Post: result = root

// int get_columns() { return columns; }
// Used: To access the private data member columns.
// Pre:
// Post: result = columns

// void set_columns(int c) { columns = c; }
// Used: To set the private data member columns.
// Pre:
// Post: columns = c


// void set_delete(tree_delete d) {should_delete = d;}
// Used: To set the private data member should_delete.
// Pre:
// Post: should_delete = d


// void get (char* prompt);
// Used: To input and insert a complete tree at the current
//       node (root for new trees).
// Pre:  Prompt is the string used to prompt the user for input.
// Post: Receiver = the tree read.


// virtual void parse(Input_string inputstr, int &setfirst);
// Used: To append a portion of a linear representation of a
//       tree, i.e. ( a b ( c , to an existing tree.  Setfirst
//       is TRUE if the first item in the string should become
//       the root of a new subtree.  Otherwise the first item
//       will be placed as the new right child of the current
//       node.
// Pre:  inputstr has been formatted so that spaces separate
//       morphemes
// Post: The receiver tree is built from its linear
//       representation.

// int is_leaf();
// Used: To  determine whether the current node is a leaf.
// Pre:  current != nil
```

```
// Post: current^.left_child =nil and current^.right_child=nil
//       and result = true, or result = false.


// ElementPtr store(ElementPtr m);
// Used: To change the value of the element in the current node.
// Pre:  current != nil
// Post: The value at the current node is replaced by m
//       and result = old current->e


// virtual void insert(ElementPtr eptr);
// Used: To insert element elem as the new right child of
//       the current node,
//           or as the new root of an empty tree.
// Pre:
// Post: Leaf is allocated.   Receiver is nonempty ^
//       current^.right_child^.e = elem, or
//       receiver is empty ^ current = root and current^.e
//       = elem


// ElementPtr retrieve();
// Used: To fetch the contents of the current tree node.
// Pre:  current != nil
// Post: Result = current^.e


// void step (step_type to_where);
// Used: To move the current tree node.
// Pre:  Destination node != nil
// Post: Moves current to the place designated by to_where or,
//       if undefined, leaves current where it is and sets
//       Error to true.


// virtual void traverse(traverse_type how);
// Used: To move current to the next node in the tree, either
//       preorder (breadth-first) or postorder(depth-first),
//       according to How.
// Pre:
// Post: current is moved to the next node according to strategy
//       (traverse_type = depth_first) or (traverse_type =
//       breadth_first)

// virtual void remove(tree_link delete_me);
// Used: To remove all the nodes under (and including) the
//       current tree node.
// Pre:  delete_me != nil
// Post: Deletes all nodes in the subtree whose root is the
//       delete_me.  The current node changes to the parent of
//       that node if it was in delete_me.

// void empty();
// Used: To make an entire tree empty of nodes.
// Pre:  Receiver is any tree.
```

```
// Post: Receiver is empty.  Objects of tree are deleted if
//       should_delete = tree_delete

// virtual void graft (Tree* b);
// Used: To graft another tree b onto the receiver below
//       the current node.
// Pre:
// Post: The root of b becomes the new right child of the
//       current node, and b loses its own separate identity.


// virtual int search (ElementPtr elem);
// Used: To search for elem in the receiver, and set current to
//       the node where it is found.
// Pre:
// Post: Searches the Tree in a preorder fashion, starting with
//       the root.  If elem is found, then current is set to
//       that node and result = TRUE.Otherwise, current is
//       unchanged and result = FALSE.


// virtual void display();
// Used: To display a tree.
// Pre:  display() must be called for each Tree_mode.e in
//       receiver
// Post: columns = 0 and a linear representation is shown on the
//       screen, or columns > 0 and a tabular representation
//       is shown.


// virtual void file_in(char* savename);
// Used: To retrieve a linear representaion of a tree from a
//       file andinsert it at the current node, the root for a
//       new tree.
// Pre:  savename is the source file.
// Post: receiver = appended tree.


// virtual int file_out(char* savename);
// Used: To write a linear representation of a tree to a file.
// Pre:  savename is the destination file.
// Post: Receiver is saved in the file savename and
//       result = TRUE, or save was unsuccessful and
//       result = FALSE.
```

APPENDIX **B**

C++ Program Listing

tree.cxx

```
// FILENAME:  TREE.CXX

// ******** Implementation of Tree class********

#include "tree.h"
#include <string.h>
#include <iostream.h>



int Tree::max_depth (TreePtr t)
{
    tree_link    tempnode;
    int m;
    if (t->size > 0)
    {
        m = 0;
        tempnode = t->current;
        t->set_current( NULL );
        t->set_error( FALSE );
        t->traverse(pre_order);

  // Traverse the tree and take the max of the individual levels.

        while (! t->get_error())
         {
        if (t->current->level > m)
           m = t->current->level;
        t->traverse(pre_order);
         }
         // Restore the tree to its initial state.
         t->set_current(tempnode);
         t->set_error( FALSE );
    }
    else
        m = -1;
    return m;
}

Tree::Tree() // Plant a tree.
{
    tree_link temproot;
    // Allocate memory for the tree structure.

    // Initialize the variables.
    set_size(0);          // Nobody in the family.
    height = -1;
```

```
      columns = 0;            // Output has nested parentheses
      width = MAXMORPHEME;     // and MaxMorpheme chars per column
      root = NULL;
      set_current(NULL);
      set_error( FALSE );
      should_delete = yes_delete;

}

Tree::~Tree()
{
    step(to_root);
    if (should_delete == yes_delete)
       empty(); // deallocate the elements in the heap
}


void Tree::get(char* prompt)
{
    Input_string inputstr;
    int level;
    Morpheme* lastitem;
    boolean alldone, setfirst;
      // setfirst means it is the root of a new subtree

    cout << prompt;
    char tempstr[256];
    cin.getline(tempstr,255);
    inputstr.set_val(tempstr);

    if ( (inputstr.retrieve(1)->get_val())[0] != '(' )
    {
      cout << "All Tree notation must begin with a \'(\'. "
           << endl;
      alldone = TRUE;
    }
    else
    {
      alldone = FALSE;
      level = 0;
      setfirst = TRUE;
    }


    while(!alldone)
    {
       inputstr.reformat(level);
       parse(inputstr, setfirst);
       lastitem = inputstr.retrieve(inputstr.morpheme_count());
       if (strcmp(lastitem->get_val(), "("))
        setfirst = FALSE;
       else
        setfirst = TRUE;


       if (level > 0)  // get more keyboard inputstr
       {
```

```
        cout << "more: ";
        cin >> tempstr;
        inputstr.set_val(tempstr);
        }
        else
        alldone = TRUE;
    } // end while



    height = max_depth(this);
}



void Tree::parse (Input_string &inputstrb, boolean &setfirst)
{
    int i = 1;
    Morpheme* e, dummy;
    int parsed = FALSE;
    tree_link temp;


    while (! parsed)
    {
      e = inputstrb.retrieve(i);
      if (e->get_val()[0] == '\0')
       parsed = TRUE;
      else if (!strcmp(e->get_val(), "("))
      {
      // Begin a subtree.
      insert(e);          // Create dummy node for a new child
      setfirst = TRUE;
      }
      else if (!strcmp(e->get_val(), ")"))
      {
      // Go back up to parent.
      temp = current->parent;
      if (setfirst)     // delete dummy node if an empty subtree
      {
         step(to_r_child);
         remove(current);
      }
      set_current(temp);
      }
      else if (setfirst)
      {
      if (size > 1)     // if not the root,  move to the dummy
         step(to_r_child);
      delete store(e);
      setfirst = FALSE;
      }
      else
      insert(e);
      i++;
    } // end while
}
```

```
int Tree::is_leaf()
{
    if (current != NULL)
       if ( (current->left_child == NULL) &&
             (current->right_child == NULL) )
      return TRUE;
       else
       return FALSE;
     else
        return FALSE;
}



ElementPtr Tree::store(ElementPtr m)
{
    // Change the contents of the current node.
    ElementPtr temp = current->e;
    current->e = m;
    return temp;
}

void Tree::insert(ElementPtr elem)
{
    tree_link node;
    // Insert a new node into the tree, either as the right child
    // of the current node or as the root of an empty tree.
    set_error( FALSE );
    if ((current != NULL) || (size == 0))
    {
        node = new Tree_node(elem);


        // New children are the youngest, so they may have only
        // left (older) siblings, but no right siblings or
        // children.
        node->parent = current;
        node->level = -1;

        if ((size > 0) && (current != NULL))
        {    // tree is nonempty
        node->level = current->level + 1;
        // Tell the previously youngest child about its new
        // sibling and establish the new sibling as the youngest.
        if (current->right_child != NULL)
        {
           current->right_child->right_sib = node; // Sib -> Right
           current->right_child = node;   // parent -> right_child
        }
        else                             // only child
        {
           current->left_child = node;   // parent -> left_child
           current->right_child = node;   // parent -> right_child
        }
        }
        else if (size == 0)     // insertion into an empty tree;
move current
        {
```

```cpp
            node->level = 0;
            set_current(node);
            root = current;
             }
             else
            set_error( TRUE );

             if (node->level > height)
            // new node is farthest from the root
            height = node->level;
             set_size(size + 1);
        }
        else
            set_error( TRUE );
    }

ElementPtr Tree::retrieve()
{
    // Return the current node's contents.
    if (current != NULL)
        return current->e;
    else
        return NULL;
}

void Tree::step(step_type to_where)
{
    // Move the current node pointer within the tree.
    tree_link temp;
    set_error( FALSE );
    switch (to_where)
    {
       case to_root:
        set_current( root );
        break;

        case to_parent:
        if ( (current != NULL) && (current->parent != NULL) )
            set_current( current->parent );
        else
            set_error( TRUE );
        break;

        case to_l_child:
        if (current->left_child != NULL)
            set_current ( current->left_child );
        else
            set_error( TRUE   );
        break;

        case to_r_child:
        if (current->right_child != NULL)
            set_current ( current->right_child );
        else
            set_error( TRUE );
        break;
```

```
     case to_right_sib:
     if (current->right_sib != NULL)
        set_current ( current->right_sib );
     else
        set_error( TRUE );
     break;

      case to_left_sib:
    if (current->parent != NULL)
       if (current->parent->left_child != current)
       {  //search for left sibling through the parent
          temp = current->parent->left_child;
          while (temp->right_sib != current)
          temp = temp->right_sib;
          set_current( temp );
       }
       else
          set_error( TRUE );
    else
       set_error( TRUE );
    break;
    } // switch
}

void Tree::traverse(traverse_type how)
{
   // Starting with the current node, move the current node
   // pointer to the next node in a breadth-first or depth-first
   // traversal.  For a complete traversal, current must be
   // initialized to NULL.
   set_error( FALSE );
   switch (how)
   {
     case depth_first:
     case post_order:
     if (current == NULL)
        if (size > 0)
        {
           step(to_root);
           while (! is_leaf() )
        step(to_l_child);
        }
        else
           set_error( TRUE );
     else if (current == root)      // done if now at the root
        set_error( TRUE );
     else if (current->right_sib != NULL)
         // look for right sibling
     {
        step(to_right_sib);
        while (! is_leaf() )   // look for left child's leaf
           step(to_l_child);
     }
     else
        step(to_parent);
     break;
```

```
          case breadth_first:
          case pre_order:
          if (current == NULL)
             if (size == 0)
                set_error( TRUE );
             else
                step(to_root);
          else
          {
             if (is_leaf())               // current is a leaf
                if (current->right_sib != NULL)
                {
             step(to_right_sib);
                }
                else if (current->parent != NULL)
                {
             step(to_parent);
             if (current != root)
             {  //look for a higher nonvisited rightsib
                while ((current != root) && (current->right_sib ==
                   NULL))
             set_current ( current->parent );
                if (current->right_sib != NULL)
             set_current( current->right_sib );
                else
             set_error( TRUE );
             }
             else
                set_error( TRUE );
                }
                else
             set_error( TRUE );
             else    // current is not a leaf
                step(to_l_child);
          }
        break;
     }  //case
}

void Tree::remove(tree_link delete_me)
{

     static long unsigned recursion_level = 0;
     recursion_level++;
     if (size == 0)
        set_error( TRUE );
     else
     {
        set_error( FALSE );

        if (delete_me == NULL)
        delete_me = root;
        // is it a leaf?
        while (delete_me->left_child != NULL)
        remove(delete_me->left_child);
        // This node is not a leaf, so okay to remove.
        // If not the root (i.e. a parent exists) make sure its
```

```
          // left and right children poiters remain okay.
          if (delete_me->parent != NULL)
          {
          tree_link p = delete_me->parent;
          if (p->left_child == p->right_child) // only child
          {
             p->left_child = NULL;
             p->right_child = NULL;
          }
          // not only child, see if its leftmost.
          else if (p->left_child == delete_me)
             // is leftmost, so change parent's left_child pointer
             p->left_child = delete_me->right_sib;
          else
            // not leftmost, locate the current node's *LEFT* sibling
          {
             for (tree_link left_sib = p->left_child;
               left_sib->right_sib != delete_me;
               left_sib = left_sib->right_sib) {  }
            // tell left sibling to point to current's right sibling
             left_sib->right_sib = delete_me->right_sib;

             // if current was previous right child,
             // make its left sib right child
              if (p->right_child == delete_me)
                 p->right_child = left_sib;
          }
          }
          if (delete_me->parent == NULL)
          current = root = NULL;  // empty tree;
          else if (current == delete_me)
          step(to_parent);
          delete delete_me->e;
          delete delete_me;
          size --;
       }
    recursion_level--;
    if (recursion_level == 0)
       height = max_depth(this);
} // remove

void Tree::empty()
{
    remove(root);
}

void Tree::graft(Tree* b)
{
    // Attach tree B under the current node.
    tree_link tempnode;
    int insertlevel;
    set_error( FALSE );
    if (size == 0)
    {
       root = b->root;
       set_current( b->root );
       set_size( b->size );
```

```
      height = b->height;
    }
    else if ((current != NULL) && (b->size > 0))
    {
      // If the current node is a leaf,  the root of the
      // attaching branch becomes both the left and the
     // right child.
       if (is_leaf())
       current->left_child = b->root;  // parent -> left_child
       // Otherwise the Right Child is now second to right.
       else
       current->right_child->right_sib = b->root;
          // Sib -> right_child
       current->right_child = b->root;
       b->root->parent = current;    // parent <- right_child
      // Traverse the grafted subtree and adjust all the
     //node levels.
       insertlevel = current->level + 1;
       b->set_current( NULL );
       do
       {
       b->traverse(depth_first);
       b->current->level = b->current->level + insertlevel;
       } while (!( b->current->parent == current));
       // Now B->current = B->root again
       // Recalculate the Tree's size and height.
       set_size( size + b->size );
       if (height < insertlevel + b->height )
       height = insertlevel + b->height;
       b->set_delete(no_delete); // Don't delete b's elements
       delete b;
    }
    else if (b->size > 0)
       set_error( TRUE );
}

int Tree::search(Element* elem)
{
    // Search for elem.  If found, goto the node with elem and
    // return TRUE.  Otherwise, don't move anywhere and return
    // FALSE.
    tree_link tempnode;
    int found = FALSE;

    // Record the current position.
    tempnode = current;

    // Start searching at the root.
    set_current( NULL );
    set_error( FALSE );
    traverse(depth_first);
    while ((! found) && (! get_error()))
    {
       if (!strcmp(current->e->get_class(),elem->get_class()))
       if ( *(current->e) == *elem )
          found = TRUE;
       else
```

```
          traverse(depth_first);
       else
       traverse(depth_first);
    }

    if (found)
       return TRUE;
    else
    {
       // Go back to where we were.
       set_current ( tempnode );
       return FALSE;
    }
} // TreeSearch


void Tree::display()
{
    int i;
    char blank[256];
    tree_link tempnode;
    int temp_error = get_error();

    if (height >= 0)
    {
      if (columns == 0)        //display in parenthesized style
      file_out("\0");
      else                     // display in columnar style
       {
      blank[0] = 0;
      for (i = 0; i <= height; i++)
      {
         cout << "(";
         cout.width(6);
         cout << i << " )" ;
         cout.width(width - 9);
         cout << blank;
      }
      cout << endl;
      set_error( FALSE );
      tempnode = current;
      set_current(NULL);
      traverse(pre_order);
      while (! get_error())
      {
         for (i = 1; i <= current->level; i++)
         {
            cout.width(width);
            cout << blank;
         }
         if (current == tempnode)
            cout << "> ";
         else
            cout << "  ";
         current->e->display();
         cout << endl;
         traverse(pre_order);
```

```cpp
      }

      // Go back to where we were.
      set_current(tempnode);
       }
    }
    else
       cout << "Tree is empty.\n\r";
    set_error(temp_error);
}


void Tree::file_in(char* savename)
{
    Input_string inputstr;
    ifstream filename;
    int level;
    Morpheme* lastitem;
    boolean alldone, setfirst;
      // setfirst means it is the root of a new subtree
    char tempstr[256];


    filename.open(savename, ios::in | ios::nocreate);
    if(filename.fail())
    {
      cout << "File of name " << inputstr.get_val() <<
        " does not exist" << endl;
      alldone = TRUE;
    }
    else
    {
      inputstr.set_val(savename);
      alldone = FALSE;
      level = 0;
      setfirst = TRUE;
    }


    while(!alldone)
    {
       inputstr.reformat(level);
       parse(inputstr, setfirst);
       lastitem = inputstr.retrieve(inputstr.morpheme_count());
       if (strcmp(lastitem->get_val(), "("))
      setfirst = FALSE;
       else
      setfirst = TRUE;


       if (!filename.eof())
       {
      filename >> tempstr;
      inputstr.set_val(tempstr);
       }
       else
```

```
      alldone = TRUE;
   } // end while
   filename.close();

   height = max_depth(this);
}


int Tree::file_out(char* savename)
{
   ofstream filename;
   char outputstr[256];
   tree_link tempnode;
   int level = 0;

   outputstr[0] = 0;
   level = 0;
   if (savename[0] != 0)
      filename.open(savename);

   int file_error = filename.fail();
   if (!file_error)
   {
      tempnode = current;
      set_current(NULL);
      set_error( FALSE );
      traverse(pre_order);
      while (! get_error())
      {
      // If has children or is root  { tree delimeter.
      if ((current == root) || (current->left_child != NULL))
      {
         strcat(outputstr,"(");
         level++;
      }

      // App the current node contents if tree not empty.
      if (size > 0)
      {
       strcat(outputstr, ((Morpheme*)(current->e))->get_val() );
       strcat(outputstr, " ");
      }

      // If no children and no right siblings, tree delimeter.
      if (is_leaf() && (current->right_sib == NULL))
      {
         traverse(pre_order);
         while (current->level < level)
         {
            strcat(outputstr,") ");
            level--;
         }
      }
      else
         traverse(pre_order);

      // If result is long enough,  output it.
```

```cpp
         if (strlen(outputstr) > 63)  // Flush!
         {
            if (savename[0] != '\0')
               filename << outputstr << endl;
            else
               cout << outputstr << endl;
            outputstr[0] = 0;
         }
      }

      set_current(tempnode);

      // Balance the parentheses.
      while (level > 0)
      {
      strcat(outputstr, ") ");
      level--;
      }

      // Output the remaining result.
      if (savename[0] != 0)
      {
      filename << outputstr;
      filename.close();
      file_error = filename.fail();
      }
      else
      cout << outputstr << endl;
   }
   return (file_error == 0); // If file_error is zero, no error:
return TRUE;
}
```

C++ Program Listing
bintree.h

```cpp
// Filename BINTREE.H
#ifndef Bintree_h
#define Bintree_h

#include "elements.h"
#include "tree.h"

class BinaryTree : public Tree
{
  public:
  virtual void insert(ElementPtr elem);
  void insert_left(ElementPtr elem);
  void insert_right(ElementPtr elem);
  virtual void parse(Input_string &inputstr, boolean &setfirst);
  virtual void get(char* prompt);
  virtual int search (ElementPtr elem);
  virtual void graft(BinaryTree* b);
  void remove(tree_link delete_me);
  void step (step_type to_where);
  virtual int empty_leaf(tree_link t);
};


typedef BinaryTree* BinaryTreePtr;

#endif

// ********  Formal Specifications for class BinaryTree ********


// virtual void insert(ElementPtr elem);
// Used: To Insert a new node into the tree, either as the left
// child of the current node (if current is a leaf), as the
// right child of the current node (if current has a single
// child), or as the root of an empty tree .
// Pre: Receiver is empty or current has no more than one child
// Post: Receiver's size=1 and root=elem, or current has elem as
//       its only child, or current has elem as its new right
//       child, respectively.

// void insert_left(ElementPtr elem);
// Used: To insert element elem as the new left child of the
//       current node, or as the new root of an empty binary
//       tree.
// Pre:  Receiver is empty, or current^.LeftChild is empty
// Post: Leaf is allocated.  Receiver is nonempty ^
//       current^.LeftChild^.e = elem, or receiver is empty ^
```

```
//          current = root and current^.e = elem

// void insert_right(ElementPtr elem);
// Used: To insert element elem as the new right child of the
//       current node, or as the new root of an empty binary
//       tree.
// Pre:  Receiver is empty, or current^.RightChild is empty
// Post: Leaf is allocated.  current is a leaf and
//       current^.LeftChild = () and current^.RightChild = elem,
//       or current^.RightChild = elem, or receiver is empty ^
//       current = root and current^.e = elem

// virtual parse(Input_string inputstr, int &setfirst);
// Used: To append a portion of a linear representation of a
//       binary tree, i.e. ( a b ( c , to an existing binary
//       tree.  Setfirst is TRUE if the first item in the string
//       should become the root of a new subtree.  Otherwise the
//       first item will be placed as the new right child of the
//       current node.
// Pre:  inputstr has been formatted so that spaces separate
//       morphemes
// Post: The receiver binary tree is built from its linear
//       representation.

// virtual void get(char* prompt);
// Used: To input and insert a complete binary tree at the
//       current node (root for new trees).
// Pre:  Prompt is the string used to prompt the user for input.
// Post: Receiver = the binary tree read.

// virtual int search (ElementPtr elem);
// Used: To search for elem in the receiver, and set current to
//       the node where it is found.
// Pre:
// Post: Searches the binary tree in a breadth-first fashion,
//       starting with the root.  If elem is found, then current
//       is set to that node and result = TRUE. Otherwise,
//       current is unchanged and result = FALSE.

// virtual void graft(TreePtr b);
// Used: To graft another binary tree B onto the receiver below
//       the current node.
// Pre:
// Post: The root of B becomes the new right child of the
//          current node, and B loses its own separate identity.
```

C++ Program Listing

bintree.cxx

```
// FILENAME: BINTREE.CXX

#include "bintree.h"
#include <iostream.h>
#include <string.h>

void BinaryTree::get(char* prompt)
{
   BinaryTreePtr temp_tree = new BinaryTree;
   temp_tree -> Tree::get(prompt);
   if (!temp_tree->get_error())
      graft(temp_tree);
}


void BinaryTree::parse (Input_string &inputstr,
                        boolean &setfirst)
{
   int i = 1;
   MorphemePtr e, dummy;
   int parsed = FALSE;
   i = 1;
   error = FALSE;
   while (!parsed && !error)
   {
     e = inputstr.retrieve(i);
     if (e->get_val()[0] == 0)
    parsed = TRUE;
     else if (e->get_val()[0] == '(' )
     {                                      //  a subtree.
    insert(e);
    setfirst = TRUE;
     }
     else if (e->get_val()[0] == ')' )
     {
    if ( setfirst )
     // mark dummy left child if an empty subtree
     {
        step(to_l_child);
        ((MorphemePtr)(current->e))->set_val("()");
        size = size - 1;
         // dummy node doesn't contribute to the size
        setfirst = FALSE;
     }
    if (current != root )
       current = current->parent;
     }
```

```
                else if ( setfirst )
                {
                if ( size > 1 )   // if not the root, ) move to the dummy
                 if
                 (((MorphemePtr)(current->left_child->e))->get_val()[0]
                   == '(')
                       step(to_l_child);
                   else
                       step(to_r_child);
                delete store(e);
                setfirst = FALSE;
                }
                else
                 insert(e);
                i++;
           }
    }

    void BinaryTree::insert(ElementPtr elem)
    // Insert a new node into the tree, either as the left child
    // of the current node (if current is a leaf), as the right
    // child of the current node (if current has a single left
    // child), or as the root of an empty tree .
    {
       tree_link node;
       error = FALSE;
       if (size == 0)
       {  // tree is empty, insert as root
          node = new Tree_node(elem);
          node->level = 0;
          current = node;
          root = current;
       }
       else if (current != NULL )
       {
          if (is_leaf() || (current->left_child ==
               current->right_child))
          { // current has no children or has a non-empty left_child
          node = new Tree_node(elem);
          node->parent = current;
          node->level = current->level + 1;


          if (is_leaf() )   // if it has no children add to the left
          {
            current->left_child = node;
            current->right_child = node;
          }
          else // add to the right
          {
            current->right_child = node;
            current->left_child->right_sib = node;
          }
          }
          else if (empty_leaf(current->left_child))
           // if left_child is empty
           {
```

```
         current = current->left_child;
         delete store(elem);
         node = current;
             step(to_parent);
          }
          else
          {
        error = TRUE;
        cout << "attempt to add a third child to a binary tree\n";
          }
      }
      else
      {
          error = TRUE;
          cout << "Error: Tree size != 0 but root = NIL\n";
      }


      if (!error )
      {
         if (node->level > height )
         // new node is farthest from the root
         height = node->level;
         size++;
      }
}

void BinaryTree::insert_left(ElementPtr elem)
    // Insert a new node into the tree as the left child
    // of the current node.
{
   tree_link node;
   error = FALSE;
   if (current != NULL )
      if (is_leaf() )
      insert(elem);
       else if (empty_leaf(current->left_child))
       {
      current = current->left_child;
      delete store(elem);
      step(to_parent);
      size++;
       }
       else
      error = TRUE;
   else
       error = TRUE;
}

void BinaryTree::insert_right(ElementPtr elem)
    // Insert a new node into the tree as the right child
    // of the current node.
{
   tree_link node;
   error = FALSE;
   if (current != NULL )
      if (is_leaf() )
```

```
              {    // add a dummy left child if not there
              MorphemePtr temp_morph = new Morpheme;
              temp_morph->set_val("()");
              insert (temp_morph);
                 size--;
               insert(elem);
               }
              else if (current->left_child == current->right_child )
              insert(elem);
               else
              error = TRUE;
           else
                error = TRUE;
      }


      void BinaryTree::graft(BinaryTreePtr b)
          // Attach binary tree B under the current node.
      {
         tree_link tempnode;
         int insertlevel;
         error = FALSE;
         if (size == 0 )
            Tree::graft(b);
         else if (current != NULL)
            if (is_leaf() || (current->left_child ==
               current->right_child) )
            Tree::graft(b);
             else if (empty_leaf(current->left_child))
             {
             tree_link org_right_child = current->right_child;
             delete current->left_child->e;
             delete current->left_child;
             current->right_child = current->left_child = NULL;
             Tree::graft(b);
             current->left_child->right_sib = org_right_child;
             current->right_child = org_right_child;
             }
             else
             error = TRUE;
      }



      int BinaryTree::search(ElementPtr elem)
          // Search for elem.  If found, goto the node with elem and
          // return TRUE.  Otherwise, don't move anywhere and return
          // FALSE.
      {
         tree_link tempnode;
         int found = FALSE;

         // Record the current position.
         tempnode = current;

         // Start searching at the root.
         current = NULL;
         error = FALSE;
         traverse(pre_order);
```

```
      while (!found && !error)
      {
         if (!strcmp(current->e->get_class(),elem->get_class()))
         if ( *(current->e) == *elem )
            found = TRUE;
         else
            traverse(pre_order);
          else
         traverse(pre_order);
      }

      if ( found )
         return TRUE;
      else
      {
         // Go back to where we were.
         current = tempnode;
         return FALSE;
      }
} // Search


void BinaryTree::remove(tree_link delete_me)
{
   // make sure it's not the root
   if (delete_me->parent != NULL)
      // make sure it's not an only child
      if (delete_me->parent->left_child !=
         delete_me->parent->right_child)
      // see if it's right sibling
      if (delete_me == delete_me->parent->right_child)
         // See if left_sibling is empty, i.e. "()"
         if (empty_leaf(delete_me->parent->left_child))
      // delete_me is a right child with an empty left sib, so:
            remove(delete_me->parent->left_child);


   if ( empty_leaf(delete_me))
      size++;
     // Its an empty node, so since it wasn't counted as a node
     // you need to add it back so because size is about to be
     // decremented.
   Tree::remove(delete_me);

} // remove


void BinaryTree::step(step_type to_where)
{
   // This is same as Tree::step, except you can't visit an
   // empty node.
   tree_link temp = current;
   Tree::step(to_where);
   if (empty_leaf(current))
      current = temp;
}
```

```cpp
int BinaryTree::empty_leaf(tree_link t)
{
   // determine if node t is empty
   if (!strcmp(t->e->get_class(), "Morpheme"))
      if (!strcmp( ((MorphemePtr)t->e)->get_val(), "()"))
      return TRUE;
      else
      return FALSE;
   else
      return FALSE;
}
```

CHAPTER 6

IMPLEMENTATION OF CLASSES

(TEAM) LABORATORY EXERCISE—ARRAY IMPLEMENTATION FOR BINARY TREES

In the text, we have implemented the class `BinaryTree` as a subclass of the more general class, `Tree`. Alternatively, the `BinaryTree` class could have been implemented by an entirely separate strategy, using an array as the basic storage mechanism, as suggested in Chapter 5 of the text. This exercise asks you to develop and implement the class `BinaryTree` using that array implementation strategy. A special case of a binary tree (the heap) was implemented in Chapter 3 of the text. For this exercise, you should try to reuse appropriate portions of the code for the linked implementation of `Tree` and `BinaryTree`. That code is provided on the distribution disk, or in the system directory for this course, in the files `tree.h`, `tree.cxx`, `bintree.h`, and `bintree.cxx`.

Part 1 — Design the Implementation Strategy

Declare the appropriate data members that will be useful for implementing the `BinaryTree` class using an array. Good guidance can be gained from looking at the declarations of the data members for the multilinked implementation of `Tree`, together with the array implementation of `Sequence` (see the files `tree.h` and `sequence.h` on the distribution disk, in the system directory for this course, or in the Appendices to Lab Chapters 5 and 4, respectively).

Which among the `Tree` member functions can be reused with minor modifications? Which of the `Tree` member functions are unnecessary for the `BinaryTree` class?

Part 2 — Reimplement the `Tree` and `BinaryTree` Member Functions

Now implement the essential `BinaryTree` member functions using the array storage strategy that you have designed.

Part 3 — Test the Resulting Implementation

Test the correctness of this implementation by running the binary tree driver program, in the file named `btreedrv.cxx`, that is provided on the distribution disk or in the system directory for this course, for several different input trees.

In particular, input each of the following binary trees and ensure that all the above functions work properly with them:

```
a.   ( + A ( * B C ) )
b.   ( + A ( * ( + B C ) ) D ) )
c.   ( )
d.   ( + ( ) B )
e.   ( + A )
```

Worksheet for Laboratory Exercise—
Array Implementation of the class `BinaryTree`

```
// Filename: arrbintree.h

#include "                 "

class BinaryTree
{
   public:
   virtual void insert(ElementPtr elem);




}


// *****Formal Specifications for class BinaryTree*****


// Filename: arrbintree.cxx

#include "arrbintree.h"

void BinaryTree::get(char* prompt)
{


}
void BinaryTree::
```

(TEAM) LABORATORY EXERCISE—LINKED BINARY TREE IMPLEMENTATION

In the text, we have implemented the class `BinaryTree` as a subclass of the more general class, `Tree`. Alternatively, the `BinaryTree` class could have been implemented by an entirely separate strategy, using a simpler linked structure as the basic storage mechanism. In this way, we can avoid some of the overhead that is needed for trees but not for binary trees, such as the need to accommodate an arbitrary number of children at any node. That is, the node structure of binary trees is intrinsically simpler than that for general trees; each node needs only to have a left and right child pointer, along with a parent pointer (see Figure 6–1). The sibling pointer can be ignored, since the number of siblings for any node is either one or zero.

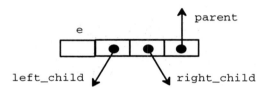

FIGURE 6–1   Node structure for a binary tree.

To test this implementation, a driver program such as the one provided on the distribution disk in the file `btreedrv.cxx`, can be used. Before starting this lab, readers should review the `Tree` and `BinaryTree` class headers, as well as the implementation of `Trees` that is discussed in Chapter 5 of the text.

Part 1 — Design the Implementation Strategy

The `BinaryTree` class can be implemented using the following definition of a node, as suggested in Figure 6–1.

```
struct BinaryTree_node          // A single node in the binary
{                               // tree, with an element and
   ElementPtr e;                // three pointers to the left
   BinaryTree_node * left_child; // child, right child, and
   BinaryTree_node * right_child;// parent.
   BinaryTree_node * parent;
};
```

This design allows us to move directly from a single node to either its leftmost child, its rightmost child, or its parent, by selecting one of the pointer values `left_child`, `right_child`, or `parent`, respectively. Such a structure is illustrated in Figure 6–2 for the simple binary tree (A B C). .

In implementing the class `BinaryTree` using this simpler linked structure, a great deal of the code in the implementation of general trees can be reused in

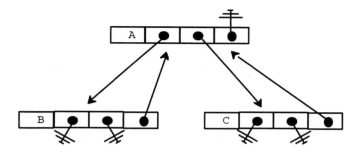

FIGURE 6–2   Linked structure representing the binary tree (A B C).

this exercise, and readers are encouraged to do that. That code is provided on the distribution disk, or in the system directory for this course, in the files `tree.h`, `tree.cxx`, `bintree.h`, and `bintree.cxx`.

Which among the `Tree` member functions can be reused with minor modifications? Which of the `Tree` member functions are unnecessary for the `BinaryTree` class?

Part 2 — Reimplement the `Tree` and `BinaryTree` Member Functions

Now implement the essential `Tree` and `BinaryTree` member functions using the new linked storage strategy. Working as a team, divide responsibilities for implementing these functions among you, so that everyone has a function or two to implement and test.

Part 3 — Test the Resulting Implementation

Test the correctness of this implementation by running the `BinaryTree` driver program, in the file named `btreedrv.cxx` that is provided on the distribution disk, or the system directory for this course, for several different input trees.

In particular, input each of the following binary trees and ensure that all the above functions work properly with them:

a. (+ A (* B C))
b. (+ A (* (+ B C)) D))
c. ( )
d. (+ ( ) B)
e. (+ A)

Worksheet for Laboratory Exercise—
Linked Implementation of the class BinaryTree

```cpp
// Filename: linkedbintree.h

#include "                    "

class BinaryTree
{
   public:
   virtual void insert(ElementPtr elem);




}


// *****Formal Specifications for class BinaryTree*****



// Filename: linkedbintree.cxx

#include "linkedbintree.h"

void BinaryTree::get(char* prompt)
{


}
void BinaryTree::
```

(TEAM) LABORATORY EXERCISE—LINKED IMPLEMENTATION OF LISTS

Implement the List class using a single-linked chain as the storage method, and then test this implementation using the list driver program (called ltest.cxx) that is provided on the distribution disk or in the system directory for this course. Both the class Sequence and the class List should be reimplemented including the following member functions (see the Appendices to Lab Chapter 4 for their specifications).

```
Sequence::Sequence()   // the constructor
List::retrieve
List::store
List::insert
List::remove
List::swap
```

Part 1 — Examine the List class

Look at sequence.h, sequence.cxx, list.h, list.cxx on the distribution disk, the system directory for this course or the Appendices to Lab Chapter 4. Notice that the class List is implemented using an array as the storage mechanism for individual elements. The text suggests an alternative strategy, using a single-linked chain to store individual elements, and then goes on to implement most of the above methods. Recall the following declarations from Chapter 6 in the text.

```
struct seqnode
  { ElementPtr e;   // pointer to element at this node
    seqnode* next;  // pointer to next node in sequence
   };

class Sequence
{  protected:
       seqnode* first;    // pointer to header node of sequence
       int size;          // number of elements
    ....
  }  // end Sequence

class List : public Sequence
{
    ...
```

Insertions and deletions at the i-th entry of a linked chain require a loop starting at the header node to locate the position for the insertion or deletion. Add two additional data members, currentptr and currentind to the List class. currentptr will be a pointer to the most recently accessed List node and currentind will be the index of that node. Then if a List access is desired at location `i`, and if `i` is greater than or equal to `currentind`, the search for position `i` can begin at `currentptr` instead of `first`. All member functions should be modified to exploit this possibly shorter search. Attention must also be paid to handling errors in cases where a member function would disrupt the integrity of the chain (like making a deletion at an undefined position in the `List`). In general, in converting from an array to a linked representation, we are gaining storage flexibility and losing some efficiency of access.

Part 2 — Revise and Test the `List` Class

Using the member functions that are developed in Chapter 6 of the text, complete the linked implementation of the `List` class. Test the correctness of your changes by using the test program called `ltest.cxx` from the distribution disk or the system directory for this course and exercising all the member functions that you developed or changed.

Questions

1. Comment on the amount of reprogramming that was required by this change. That is, what functions in `Sequence` and `List` were changed, and what is the extent of the changes?
2. Comment on the process of testing your changes using the test program. Was it useful? To what extent do you think your testing has caught all the errors that might have been created in this exercise?

Worksheet for Laboratory Exercise—
Linked Implementation of the class `List`

```
// Filename: sequence.h
// Class description:

#include "elements.h"

class Sequence
{
    // DATA MEMBERS

    // MEMBER FUNCTIONS


//*******Specifications for the Sequence class***********

// Filename: sequence.cxx
#include "sequence.h"
```

```
// Filename: list.h
// Class description:

class List: public Sequence
{
// MEMBER FUNCTIONS


//*******Specifications for the List class*********

// Filename: list.cxx
#include "list.h"
```

Notes for Answers to Questions

1.

2.

(TEAM) LABORATORY EXERCISE—COMPARISON OF LIST IMPLEMENTATIONS

Experimentally corroborate the differences in complexity between the linked and array implementations of the List class by establishing a fairly large list (perhaps containing, say, 1000 random numbers), performing a large number of insertions and deletions (say 1000), and measuring the actual run times for each case under each of the linked and array implementations. This kind of test, for example, can be made by using a simple insertion sort on the same list of 1000 random numbers, varying only the implementation strategy for the List class from one run of the program to the other.

Part 1 — Design a Test Case

Design a basis for objectively comparing the array and linked implementations of the List member functions. For example, write a program that will measure the run time for the linear search or the insertion sort. Recall the techniques for timing program runs from Lab Chapter 3.

Part 2 — Measure the Efficiency of This Revision

Run this program with the linked implementation of the List class and an input list of 1000 random numbers, and measure the run time. Now, change the implementation from linked to array, and rerun the same program with the same input list, and measure the run time again. Repeat these two runs with each of a variety of input list sizes, recording the run times for each pair of runs.

Questions

1. Does the run time of the array implementation grow linearly with the size of the input n? What about the run time for the linked implementation?
2. What differences do you see between the original array implementation of the List class and your new linked implementation, with respect to the execution time of a linear search or an insertion sort?
3. Try the linked implementation both with and without currentptr and currentind. How much do they help? How much do they cost?

Worksheet for Laboratory Exercise—
Comparison of List Implementations

```
// Filename: listcompare.cxx
```

Notes for Answers to Questions

1.

2.

3.

CHAPTER 7

OPERATING SYSTEMS
AND SOFTWARE DESIGN

This chapter contains laboratory exercises designed to enhance your understanding of the UNIX operating system, the design of certain components of an operating system, the use of simulation in the study of physical systems, and the process of large software system design and modification. Some of these exercises require you to perform empirical analyses using the methodology from Chapter 3 to support real-world types of decision making.

UNIX COMMANDS AND DIRECTORY STRUCTURE

The UNIX operating system is supported by an underlying directory structure that has the shape of a general tree. Each node of the tree has a name and contains a list of files as well as the names of all nodes that are direct descendents of that node. Examples are given in Chapter 5 of the text.

Each authorized user of a particular UNIX system is assigned a node in this tree. Whenever that user logs in for a working session, the system automatically places the user at this node representing the "home directory" for the particular user. From that node in the tree, the user can create subdirectories and files as new descendent nodes, "navigate" around inside the tree, and display information about any node within this directory structure. The UNIX commands that are available to the user for accomplishing these activities are simultaneously arcane and invaluable. Figure 7–1 provides a list of some of the key UNIX commands and brief descriptions of their different meanings.

`login`	start a UNIX session
`passwd`	change your password
`pwd`	display the current "working" directory
`cd`	change the current directory
`rm`	remove (erase) a file from the current directory
`cp`	copy a file from one directory to another
`mv`	move a file from one directory to another
`ls`	list all the files and subdirectories in the current directory
`mkdir`	make (create) a new subdirectory below the current one
`rmdir`	remove a directory
`help`	display all the UNIX commands that are available
`man`	display a page in the reference manual that explains a command
`logout`	end a UNIX session

FIGURE 7–1   Some UNIX file system commands.

Readers who are not familiar with these commands may wish to obtain an account on a UNIX system and experiment with them independently. A number of excellent introductions to the UNIX system and commands are also available. Several popular ones are listed in the References section at the end of this chapter.

(TEAM) LABORATORY EXERCISE—SIMULATING UNIX COMMANDS

All of the UNIX commands summarized in the previous section can be visualized as individual activities with respect to the tree that is the UNIX directory structure itself. This exercise gives you an opportunity to utilize the `Tree` class as you design a program to simulate the effect of these commands as one navigates around a UNIX directory structure and makes individual changes in the shape of the directory tree itself.

Part 1 — Exercise Your Local UNIX System

Using an appropriate UNIX Guide as a reference, log onto your local UNIX machine and perform the following basic operations.

1.   Set your password using the `passwd` command.
2.   Move to the root of the directory tree using the `cd` command.
3.   Change the current directory to each of four or five different subtrees and display the corresponding contents and locations in the tree, using

the cd, ls, and pwd commands, respectively. One of those directories should be your "home" directory and another should be the UNIX root directory /.

4. Display a copy of the contents of the root directory on a local printer <printer name>, using the following commands:

cd /
ls | lpr -P<printer name>

5. Move back to your home directory and send a message to a colleague in the class, using the local UNIX mail command and the help subcommand within mail. Read your mail, and then exit from the mail command.

6. While in your home directory, create two subdirectories, called A and B, using the mkdir command, and then move to each of them.

7. Log out.

Part 2 — Design of a UNIX File System Simulation Program

Use the Tree class described in Chapter 5 of the text to design and implement, in C++, a simple UNIX file system simulator. Your program should begin to simulate a UNIX session in response to the command, "login" which will read in a skeleton UNIX directory tree from a file. Use the file named unix.dat on the distribution disk or in the file system directory for this course to develop and test your program. Your program should provide for simulated execution of the following UNIX file system commands:

1. pwd — display the current "working directory"
2. cd — change the current directory
3. rm — remove file from the current directory
4. mv — move a file from one directory to another
5. ls — list all the files and subdirectories in the current directory
6. mkdir — create a new subdirectory below the current directory
7. logout — stop the simulated UNIX session.

Part 3 — Exercise your UNIX File System Simulator Program

Use the simulator program developed in Part 2 to accomplish the following steps.

1. Read the skeleton UNIX directory tree from the file named unix.dat on the distribution disk.
2. Move to the root of the directory tree using the cd command.
3. Change the current directory to each of four or five different subtrees and display its contents and locations in the tree, using the cd, ls, and pwd commands. One of those directories should be the UNIX root directory, /.
4. Add to this directory several subtrees, using the printout that you obtained in Part 1 as a guide.

5.   Save this modified directory on your floppy disk, or in your directory for this course, in the file named `unixnew.dat`.

Part 4 — Modify the UNIX File System Simulator Program (Extra Credit)

Modify your program so that it will accept the login command as its first command, complete with password checking. It should use a separate password file in your directory for this course, called `passwd.dat` and created independently, in order to check that the person "logging in" to the Simulator program is a registered user and is using the correct password. No other simulator commands should be accessible to the user until he/she has logged in properly. After a proper login, the simulator program should function just as it previously did.

Worksheet for Laboratory Exercise—
Simulating Unix Commands

```
/* -- Program name:
   -- Programmer:
   -- Date:
   -- ** Overview
            .
            .
            .
                 */

#include < ... >

// GLOBAL CONSTANTS AND TYPEDEF'S

// GLOBAL FUNCTION PROTOTYPES

main()
{
   // FUNCTION PROTOTYPES


   // LOCAL DATA


   // STATEMENTS




}
//Function:
//Purpose:
//Pre:
//Post:
return-type function-name1(formal arguments)
{


}// end function-name1

   .
   .
   .
```

LABORATORY EXERCISE—OPERATING SYSTEM SIMULATION

In this project, you will exercise the operating system simulator described in Chapter 7 of the text and listed in the Appendix to this chapter. Once you are familiar with the structure and operation of the simulator, you shall use it to simulate the effects of several possible hardware upgrades to the system such as adding more memory and/or disk space. We will also see that the simulator can be used to assess the consequences of changes in the parameters of the operating system itself, such as changing the page size. Finally, we show that such a simulator can be used to provide helpful information for the process of computer system selection by facilitating the generation and collection of performance statistics for various potential workloads. (A *workload* is some representation of the set of applications to be run on a proposed system).

Part 1 — Exercise the Simulator

The purpose of this part is to familiarize you with the structure and operation of the Operating System Simulator.

1. Study the C++ code for the simulator in the Appendix (a copy of the Simulator is in the directory `chap7` on the distribution disk or in the system directory for this course). Be sure that you understand the basic components of the system such as the virtual and main memories, process control blocks, page tables, and the input, ready and block queues, and how these are represented as object classes. Continue your study by looking closely at the `OSObj` object and its methods `scheduler`, `dispatcher`, `timeslicer`, `blockio`, and `pagefault`. A review of the related discussions in Chapter 7 of the main text will provide additional clarification.
2. Make a copy of the simulator driver program (file `simdrv.cxx`) from your network server or the distribution disk.
3. Run the program using the test data supplied in file `testi`.
4. Study the simulator output until you understand what it represents.

Part 2 — Assess the Effects of Changes in the System

The purpose of this part is to use the simulator to assess the consequences of changes in the system hardware and/or software parameters. Each of the following tasks should be performed independently of the others.

1. Assess the consequences of increasing the size of main memory from its current 32K to 48K. Use the same test data as in Part 1.
2. Assess (independently of 1 above) the consequences of adding enough disk space to increase the virtual memory from its current 64K to 144K. Use the same test data as in Part 1.
3. Assess (independently of 1 and 2 above) the consequences of increasing the page size from 2K to 4K. Use the same test data as in Part 1.

Part 3 — Changing the System Page Replacement Policy

As you know, the simulated system currently uses the First-In-First-Out algorithm as a page replacement policy. This means that during a page fault, when a page frame is needed for an incoming page and no empty page frame is available, the page which has been in the system the longest is selected for replacement. However, as you can imagine, the "oldest" page is not necessarily the best page to replace. That is, it just might be needed again soon, causing yet another page fault. Ideally, we would like to replace the page which will not be needed for the longest time in the future. But without an accurate vision of what is to come in the future, this is a hopeless wish. However, we can approximate this ideal by assuming that if a page has not been *used* for a long time, it is unlikely to be needed again soon. So, if we can devise a method of keeping track of use of various pages, we can develop an algorithm for replacing the *L*east *R*ecently *U*sed page. This is called the *LRU* algorithm.

In reality, operation of the LRU scheme is prohibitively time-consuming without hardware assistance. The solution requires a hardware bit to be associated with each page frame in main memory, along with a system counter. That bit is automatically turned on when the corresponding page is referenced. We can now modify the main memory object, MM, to include an entry, time_interval, representing the number of intervals (using the system counter) since the last reference to that page. Then, after some fixed interval of time, we can simulate a process to sample the reference bits and increment the number of time intervals in MM for any page not referenced during that interval. Then, when a page frame is needed, the system page table is referenced and the page not referenced for the largest number of time intervals is selected for replacement.

For this project, you are to add the reference bit list and interval counter, and code the algorithm to replace the fifo member function in OSObj. Make the necessary changes in *your* copy of the simulator and run the program with the test data used in Part 1. Assess the differences in system performance between the system with a FIFO page replacement algorithm and with an LRU page replacement algorithm.

Questions

1. A number of assumptions have been made and incorporated into the simulator. Do you believe that these assumptions are realistic? If not, suggest one or more alternatives and present a justification for your suggestions.
2. Compare the performance improvements, if any, that you observed when you changed the size of main memory, the amount of disk space, and the page size.
3. Create two additional test suites of data reflecting different workload characteristics. That is, create a workload environment of compute-bound jobs (i.e., jobs with heavy CPU requirements and light I/O requirements), and compare this with a job mix where I/O-bound jobs

(those with heavy I/O but relatively light computational requirements) are predominant.

Worksheet for Laboratory Exercise—
Implementation of the LRU Page Replacement Algorithm

```
// Function OSObj::lru()
// Purpose:

// Pre:

// Post:

void OSObj::nru(){
```

```
}// end OSObj::lru()
```

Notes for Answers to Questions

1.

2.

3.

(TEAM) LABORATORY EXERCISE—JOB SCHEDULING

One of the functions of an operating system is to manage the scheduling of jobs as they enter and leave each of the active queues in the system. To illustrate some of these dynamics, assume that we have an operating system that manages a single batch job queue and a single print queue, as pictured in Figure 7–2.

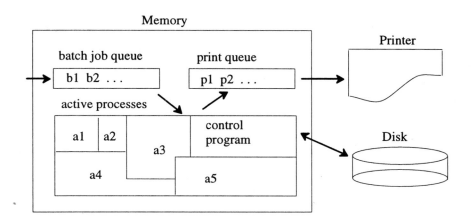

FIGURE 7–2 Simple model of operating system queues.

A job may enter either of these queues at any time, as keyed by one of the following requests:

```
J jobno priority memorysize    P jobno
```

Here, `jobno` is a preassigned identifying number for the job, `priority` is an integer from 1 to 5, identifying the job's priority, and `memorysize` is an integer from 1000 to 100,000 indicating the memory requirements for initiating the job as an active process in the system.

Moreover, the active processes in the system are allocated fixed blocks of memory for their duration (called an "address space"), and a linked list of these processes and their respective address spaces is also maintained by the operating system. In conjunction with this, a linked list called the "available space list" is maintained to keep track of all available (unused) contiguous blocks of memory in the system. Whenever an active process terminates, the following message is sent to the operating system:

```
T jobno
```

This is a signal to the operating system to delete a job from the active processes list, return its address space to the available space list, and search the batch job queue to find one or more new jobs that can now be initiated. This search is made with respect to priorities. If one or more such jobs are found, they are removed from the queue, allocated appropriate address spaces (in accordance with their memory requirements), and the available (free) space list is updated accordingly.

The other event that can occur is the termination of a print job, in which case the printer sends the following signal to indicate that it is ready to accept the next job in the print queue.

R

In this event, the operating system removes the next job from the head of the print queue and passes it to the printer.

These events can occur in any sequence and in any number. Moreover, the occurrence of such an event does not guarantee that it will receive immediate satisfaction. For example, the signal R may occur before any jobs have entered the print queue, or the signal T may result in termination of a job and the freeing of insufficient memory space to satisfy *any* jobs waiting in the batch job queue. A typical stream of events in this setting is given in Figure 7–3, along with some initial queue and list contents. The final contents of the queues and lists for these events are shown in Figure 7–4.

Part 1 — Design the Model Using Queues and Lists

Design the operating system queue management process simulation described above. Note the the Queue class needs to be adapted so that its general element has type batch/print job, and that the List class needs to be adapted so that its general element is (a single process with) a storage address range. Also assume that, in addition to the four events that are described above, the signal D indicates that the contents of all active queues and lists be displayed.

```
J 12 8 10000
J 13 5 40000
J 14 7 20000
T 13
P 10
R
J 15 8 2000 0
J 16 5 3000 0
P 11
T 12
P 12
J 17 7 2000 0
```

batch job queue
  11 5 10000
print queue
  7
  8
  9
active processes
  10 (5000–19999)
available space list
  (0–4999)
  (20000–100000)

(a)   *(b)*

FIGURE 7–3 *(a)* A typical stream of events; *(b)* initial queue and list contents.

batch job queue   active processes

   15 8 20000   10 (5000-19999)
   17 7 20000   11 (20000-29999) 16

print queue   (30000-59999)
                             14 (70000-89999)

    8   available space list
    9
   10   (0-4999)
   11   (60000-69999)
   12   (90000-100000)

FIGURE 7–4   Final queue and list contents for this stream of events.

Part 2 — Implement and Test the Model

Implement the model and exercise it using the stream of events that appears in Figure 7–3, demonstrating that your program gives the queue contents that are indicated after each event is served by the system. Then add more events to the stream, testing especially how the system responds when such an event cannot be served immediately (e.g., an occurrence of a P event and an empty print queue).

Worksheet for Laboratory Exercise—
Job Scheduling

```
/* -- Program name:
   -- Programmer:
   -- Date:
   -- ** Overview
           •
           •
           •
                 */

#include < ... >

// GLOBAL CONSTANTS AND TYPEDEF'S

// GLOBAL FUNCTION PROTOTYPES

main()
{
   // FUNCTION PROTOTYPES


   // LOCAL DATA


   // STATEMENTS




}
// Function:
// Purpose:
// Pre:
/ /Post:
return-type function-name1(formal arguments)
{


}// end function-name1

   •
   •
   •
```

References

[1]   Bourne, S. R., *The UNIX System*, Addison-Wesley Publishing Company, Reading, Massachusetts, 1983, 351 pages.

[2]   Christian, Kaare, *The UNIX Operating System*, John Wiley & Sons, New York, 1983, 318 pages.

[3]   Kernighan, Brian W. and Rob Pike, *The UNIX Programming Environment*, Prentice-Hall, Inc., Englewood Cliffs, NJ, 1984, 357 pages.

[4]   Waite, Mitchell, Donald Martin, and Stephen Prata, *UNIX Primer Plus*, Howard W. Sams & Co., Inc., Indianapolis, Indiana, 1983, 414 pages.

[5]   Wang, Paul S., *An Introduction to Berleley UNIX*, Wadsworth Publishing Company, Belmont, California, 1988, 512 pages.

[6]   Wilson, James, *Berkeley UNIX: A Simple and Comprehensive Guide*, John Wiley & Sons, Inc., New York, NY, 1991.

C++ Program Listing
The Operating System Simulator
The Header Files

```
// This is a header file for OS simulators constants.
//
//
// NOTE: 1.PSIZE must be a power of 2.
//       2.In general virtual memory size(VMSIZE) >= main
//         memory size (MMSIZE), else you are wasting
//         main memory.
//       3.The size of the operating system(OSSIZE) must be
//         less than main memory size(MMSIZE) or there
//         will be no room for programs other than the OS.


#ifndef OSC_H
#define OSC_H


const int PSIZE =  2048; // (bytes) size of a page in main and
                         // virtual memory
const long VMSIZE = 64;  // (Kbytes) size of virtual memory
const long MMSIZE = 32;  // (Kbytes) size of main memory
const long OSSIZE = 4;   // (Kbytes) size of the
                         // operating system
const int SNAPINTV = 50; // number of passes through
                         // OSObj::dispatcher()
                         // between printing reports
const int TABLESIZE = (VMSIZE * 1024)/PSIZE;
                         // (pages) size of a
                         // pagetable and virtual memory
const int MMTABLESIZE = ((MMSIZE - OSSIZE)* 1024)/PSIZE;
                         // (pages) size of avaliable memory



#endif



// This is the header file for the OSObj(Operating System)

//  class.  This class represents the operating system(OS).


#ifndef OSOBJ_H
#define OSOBJ_H
```

```cpp
#include <iostream.h>
#include <iomanip.h>
#include <stdlib.h>
#include "strg.h"
#include "standobj.h"
#include "random.h"
#include "osconsts.h"
#include "jobspecq.h"
#include "pagetab.h"
#include "pcb.h"
#include "pcbq.h"
#include "vm.h"
#include "mm.h"


class OSObj
{
  private:
    // GLOBAL DEFINITIONS ...
    enum os_call {_scheduler_,_dispatcher_,_timeslicer_,
                  _blockio_,_pagefault_};
    enum last_event {nada, page_fault, page_swap, idle, exec};


    // DATA MEMBERS ...
    // system clock
    long systemtime;


    // accounting - how many times were these functions used
    int scheduler_cnt;
    int dispatcher_cnt;
    int timeslicer_cnt;
    int blockio_cnt;
    int pagefault_cnt;
    int page_replacement_cnt;


    // sytem flags
    os_call taskflag;       // Which function is called next?


    last_event eventflag;
// the last action of the current process
// used to determine how much time has passed
// for processes on the blockq


    boolean lastflag;
// the last job in the system has completed execution


    // object pointers
    JobSpecQ* job_inputq_ptr;
    VM* virtual_memory_ptr;
```

```cpp
        MM* main_memory_ptr;
        PCBQ* readyq_ptr;
        PCBQ* blockq_ptr;
        PCB* current_proc_ptr;


        // MEMBER FUNCTIONS ...
        // OS tasks
        void scheduler();
        void dispatcher();
        void timeslicer();
        void blockio();
        void pagefault();


        // OS support functions
        void test_system_parameters();
        int calc_size_in_pages(JobSpec*);
        void check_blockq();
        void fifo();


    public:
      //MEMBER FUNCTIONS
      // constructor - destructor
      OSObj::OSObj();
      virtual OSObj::~OSObj();


      // display
      void display();


      // access - modify
      void execute(string);
    };


#endif




// This is the header file for the MM (Main Memory) class
// that is a descendent of the Element class.  This class
// represents the physical memory of the system - your RAM.


#ifndef MM_H
#define MM_H


#include <iostream.h>
#include <iomanip.h>
#include "queue.h"
```

```cpp
#include "standobj.h"
#include "osconsts.h"
#include "pagetab.h"
#include "pcb.h"
#include "elements.h"


class MM:public Element // Main Memory
{
 private:
  // DATA MEMBERS ...
  struct pageframe
  {
    int jobnumber;
    int jobpage;
    long loadtime;
  };


  pageframe* pageframe_array[MMTABLESIZE];

  Queue* mm_free_list_ptr;
  float mm_utilization;
  float mm_inst_utilization;

 public:
  // MEMBER FUNCTIONS ...
  // constructor - destructors
  MM::MM();
  MM::~MM();


  // display
  void display();


  // access - modify
  int get_jobnumber(int);
  void set_jobnumber(int,int);
  int get_jobpage(int);
  void set_jobpage(int,int);
  long get_loadtime(int);
  void set_loadtime(int,long);
  Queue* return_mm_free_list_ptr();
  int find_oldest_frame();
  void release_memory(PCB*);
  void calc_mm_utilization();
}; // end class MM


#endif



// This is the header file for the VM (Virtual Memory) class
// that is a descendent of the Element class.  This class
// represents your disk or other mass storage device.
```

```
#ifndef VM_H
#define VM_H


#include <iostream.h>
#include <iomanip.h>
#include "strg.h"
#include "osconsts.h"
#include "elements.h"
#include "pagetab.h"
#include "pcb.h"


class VM:public Element // Virtual Memory
{
 private:
   // DATA MEMBERS ...
   struct vpage
   {
     int jobnumber;
     int jobpage;
   };


   vpage* virtual_page_array[TABLESIZE];
   int vm_free;


  public:
    // MEMBER FUNCTIONS ...
    // constructor - destructor
    VM();
    ~VM();

    // display
    virtual void display();


    // access - modify
    int get_vm_free();
    void load_proc_to_vm(PCB*);
    void remove_proc_from_vm(PCB*);
  }; // end VM class


#endif



// This is the header file for the random() function, however it
// is implemented on your system.


#ifndef RANDOM_H
#define RANDOM_H
```

```
// Function:  random()
// Purpose:   Generate a random floating point
//            number between 0 and 1.
// Pre:       Seed the random number generator with a value
//            on the first use of the function.
// Post:      random() = (0 <= value <= 1) and seed is reset.
//            The sequence of random values will always be the
//            same for a given seed.  For greater randomness on
//            a unix system try obtaining the seed from the
//            gettime() function initially.


float random();


#endif



// This is the header file for the JobSpec class
// that is a descendent of the Element class.  The
// class represents programs submitted to the computer
// for execution.


#ifndef JOBSPEC_H
#define JOBSPEC_H


#include <iostream.h>
#include <iomanip.h>
#include "strg.h"
#include "elements.h"


class JobSpec:public Element
{
  protected:
     // DATA MEMBERS ...
     int jobnumber;
     int jobtime;
     long jobsize;
     float blockrate;

  public:
     // MEMBER FUNCTIONS ...
     // constructors - destructors
     JobSpec();
     JobSpec(int,int,long,float);
     JobSpec(int,ifstream&);
     virtual ~JobSpec();


     // display
     virtual void display();
```

```
      // access
      virtual int get_jobnumber();
      virtual int get_jobtime();
      virtual long get_jobsize();
      virtual float get_blockrate();


      // file in - file out
      virtual void file_in(ifstream&);
}; // end class JobSpec


#endif




// This is the header file for the JobSpecQ class
// that is a descendent of the Queue class.  This
// class represents the queue of waiting jobs in a
// batch system, much like a card reader or job spool.


#ifndef JOBQ_H
#define JOBQ_H


#include <fstream.h>
#include <stdlib.h>
#include <iostream.h>
#include <iomanip.h>
#include "strg.h"
#include "osconsts.h"
#include "jobspec.h"
#include "queue.h"


class JobSpecQ : public Queue
{
 public:
      // DATA MEMBERS ...
      int number_of_jobs;

      // MEMBER FUNCTIONS
      // constructors - destructors
      JobSpecQ();
      // ~JobSpecQ() - inhierited from Queue


      // display
      void display();


      // access - modify
      int get_number_of_jobs();
      void load_jobq(string);
}; // end class JobSpecQ
```

```
#endif


// This is the header file for the PCB(Process Control Block)
// class that is a descendent of the JobSpec class.  This class
// represents a programming job in execution - a process.


#ifndef PCB_H
#define PCB_H


#include <iostream.h>
#include <iomanip.h>
#include <string.h>
#include "osconsts.h"
#include "strg.h"
#include "pagetab.h"
#include "random.h"
#include "jobspec.h"


class PCB:public JobSpec  // Process Control Block
{
  protected:
     // DATA MEMBERS ...
     int size_in_pages;
     string state;
     int current_vpage;
     int blocktime;
     PageTable* pcb_page_table;


  public:
     // MEMBER FUNCTIONS
     // constructors - destructors
     PCB(JobSpec*,int);
     virtual ~PCB();


     // display
     virtual void display();


     // access - modify
     void decr_jobtime(int);
     int get_size_in_pages();
     char* get_state();
     void set_state(string);
     int get_current_vpage();
     void set_current_vpage(int);
     int get_blocktime();
     void set_blocktime(int);
     void decr_blocktime(int);
```

```
      PageTable* return_page_table_ptr();
      boolean check_for_blocked_IO();
      boolean check_for_new_current_vpage();
      boolean test_if_page_in_MM();
      void select_new_current_vpage();
}; // end class PCB


#endif



// This is the header file for the PCBQ (Process Control Block
// Queue) class that is a descendent of the Queue class.  This
// class supports the abstraction of a ready queue and block
// queue in the OS.


#ifndef PCBQ_H
#define PCBQ_H


#include<iostream.h>
#include<iomanip.h>
#include "strg.h"
#include "osconsts.h"
#include "pagetab.h"
#include "pcb.h"
#include "queue.h"


class PCBQ : public Queue // Process Control Block Queue
{
  public:
    // MEMBER FUNCTIONS
    // constructor - destructor
    // inheirted from Queue


    // display
    virtual void display();


    // access - modify
    int enter(PCB*);
    boolean search_q(int,PCB*&);
};


#endif



// This is the header file for the PageTable class
// that is a descendent of the Element class.  The class
// supports the PCB class by mapping the use of main memory.
```

```cpp
#ifndef PAGETAB_H
#define PAGETAB_H


#include <iostream.h>
#include <iomanip.h>
#include "osconsts.h"
#include "elements.h"


class PageTable:public Element
{
  private:
    // DATA MEMBERS
    struct page
    {
      int page_frame_num;
      boolean presence_bit;
      long loadtime;
    };


    page* page_table[TABLESIZE];


  public:
    // MEMBER FUNCTIONS
    // constructors - destructors
    PageTable();
    virtual ~PageTable();

    // display
    void display();


    // access/modify
    int get_page_frame_num(int);
    void set_page_frame_num(int,int);
    boolean get_presence_bit(int);
    void set_presence_bit(int,boolean);
    long get_loadtime(int);
    void set_loadtime(int,long);
}; // end class PageTable


#endif
```

C++ Program Listing
The Operating System Simulator
The Implementation Files

```
/* Program: simdrv.cxx
```

This program is the driver for the Operating Systems Simulator. The simulation is modelled on a batch processing system that reads in a set of jobs, then executes each one as there is room in the virtual memory of the computer. The model uses a paged memory system and generally assumes that main memory is much smaller than virtual memory.

The program works by reading in a text file containing a set of job descriptions of the form:

```
    1524     - CPU time required in milliseconds
    12400    - job size in bytes
    0.82     - blockrate: the chance the job will request I/O on
               each of its time slices on the CPU.
               0.0 <= blockrate <= 0.99
```

The program will remove from the job input queue any job whose blockrate is negative or >1, and any job whose size is larger then virtual memory or <=0. The program will prompt you for a file name in your local directory.

The program's output is of several types:
1. A list of accepted jobs and their specifications.
2. The time in milliseconds that each job enters and leaves virtual memory.
3. "Snapshots" of the contents of the main and virtual memories, and a measure of main memory utilization.
4. A summary table of the number of times each of the major operating system (OS) tasks were called in the execution of the program.

The characteristics of the system are determined by 5 constants defined in the file "osconsts.h." They are:

PSIZE   Size of a virtual memory page and a main memory page frame in bytes. Always a power of 2.

VMSIZE Size of virtual memory (VM) in Kbytes. Jobs must be
smaller than VMSIZE or they will not fit.
The size of your addressable memory space.

MMSIZE Size of main memory (MM) in Kbytes. The size
of the physical memory.

OSSIZE The size of the program that represents the
operating system (OS) itself, in Kbytes. The OS
is a program that must be running in MM to do
its work.

SNAPINTV An integer number of passes through the Dispatcher
between "snapshot" of the contents of the MM and VM.

These parameters may be changed for experimentation.
*/


```cpp
#include <iostream.h>
#include <iomanip.h>
#include "strg.h"
#include "osobj.h"


void main(){
  cout << setw(30) << "The OS Simulator" << endl;
  OSObj OSSys;
  string job_file_name;
  cout << "enter filename : ";
  read_string(job_file_name,20);
  cout << endl;
  OSSys.execute(job_file_name);
}
```


/* This is the implementation file for the OSObj class.

The OSObj represents the OS itself and is the heart of the
simulation. It initializes and maintains pointers to all the major elements of the system – the job input queue, main and
virtual memory, the block and ready queues, as well as the current process. This object also maintains the system clock.

Note: There are 5 fixes to this file for use with the Micro-
soft C/C++ 7.0 compiler. If you are using this compiler uncom-
ment the code after the words "MS7.0 compiler fix" and comment

```
out the next line.
*/


#include "osobj.h"


// ****** PUBLIC ******


//
// constructor - destructors
//


//    Constructor: OSObj::OSObj()
//    Purpose: Initalize receiver with default values.
//    Pre:      None
//    Post:     my_class = "MM" and receiver is initialized
//              with default values
OSObj::OSObj()
{
  test_system_parameters();
  systemtime = 0;
  scheduler_cnt = 0;
  dispatcher_cnt = 0;
  timeslicer_cnt = 0;
  blockio_cnt = 0;
  pagefault_cnt = 0;
  page_replacement_cnt = 0;


  eventflag = nada;
  lastflag = FALSE;
  taskflag = _scheduler_;


  job_inputq_ptr = new JobSpecQ();
  virtual_memory_ptr = new VM();
  main_memory_ptr = new MM();
  readyq_ptr = new PCBQ();
  blockq_ptr = new PCBQ();
  current_proc_ptr = NULL;
} // end OSObj::OSObj()


// Destructor:  OSObj::~OSObj()
// Purpose:To destroy the receiver.
// Pre:     Receiver is initialized.
// Post:    Receiver is destroyed.
OSObj::~OSObj()
{
  delete job_inputq_ptr;
  delete virtual_memory_ptr;
  delete main_memory_ptr;
```

```cpp
    delete readyq_ptr;
    delete blockq_ptr;
} // end OSObj::~OSObj()



//
// display
//


// Function: OSObj::display()
// Purpose:  To display a summary of system task calls
//           at the computer screen with a header.
// Pre:      OSObj is initalized and output = oldStuff
// Post:     output = oldStuff header summary \n
void OSObj::display(){
  cout << endl;
  cout << "********** Summary Table **********" << endl;
  cout << "Number of jobs that entered the system: ";
  cout << setw(3) << job_inputq_ptr->get_number_of_jobs();
  cout << endl;
  cout << "Number of calls to the scheduler   :";
  cout << setw(4) << scheduler_cnt << endl;
  cout << "Number of calls to the dispatcher  :";
  cout << setw(4) << dispatcher_cnt << endl;
  cout << "Number of calls to the timeslicer  :";
  cout << setw(4) << timeslicer_cnt << endl;
  cout << "Number of calls to the blockio     :";
  cout << setw(4) << blockio_cnt << endl;
  cout << "Number of calls to the pagefault   :";
  cout << setw(4) << pagefault_cnt << endl;
  cout << "Number of calls to page replacement:";
  cout << setw(4) << page_replacement_cnt << endl;
  cout << endl;
  cout << "STRIKE RETURN";
  char ch;
  cin.get(ch);
  cout << endl;
} // end OSObj::display()



//
// access - modify
//


// Function: OSObj::execute(string in_filename)
// Purpose:  To start the simulation.
// Pre:      The receiver is initialized.
// Post:     The job_inputq is initalized from the text file
//           in_filename
//           and the taskflag function is called. This continues
//           until the last job on the job_inputq completes
//           execution; then display() is called.
void OSObj::execute(string in_filename){
  // cout << "In execute" << endl;
```

```
    cout << setw(30) << "Operating System Simulator" << endl;
    job_inputq_ptr->load_jobq(in_filename);
    job_inputq_ptr->display();
    char ch;
    cout << endl;
    cout << "STRIKE RETURN";
    cin.get(ch);
    cout << endl;
    while(!lastflag){
      switch(taskflag){
      case _scheduler_:
        scheduler();
        break;
      case _dispatcher_:
        dispatcher();
        break;
      case _timeslicer_:
        timeslicer();
        break;
      case _blockio_:
        blockio();
        break;
      case _pagefault_:
        pagefault();
        break;
      }
    }
    display();
    cout << "End of Run" << endl;
} // end OSObj::execute(string)



// ****** PRIVATE ******



//
// OS tasks
//



// Function:  OSObj::scheduler()
// Purpose:   To load programs into virtual memory.
//            To load jobs from the job input queue into virtual
//            memory as there is space available and the entire
//            job will fit.
// Pre:       The size of job_inputq = N, N>=0, and VM is not
//            full with M, M>=0 processes.
// Post:      The size of job_inputq = N - X, (N - X)>=0, and VM
//            now has N + X processes OR job_inputq is empty.
void OSObj::scheduler()
{
  JobSpec* current_job_ptr;


  // cout << "in scheduler" << endl;
  scheduler_cnt++;
```

```
                boolean a_proc_will_fit = TRUE;
                boolean repeat_flag = FALSE;
                int repeat_jobnumber = -1;

                while(a_proc_will_fit){
                  if(!job_inputq_ptr->is_empty()) // there are jobs
                    current_job_ptr = (JobSpec*)job_inputq_ptr->front();
                  else{
                    // cout << "job_inputq empty" << endl;
                    a_proc_will_fit = FALSE;
                  }

                  if(repeat_flag && (current_job_ptr->get_jobnumber()==
                  repeat_jobnumber)){
                    // The entire job_inputq has been examined.
                    //cout << repeat_jobnumber << " did not fit and
                    // has been seen";
                    //cout << " twice, stop" << endl;
                    a_proc_will_fit = FALSE;
                  }

                  if(a_proc_will_fit){
                    int proc_size_in_pages =
                     calc_size_in_pages(current_job_ptr);
                    if((virtual_memory_ptr->get_vm_free()
                        - proc_size_in_pages)>=0){
                  // the proc does fit
                      cout << "Job: " << setw(3) <<
                      current_job_ptr->get_jobnumber();
                  cout << " enters system at " << setw(8) << systemtime;
                  cout << " ms." << endl;
                  PCB* new_proc_ptr =
                    new PCB(current_job_ptr,proc_size_in_pages);
                  virtual_memory_ptr->load_proc_to_vm(new_proc_ptr);
                  readyq_ptr->enter(new_proc_ptr);
                  job_inputq_ptr->remove();
                    }
                    else{
                  // proc did not fit in available VM
                  if(!repeat_flag){
                    // mark first job not to fit
                    repeat_flag = TRUE;
                    repeat_jobnumber = current_job_ptr->get_jobnumber();
                    // cout << "first no fit, jobnumber: ";
                    // cout << setw(8) << repeat_jobnumber << endl;
                  }
                      job_inputq_ptr->rotate();
                    } // else
                  } // if(a_proc_will_fit)
                } // while
                //cout << "call dispatcher from scheduler" << endl;
                taskflag = _dispatcher_;
              } // end OSObj:::scheduler()


              // Function: OSObj::dispatcher()
              // Purpose:  To allocate the CPU to the first ready process.
```

```
//              To set the current process to the first available
//              one on the readyq. The function also checks the
//              blockq for new ready processes and produces snap-
//              shots of the system state.
// Pre:        readyq, blockq and current_proc_ptr are initialized
// Post:       Any process with blocktime <= 0 is placed on the
//              rear of the readyq by check_blockq. If readyq is
//              not empty then current_proc_ptr = readyq.front().
//              If SNAPINTV passes have occurred through the
//              dispatcher - display a map of MM and VM. If there
//              are still jobs taskflag =_timeslicer_ else lastflag
//              = TRUE and control returns to the dispatcher().
void OSObj::dispatcher()
{
  // cout << "in dispatcher" << endl;
  dispatcher_cnt++;
  if((!job_inputq_ptr->is_empty())||
     (!readyq_ptr->is_empty())||
     (!blockq_ptr->is_empty())){
    // cout << "There are still proc in the system." << endl;


    if(!blockq_ptr->is_empty())
      check_blockq();
    /*else
      cout << "blockq empty at dispatcher" << endl;*/
    eventflag = nada;


    if(dispatcher_cnt % SNAPINTV == 0){
      // time for a picture of the system
      cout << endl;
      cout << "Systemtime: " << setw(8) << systemtime << endl;
      virtual_memory_ptr->display();
      main_memory_ptr->display();
    }
    else
      main_memory_ptr->calc_mm_utilization();


    if(!readyq_ptr->is_empty()){
      // cout << "new running process" << endl;
      current_proc_ptr = (PCB*)readyq_ptr->front();
      // MS7.0 compiler fix for the failure to
      // promote a char[8] to char[21].
      // string tmp;
      // strcpy(tmp,"running");
      // current_proc_ptr->set_state(tmp);
      current_proc_ptr->set_state("running");
      readyq_ptr->remove();
    }
    /*else
      cout << "readyq is empty at dispatcher" << endl;*/


    // cout << "Call timeslicer from dispatcher." << endl;
    taskflag = _timeslicer_;
```

```
      }
      else{
        // cout << "System is out of work." << endl;
        lastflag = TRUE;
      }
} // end OSObj::dispatcher()


// Function: OSObj::timeslicer()
// Purpose:   To simulate the actions of the CPU cycle.
//            If there is a current process in the "running"
//            state, can it continue to execution? It may be
//            suspended if the current piece of code needed is
//            not in MM with a pagefault() or for input/output
//            with a call to blockio().  If yes, then decrement
//            the process' runtime. If runtime is = 0, then
//            process has completed and it is removed from the
//            system else it is placed on the rear of the readyq.
// Pre:       systemtime = T ; current_proc-ptr, readyq and
//            blockq are initailized.
// Post:      If there is no current_proc with state = "running"
//            then systemtime = T + 100ms and call dispatcher()
//            else if the current vpage is not in memory
//                call pagefault()
//            else if process blocks for I/O
//                call blockio()
//            else if jobtime <= 0, proc finished
//                systemtime = T + 100
//                remove proc from system
//                call scheduler()
//            else jobtime > 0
//                jobtime -= 100ms
//                place current_proc on readyq.rear()
//                systemtime = T + 100ms
//                call dispatcher()
//
void OSObj::timeslicer()
{
  char ch;


  // cout << "In timeslicer" << endl;
  timeslicer_cnt++;
  if((current_proc_ptr == NULL) ||
     (readyq_ptr->is_empty() &&
     (strcmp(current_proc_ptr->get_state(),"running")!=0))){
    // cout << "In timeslicer with no processes to execute, call
    // dispatcher." << endl;
    systemtime += 100;
    eventflag = idle; // No work for the CPU
    taskflag = _dispatcher_;
  }
  else{
    // cout << "In timeslicer with a running process." << endl;
    if(current_proc_ptr->get_current_vpage() == -1){
      // cout << "first time slice, install page 0" << endl;
      current_proc_ptr->set_current_vpage(0);
```

```
         taskflag = _pagefault_;
      }
    else{
      if(current_proc_ptr->check_for_new_current_vpage()){
      current_proc_ptr->select_new_current_vpage();
      if(!current_proc_ptr->test_if_page_in_MM()){
        // cout << "page fault in timeslicer, new page not in MM"
<< endl;
        taskflag = _pagefault_;
          }
      /*else{
        cout << "new page in MM" << endl;
      }*/
      }
      else{
      // cout << "Remaining on the current page." << endl;
      if(!current_proc_ptr->test_if_page_in_MM()){
      // cout << "page fault in timeslicer, ";
      // cout << "current page not in MM" << endl;
        taskflag = _pagefault_;
      }
      /*else{
        cout << "current page in MM" << endl;
      }*/
        }// else remaining on current page
      }// else in timeslicer with a running process


    if(taskflag != _pagefault_){
      if(current_proc_ptr->check_for_blocked_IO()){
      // cout << "blockio called from timeslicer" << endl;
      taskflag = _blockio_;
        }
        else{
      // cout << "proc did not block in execution" << endl;
      systemtime += 100;
      current_proc_ptr->decr_jobtime(100);
      eventflag = exec;
      if(current_proc_ptr->get_jobtime() <= 0){
        cout << "Process ID: " << setw(8) <<
        current_proc_ptr->get_jobnumber();
        cout << " completed execution at " << setw(8) <<
        systemtime;
        cout << "ms" << endl;
        cout << "STRIKE RETURN" << endl;
        cin.get(ch);
        virtual_memory_ptr->
        remove_proc_from_vm(current_proc_ptr);
        main_memory_ptr->release_memory(current_proc_ptr);
        delete current_proc_ptr;
          current_proc_ptr = NULL;
        // cout << "call scheduler from timeslicer" << endl;
        taskflag = _scheduler_;
        }
      else{
        // cout << "Current proc did not finish" << endl;
        // MS7.0 compiler fix
```

```
          // string tmp;
          // strcpy(tmp,"ready");
          // current_proc_ptr->set_state(tmp);
          current_proc_ptr->set_state("ready");
          readyq_ptr->enter(current_proc_ptr);
          // cout << "Call dispatcher from timeslicer" << endl;
          taskflag = _dispatcher_;
        }// else current proc did not finish
       }// else proc did not block
     }// if(taskflag! = _pagefault_)
   }// if in timeslicer without a running process
} // end OSObj::timeslicer()


// Function: OSObj::blockio()
// Purpose:  To simulate the waiting for I/O. Typically a disk
//           read or write. The function determines the amount
//           of time to assign to a proc's blocktime - how long
//           it must spend on the blockq and places it there.
// Pre:      current_proc_ptr->blocktime = 0, state = "running"
// Post:     blocktime = (0 to 0.5*jobtime)+100 ms, state =
//           "blocked", and call dispatcher().
void OSObj::blockio(){
  // cout << "In blockio" << endl;
  blockio_cnt++;
  int block_time =(int)(random() * 0.5 *
        current_proc_ptr->get_jobtime()) + 100;
  // cout << "Set blocktime to - " << block_time << " ms" <<
     endl;
  current_proc_ptr->set_blocktime(block_time);
  // MS7.0 compiler fix
  // string tmp;
  // strcpy(tmp,"blocked");
  // current_proc_ptr->set_state(tmp);
  current_proc_ptr->set_state("blocked");
  blockq_ptr->enter(current_proc_ptr);
  // cout << "call to dispatcher from blockio" << endl;
  taskflag = _dispatcher_;
} // end OSObj::blockio()


// Function: OSObj::pagefault()
// Purpose:  A piece of needed code is copied into main memory.
//           To place a page for the current process in main
//           memory from virtual memory. If the number of free
//           page frames is > 0, the proc's current_vpage is
//           placed in MM, else a page replacement policy is
//           called. In this version that policy is FIFO: first
//           in - first out, to remove from memory a page of
//           some proc to make room. A single page move is
//        assumed to take 100ms.
// Pre:      MM has an initial set of pages in its pageframes
//           and current_proc_ptr->current_vpage = i.
//           free_frame_list is an initial list of unoccupied
//        pageframe numbers.
// Post:     If size of free_frame_list < 0 then
//             call page replacement policy and add a page to
```

```
//              mm_free. In the first empty pageframe in
//              free_frame_list place i and change the
//              current_vpage's presence bit to reflect that it is
//              now in MM.  systemtime += 100ms.
//          Call dispatcher().
void OSObj::pagefault()
{
  // cout << "In pagefault" << endl;
  pagefault_cnt++;
  eventflag = page_fault;

  if(main_memory_ptr->return_mm_free_list_ptr()->is_empty()){
    // cout << "There are no empty pageframes, ";
    // cout << "go to page replacement";
    // cout << endl;
    page_replacement_cnt++;
    fifo();
    eventflag = page_swap;
  }
  /*else
    cout << "There are unused frames in memory." << endl;*/


    // That is frames that have never been used or contain
    // pages for processes that have completed execution
    // or a page released by the page replacement policy.


  Queue* free_frame_list = main_memory_ptr->re-
turn_mm_free_list_ptr();
  int empty_frame = ((In-
tObj*)(free_frame_list->front())) ->get_val();

  int newpage = current_proc_ptr->get_current_vpage();


  main_memory_ptr->set_jobnumber(empty_frame,
            current_proc_ptr->get_jobnumber());
  main_memory_ptr->set_jobpage(empty_frame,newpage);
  main_memory_ptr->set_loadtime(empty_frame,systemtime);


  PageTable* cp_table = current_proc_ptr->
    return_page_table_ptr();
  cp_table->set_page_frame_num(newpage,empty_frame);
  cp_table->set_presence_bit(newpage,TRUE);
  cp_table->set_loadtime(newpage,systemtime);


  free_frame_list->remove();
  systemtime += 100;


  // MS7.0 compiler fix
  // string tmp;
  // strcpy(tmp,"ready");
```

```
  // current_proc_ptr->set_state(tmp);
  current_proc_ptr->set_state("ready");
  readyq_ptr->enter(current_proc_ptr);
  // cout << "call to dispatcher from pagefault" << endl;
  taskflag = _dispatcher_;
} // end OSObj::pagefault()


//
// OS Support Functions
//


// Function: OSObj::test_system_parameters()
// Purpose:  To test the system parameters for acceptability.
//           Used by OSObj::OSObj()
// Pre:      Parameters are defined.
// Post:     Accept all parameters and continue or exit the
//           program.
void OSObj::test_system_parameters()
{
  // cout << "In test_sys_params" << endl;
  boolean fault_flag = FALSE;
  if(PSIZE<=0){
    cout << "Program Error: PSIZE <= 0" << endl;
    fault_flag = TRUE;
  }
  else {
    int divisor = PSIZE;
    while((divisor != 2) && ((divisor % 2) == 0))
      divisor /= 2;
    if((divisor > 2) && ((divisor % 2)!=0)){
      cout << "Program Error: PSIZE not a power of 2." << endl;
      fault_flag = TRUE;
    }
    else if(PSIZE==1)
      cout << "PSIZE = 1, pretty small." << endl;
  }
  if((OSSIZE<=0)||(MMSIZE<=0)||(VMSIZE<=0)){
    cout << "Program Error: OS, MM or VM SIZE <= 0." << endl;
    fault_flag = TRUE;
  }
  if(OSSIZE>=MMSIZE){
    cout << "Program Error: OSSIZE >= MMSIZE, no room for jobs."
      << endl;
    fault_flag = TRUE;
  }

  if(fault_flag){
    cout << endl;
    cout << "There is an error in the size of one of the base ";
    cout << "parameters found in \"oscollec.h\"." << endl;
    exit(0);
  }
} // end OSObj::test_system_parameters()


// Function: OSObj::calc_size_in_pages(JobSpec* current_job)
// Purpose:  To calculate the number of pages of memory a
```

```
//             process will require, each of PSIZE bytes.
// Pre:        current_job initalized
// Post:       calc_size_in_pages() = jobsize/PSIZE or
//             jobsize/PSIZE + 1 if jobsize % PSIZE != 0
int OSObj::calc_size_in_pages(JobSpec* current_job)
{
  int pgsize = current_job->get_jobsize() / PSIZE;


  if(current_job->get_jobsize() % PSIZE)
    return ++pgsize;
  else
    return pgsize;
} // end OSObj::calc_size_in_pages(JobSpec* current_job)


// Function: OSObj::check_blockq()
// Purpose:  To decrement the blocktime of all the processes on
//           the blockq by the elapsed time since the blockq was
//           last checked and remove any with blocktime <= 0 to
//           the readyq. The elapsed time will depend on the
//           eventflag.
// Pre:      eventflag is initalized and blockq is not empty.
// Post:     eventflag = nada and all blocktimes are
//           decremented, if a blocktime <= 0 then that proc is
//           removed and placed on the rear of the readyq.
void OSObj::check_blockq()
{
  boolean repeatflag = FALSE;
  boolean stopflag = FALSE;
  long repeat_ID = -1;
  int decr_time;
  PCB* temp_ptr;


  // cout << "In check_blockq" << endl;
  switch(eventflag){
    case nada:
      decr_time = 0;
      break;
    case page_fault:
    case idle:
    case exec:
      decr_time = 100;
      break;
    case page_swap:
      decr_time = 200;
      break;
  }


  while(!stopflag){
    if(!blockq_ptr->is_empty())
      temp_ptr = (PCB*)blockq_ptr->front();
    else{
      //cout << "Empty blockq in check_blockq()" << endl;
```

```
                                    stopflag = TRUE;
                                }


                    if(repeatflag && (repeat_ID == temp_ptr->get_jobnumber())){
                        // Have examined the entire queue
                        //cout << "Same proc ID seen twice in check_blockq" <<
                            endl;
                        stopflag = TRUE;
                    }


                    if(!stopflag){
                        temp_ptr->decr_blocktime(decr_time);


                        if(temp_ptr->get_blocktime()<=0){
                    // cout << "Removing proc: " << setw(6) <<
                        temp_ptr->get_jobnumber();
                    // cout << " from front of blockq to rear of readyq." <<
                        endl;
                    // MS7.0 compiler fix
                    // string tmp;
                    // strcpy(tmp,"ready");
                    // temp_ptr->set_state(tmp);
                    temp_ptr->set_state("ready");
                    readyq_ptr->enter(temp_ptr);
                    blockq_ptr->remove();
                        }
                        else{ // blocktime > 0
                    if(!repeatflag){
                        // cout << "First proc with blocktime > 0, mark: ";
                        // cout << setw(8) << temp_ptr->get_jobnumber() << endl;
                        repeatflag = TRUE;
                        repeat_ID = temp_ptr->get_jobnumber();
                    }
                    blockq_ptr->rotate();
                        } // else
                    } // if(!stopflag)
                } // while
            } // end OSObj::check_blockq()



// Function: OSObj::fifo()
// Purpose:  To implement the first in - first out (FIFO) page
//           replacement policy. The process with the pageframe
//           containing the oldest page in MM is freed and
//           placed on the mm_free_list. If fifo() is called you
//           are performing a page move, assumed to take 100ms.
//           That means a complete replacement with the page
//           the proc actually needs takes 200ms.
// Pre:      The size of mm_free_list = 0, MM is initalized and
//           the oldest pageframe M contains page I of proc N.
// Post:     The size of mm_free_list = 1, mm_free_list = (M)
//           and the presence_bit of page I for process N is
//           marked FALSE of process N. systemtime += 100 ms
```

```
void OSObj::fifo(){
  PCB* temp_ptr;


  // cout << "In fifo" << endl;
  int oldest_frame = main_memory_ptr->find_oldest_frame();
  int job_with_oldest_page = main_memory_ptr->
    get_jobnumber(oldest_frame);
  int oldest_page = main_memory_ptr->get_jobpage(oldest_frame);


  if(job_with_oldest_page == current_proc_ptr->get_jobnumber()){
    // cout << "oldest page belongs to current job" << endl;
    current_proc_ptr->return_page_table_ptr()->
     set_presence_bit(oldest_page,FALSE);
  }
  else{
    // cout << "oldest page belongs to non-current process" <<
      endl;
    // so search the blockq for the process
    boolean found = blockq_ptr->
     search_q(job_with_oldest_page,temp_ptr);

    if(!found){ // search the readyq for the process
      found = readyq_ptr->
       search_q(job_with_oldest_page,temp_ptr);
      if(!found){
      cout << "Program Error: Process in Main Memory can not ";
      cout << "be found on the ready or block queues." << endl;
      cout << "ProcID: " << setw(8) << job_with_oldest_page <<
       endl;
      cout << "If you get this message, "
      cout << "you are in serious trouble.";
      exit(0);
       }
    }// if(!found)
    temp_ptr->return_page_table_ptr()->
     set_presence_bit(oldest_page,FALSE);
  }// else oldest page belongs to non-current process


  // add freed frame to mm_free_list
  IntObj* new_free_frame = new IntObj(oldest_frame);
  main_memory_ptr->return_mm_free_list_ptr()->
    enter(new_free_frame);
  systemtime += 100;
} // end OSObj::fifo()



/* This is the implementation file for the MM class


  The MM class represents the physical memory of the system.
  Main memory is represented by an array of pointers to
  pageframes - each of which hold one page of a process.  A
```

```
        queue of empty pageframes is maintained, pointed to by the
        mm_free_list_ptr.  Also associated with this class is the
        system statistic memory utilization.  Memory utilization
        attempts to express how well your memory is being used as a
        percentage of its use over its capacity.
*/


#include "mm.h"


//
// constructor - destructors
//


//   Constructor:  MM::MM()
//   Purpose:      Initalize receiver with default values.
//   Pre:          None
//   Post:         my_class = "MM" and receiver is initialized
//                 with default values
MM::MM()
{
  int i = 0;

  // cout << "In MM()" << endl;
  mm_free_list_ptr = new Queue();
     // a queue of free pageframe numbers


  strcpy(my_class,"MM");


  // The following 2 pieces of code are functionally equivalent.
  // The first uses the array index and the second a pointer to
  // the array.
/*
  for(i;i<MMTABLESIZE;i++)
  {
    pageframe_array[i] = new pageframe;
    pageframe_array[i]->jobnumber = -1;
    pageframe_array[i]->jobpage = -1;
    pageframe_array[i]->loadtime = 0;


    IntObj* numptr = new IntObj(i);
    mm_free_list_ptr->enter(numptr);
  }
*/


  for(pageframe** pptr=pageframe_array;
      pptr<pageframe_array+MMTABLESIZE;pptr++)
  {
    *pptr = new pageframe;
```

```
      (*pptr)->jobnumber = -1;
      (*pptr)->jobpage = -1;
      (*pptr)->loadtime = 0;


      IntObj* numptr = new IntObj(i++);
      mm_free_list_ptr->enter(numptr);
   }


   mm_utilization = 0;
   mm_inst_utilization = 0;
   display();
} // end MM::MM()



// Destructor:  MM::~MM()
// Purpose:      To destroy the receiver.
// Pre:          Receiver is initialized.
// Post:         Receiver is destroyed.
MM::~MM()
{
   // delete the free list
   delete mm_free_list_ptr;


   // The following 2 pieces of code are functionally equivalent.
   // The first uses the array index and the second a pointer to
   // the array.


   // then delete the pageframes
/*
   for(int i;i<MMTABLESIZE;i++)
   {
     delete pageframe_array[i];
   }
*/


   for(pageframe** pptr=pageframe_array;
        pptr<pageframe_array+MMTABLESIZE;pptr++)
   {
     delete *pptr;
   }
} // end ~MM::MM()



//
// display
//


// Function: MM::display()
// Purpose:  To display a representation of the receiver
```

```
//              at the computer screen with a header.
// Pre:         MM is initalized and output = oldStuff
// Post:        output = oldStuff header MM \n
void MM::display()
{
  char ch;
  int k = 0;
  int OSPAGES = (OSSIZE * 1024)/PSIZE; // size of OS in pages


  calc_mm_utilization();
  cout << endl;
  cout << setw(30) << "*** Main Memory ***" << endl;
  cout << setw(26) << "memory utilization = ";
  cout << setw(6) << mm_utilization << endl;
  cout << "   pageframe    jobnumber    jobpage   loadtime" <<
     endl;

  for(int i=0;i<OSPAGES;i++)
  {
    cout << setw(10) << i;
    cout << setw(13) << "OS    0";
    cout << setw(9) << i;
    cout << setw(12) << "0" << endl;
    k++;
  }


  for(pageframe** pptr=pageframe_array;
     pptr<pageframe_array+MMTABLESIZE;pptr++)
  {
    cout << setw(10) << k;
    cout << setw(13) << (*pptr)->jobnumber;
    cout << setw(9) << (*pptr)->jobpage;
    cout << setw(12) << (*pptr)->loadtime << endl;
    k++;
    if((k%15)==0) // every 15 lines stop display
    {
       cout << "STRIKE RETURN" << endl;
       cin.get(ch);
    }
  }
  cout << "STRIKE RETURN" << endl;
  cin.get(ch);
} // end MM::display()


//
// access - modify
//


// GENERIC FUNCTION DESCRIPTION
// Function: MM::get_????????()
// Purpose:  To return the value of ????????
// Pre:      ???????? = a value
```

```
// Post:      get_???????? = value, where ???????? is
//            a data member of the object


// Function: MM::set_????????(new_value)
// Purpose:  To set the value of ???????? to value
// Pre:      ???????? has an initial value
// Post:     ???????? = new_value, where ???????? is
//           a data member of the object


int MM::get_jobnumber(int index)
{
  return pageframe_array[index]->jobnumber;
} // end MM::get_jobnumber(int)


void MM::set_jobnumber(int index,int jobnum)
{
  pageframe_array[index]->jobnumber = jobnum;
} // end MM::set_jobnumber(int,int)


int MM::get_jobpage(int index)
{
  return pageframe_array[index]->jobpage;
} // end MM::get_jobpage(int)


void MM::set_jobpage(int index,int jobpg)
{
  pageframe_array[index]->jobpage = jobpg;
} // end MM::set_jobpage(int,int)


long MM::get_loadtime(int index)
{
  return pageframe_array[index]->loadtime;
} // end MM::get_loadtime(int)


void MM::set_loadtime(int index,long time)
{
  pageframe_array[index]->loadtime = time;
} // end MM::set_loadtime(int,long)


// Function: MM::return_mm_free_list_ptr()
// Purpose:  Return the pointer to the free list.
// Pre:      mm_free_list is initalized
// Post:     return_mm_free_list_ptr() =
//           (Queue*)mm_free_list
Queue* MM::return_mm_free_list_ptr()
{
  return mm_free_list_ptr;
} // end MM::return_mm_free_list_ptr()
```

```
// Function: MM::find_oldest_frame()
// Purpose:  Return the pageframe number with the oldest
//           loadtime.
// Pre:      Receiver is initalized.
// Post:     find_oldest_frame() = i, where
//           pageframe_array[i].loadtime has the smallest
//        value of all pageframes
int MM::find_oldest_frame()
{
  int oldest_frame = 0;
  long min_time = pageframe_array[0]->loadtime;
  long tmp_time;
  for(int i = 1;i<MMTABLESIZE;i++)
  {
    tmp_time = pageframe_array[i]->loadtime;
    if(tmp_time < min_time)
    {
      min_time = tmp_time;
      oldest_frame = i;
    }
  }
  return oldest_frame;
} // end MM::find_oldest_frame()


// Function: MM::release_memory(PCB* exiting_proc_ptr)
// Purpose:  To return to use all pageframes of a process that
//           has completed execution.
// Pre:      exiting_proc_ptr is a PCB that has completed
//           execution (jobtime = 0),  the process' pagetable
//           has 1 to size_in_pages marked as present in MM and
//           mm_free_list has size = i
// Post:     All pages are marked FALSE in the presence_bit of
//           the exiting_proc's pagetable and those which were
//           TRUE are added to the mm_free_list's rear.
//           mm_free_list has size i + # of freed pageframes
void MM::release_memory(PCB* exiting_proc_ptr)
{
  PageTable* exit_table_ptr = exiting_proc_ptr->
    return_page_table_ptr();
  int job_size = exiting_proc_ptr->get_size_in_pages();
  for(int i=0;i<job_size;i++)
  {
    if(exit_table_ptr->get_presence_bit(i) == 1)
    {
      IntObj* free_block_ptr =
              new In-
tObj(exit_table_ptr->get_page_frame_num(i));
      mm_free_list_ptr->enter(free_block_ptr);
      exit_table_ptr->set_presence_bit(i,FALSE);
    } // end if
  } // end for
}// end MM::release_memory(PCB*)


// Function: MM::calc_mm_utilization()
// Purpose:  To calculate the cumalitive average use of MM.
```

```
// Pre:        calc_mm_utilization = i, initally = 0
// Post:       calc_mm_utilization = (i + mm_inst_utilization)/2
void MM::calc_mm_utilization()
{
  mm_inst_utilization = (float)(((MMSIZE * 1024) -
    (mm_free_list_ptr->get_size()
        * PSIZE)) / (MMSIZE * 1024));
  mm_utilization = (mm_utilization + mm_inst_utilization) / 2;
} // end MM::calc_mm_utilization()



/* This is the implementation file for the VM class.


   The class VM is the representaion of virtual memory in the OS
simulator.  In a real system this would be your disk drive, a
place where a copy of your program resides and pages of it are
copied into main memory for execution.  There is a limit to size
of addressable memory any system has.  The implementaion
consists of an array of pointers to virtual pages and a counter
of free pages in that array.
*/


#include "vm.h"


//
// constructor - destructors
//


//    Constructor: VM::VM()
//    Purpose:     Initalize the receiver to default values.
//    Pre:         None
//    Post:        my_class = "VM" and receiver is initalized
//                 to default values
VM::VM()
{
  //cout << "In VM " << endl;
  strcpy(my_class,"VM");
  vm_free = TABLESIZE;
  for(vpage** pptr=virtual_page_array;
    pptr<virtual_page_array+TABLESIZE;
    pptr++)
  {
    *pptr = new vpage;
    (*pptr)->jobnumber = -1;
    (*pptr)->jobpage = -1;
  }
  display();
} // end VM::VM()


// Destructor: VM::~VM()
// Purpose:    To destroy the receiver.
```

```
//   Pre:      Receiver is initialized.
//   Post:     Receiver is destroyed.
VM::~VM()
{
  for(vpage** pptr=virtual_page_array;
      pptr<virtual_page_array+TABLESIZE;
      pptr++)
  {
     delete *pptr;
  }
} // end VM::~VM()




//
// display
//


// Function: VM::display()
// Purpose:  To display a representation of the receiver
//           at the computer screen with a header.
// Pre:      VM is initalized and output = oldStuff
// Post:     output = oldStuff header VM \n
void VM::display()
{
  char ch;
  int k = 0;

  cout << setw(27) << "*** Virtual Memory ***" << endl;
  cout << setw(6) << vm_free << " pages of VM free, each of size
";
  cout << setw(4) << PSIZE << " bytes" << endl;
  cout << " vpage   jobnumber   jobpage" << endl;
  for(vpage** pptr=virtual_page_array;
      pptr<virtual_page_array+TABLESIZE;
      pptr++)
  {
     cout << setw(6) << k;
     cout << setw(9) << (*pptr)->jobnumber;
     cout << setw(9) << (*pptr)->jobpage << endl;
     k++;
     if((k%15)==0) // stop display every 15 lines
     {
       cout << "STRIKE RETURN" << endl;
       cin.get(ch);
     }
  }
  cout << "STRIKE RETURN" << endl;
  cin.get(ch);
} // end VM::display()



//
// access - modify
//
```

```
// Function: VM::get_vm_free()
// Purpose:  To return the value of vm_free
// Pre:      vm_free = value
// Post:     get_vm_free() = value
int VM::get_vm_free()
{
  return vm_free;
} // end VM::get_vm_free()


// Function: VM::load_proc_to_vm
// Purpose:  To load a process to VM and decrement the vm_free
//           counter
// Pre:      VM has N jobs present and vm_free = i. proc_ptr is
//           j pages in size and vm_free -j >= 0
// Post:     VM has N+1 jobs present and vm_free = i - j. The
//           virtual pages used need not be in consequtive
//           order.
void VM::load_proc_to_vm(PCB* proc_ptr)
{
  //cout << "IN VM::load_proc_to_vm" << endl;
  vpage** pptr = virtual_page_array;
  int j = 0;
  int job_size_pgs = proc_ptr->get_size_in_pages();
  int jobnum = proc_ptr->get_jobnumber();


    while((pptr<virtual_page_array+TABLESIZE) && (j<job_size_pgs))
    {


      if((*pptr)->jobnumber == -1)
      {
        (*pptr)->jobnumber = jobnum;
        (*pptr)->jobpage = j++;
      }
      pptr++;
    }

  vm_free -= job_size_pgs;
} // end VM::get_vm_free()


// Function: VM:::remove_proc_from_vm(PCB* proc_ptr)
// Purpose:  To remove from VM a process which has completed
//           execution.
// Pre:      There are job_size_in_pages entries in VM for the
//           proc.  vm_free = i
// Post:     All of the proc's virtual pages are re-initialized
//           and vm_free = i + job_size_in_pages.
void VM::remove_proc_from_vm(PCB* proc_ptr)
{
  vpage** pptr = virtual_page_array;
  int j = 0;
  int job_size_pgs = proc_ptr->get_size_in_pages();
  int jobnum = proc_ptr->get_jobnumber();
```

```
      while((pptr<virtual_page_array + TABLESIZE) &&
         (j<job_size_pgs))
      {
        if((*pptr)->jobnumber == jobnum)
        {
           (*pptr)->jobnumber = -1;
           (*pptr)->jobpage = -1;
           j++;
        }
        pptr++;
      }


   vm_free += job_size_pgs;
} // end VM::remove_proc_from_vm(PCB*)



// RANDOM.CXX


#include "random.h"


float random()
{
  static long seed = 0;
  long val; // 0 <= val <= 32767


  seed = 25173 * seed + 13849;
  val = ((seed % 32768) + 32768) % 32768;
  return (float)val / 32767;
}



/* This is the implementation file for the JobSpec class.


   The objects of this class represent the jobs submitted to the
OS for execution - the "programs."  A descendent of JobSpec -
PCB, will transform these "programs" into "processes" executing
on the system.
 */



#include "jobspec.h"


//
// constructor - destructors
//
```

```
//   Constructor:  JobSpec::JobSpec()
//   Purpose:      Initalize receiver to default values
//   Pre:          None
//   Post:         my_class = "JobSpec" and receiver is
//                 initialized with default values
JobSpec::JobSpec()
{
  strcpy(my_class,"JobSpec");
  jobnumber = -1;
  jobtime = 0;
  jobsize = 0;
  blockrate = 0.0;
} // end JobSpec::JobSpec()



//   Constructor:  JobSpec::JobSpec(int jn, int jt, long js,
//                          float br)
//   Purpose:      Initialize receiver with all data members
//                 explicitly provided.
//   Pre:          None
//   Post:         my_class = "JobSpec" and receiver is
//                 initialized with provided values
JobSpec::JobSpec(int jn, int jt, long js, float br)
{
  strcpy(my_class,"JobSpec");
  jobnumber = jn;
  jobtime = jt;
  jobsize = js;
  blockrate = br;
} // end JobSpec::JobSpec(int,int,long,float)



// Constructor: JobSpec::JobSpec(int jn, ifstream& infile)
// Purpose:     Initialize the receiver with an explicitly
//              provided jobnumber and all other values from
//              the text file, infile.
// Pre:         None
// Post:        my_class = "JobSpec", jobnumber = jn and
//              receiver is initialized with remaining values
//              from infile.
JobSpec::JobSpec(int jn, ifstream& infile)
{
  strcpy(my_class,"JobSpec");
  jobnumber = jn;
  file_in(infile);
} // end JobSpec::JobSpec(int,ifstream&)



//   Destructor:JobSpec::~JobSpec()
//   Purpose:   To destroy the receiver.
//   Pre:       Receiver is initialized.
//   Post:      Receiver is destroyed.
JobSpec::~JobSpec()
{
  ;
} // end JobSpec::~JobSpec()
```

```
//
// display
//


// Function: JobSpec::display()
// Purpose:  To display a representation of the receiver
//           at the computer screen.
// Pre:      JobSpec is initalized and output = oldStuff
// Post:     output = oldStuff JobSpec \n
void JobSpec::display()
{
  cout << setw(10) << my_class
     << setw(8) << jobnumber
     << setw(8) << jobtime
     << setw(8) << jobsize
     << setw(8) << setprecision(4)
     << blockrate << endl;
} // end JobSpec::display()



//
// access - modify
//


// GENERIC FUNCTION DESCRIPTION
// Function: JobSpec::get_????????()
// Purpose:  To return the value of ????????
// Pre:      ???????? = a value
// Post:     get_???????? = value, where ???????? is
//           a data member of the object
int JobSpec::get_jobnumber()
{
  return jobnumber;
} // end JobSpec::get_jobnumber()


int JobSpec::get_jobtime()
{
  return jobtime;
} // end JobSpec::get_jobtime()


long JobSpec::get_jobsize()
{
  return jobsize;
} // end JobSpec::get_jobsize()


float JobSpec::get_blockrate()
{
  return blockrate;
} // end JobSpec::get_blockrate()
```

```
//
// file in - file out
//


// Function:  JobSpec::file_in(ifstream& in_file)
// Purpose:   To read in a set of values for the receiver from a
//            text file, in_file.  This function assumes that the
//            class name and jobnumber are initialized already.
// Pre:       in_file = int long float restOfFile
// Post:      in_file = restOfFile and jobtime = int,
//            jobsize = long, and blockrate = float
void JobSpec::file_in(ifstream& in_file)
{
  in_file >> jobtime >> jobsize >> blockrate;
} // end JobSpec::get_blockrate()



/* This is the implementation file for the JobSpecQ class.

   This class maintains a queue of JobSpec objects acceptable to
   the OS simulator read from your input file.  As there is room
   in VM, jobs are removed.  The class also maintains a count of
   the number of jobs accepted to the queue - number_of_jobs.
*/


#include "jobspecq.h"


//
// constructor - destructor
//


//   Constructor:  JobSpecQ::JobSpecQ()
//   Purpose:      Initalize receiver to default values
//   Pre:          None
//   Post:         The receiver is an initialized Queue with
//                 number_of_jobs = 0
JobSpecQ::JobSpecQ()
{
  // cout << "in JobSpecQ" << endl;
  Queue::Queue();
  number_of_jobs = 0;
} // end JobSpecQ::JobSpecQ()


//
// display
//


// Function:  JobSpecQ::display()
// Purpose:   To display a representation of the receiver
```

386 FUNDAMENTALS OF COMPUTING II: C++ LABORATORY MANUAL

386 FUNDAMENTALS OF COMPUTING II: C++ LABORATORY MANUAL

```
//              at the computer screen with a header.
// Pre:        JobSpecQ is initalized and output = oldStuff
// Post:       output = oldStuff header JobSpecQ number_of_jobs \n
void JobSpecQ::display()
{
  cout << endl;
  cout << setw(10) << " " << "classname";
  cout << setw(12) << " " << "jobnumber";
  cout << setw(8) << " " << "jobtime";
  cout << setw(8) << " " << "jobsize";
  cout << setw(11) << " " << "blockrate" << endl;
  Queue::display();
  cout << "Job Count = " << number_of_jobs << endl;
} // end JobSpecQ::display()


//
// access - modify
//


// Function: JobSpecQ::get_number_of_jobs()
// Purpose:  To return the value of number_of_jobs
// Pre:        number_of_jobs = a value
// Post:       get_number_of_jobs() = value,
int JobSpecQ::get_number_of_jobs()
{
  return number_of_jobs;
} // end JobSpecQ::get_number_of_jobs()


// Function: JobSpecQ::load_jobq(string filename)
// Purpose:  To open a text file, filename, if it exists
//           and read in a stream of JobSpec parameters.
//           Those JobSpec with valid parameters are accepted
//          and entered into the receiver and all others are
//           deleted.
// Pre:        The receiver is initalized.
// Post:       The receiver has size = number_of_jobs
void JobSpecQ::load_jobq(string filename)
{
  int i = 1; // assigned job number
  char ch;


  // open an input file stream, only if the
  // file already exists
  ifstream infile(filename,ios::in|ios::nocreate);
  if(infile.bad())
  {
    cout << "File named : " << filename << " not found";
    cout << endl << "STRIKE RETURN" << endl;
    cin.get(ch);
    exit(0);
  }
  else
```

```
{
  infile >> ws; // ignore leading white spaces
  while((!infile.eof())&&(!is_full()))
  {
    JobSpec* job = new JobSpec(i,infile);
    infile >> ws;
    if((job->get_jobsize() > (1024*VMSIZE)) ||
        (job->get_jobsize() <=0))
    {
  cout << "JobSpec # " << setw(4) << job->get_jobnumber();
  cout << " rejected due to illegal size" << endl;
  delete job;
    }
    else if((job->get_blockrate() >= 0.99) ||
        (job->get_blockrate() < 0.0))
    {
      cout << "JobSpec # " << setw(4) << job->get_jobnumber();
      cout << " rejected due to bad blockrate" << endl;
      delete job;
    }
    else if(job->get_jobtime() <= 0)
    {
      cout << "JobSpec # " << setw(4) << job->get_jobnumber();
      cout << " rejected due to jobtime <= 0" << endl;
      delete job;
    }
    else // job accepted
    {
  enter(job);
  i++;
    }
  } // end while
  number_of_jobs = --i;
  } // else
} // end JobSpecQ::load_jobq(string)



/* This is the implementation file for the PCB class
```

    The class PCB implements the process control block, a record
by which the system tracks the state of a process. In the
simulation it also represents the process itself. The class PCB
is descended from the JobSpec class and inherits all of that
class's fields and methods. Each instance of a PCB creates an
instance of a PageTable to record the location of pages in main
memory.

```
*/


#include "pcb.h"


//
// constructor - destructors
//
```

```
//   Constructor: PCB::PCB(JobSpec* new_job_ptr, int size)
//   Purpose:     Initalize receiver for a given JobSpec.
//   Pre:         An initialized JobSpec and size.
//   Post:        my_class = "PCB" and receiver is initialized
//                with values from a JobSpec and a calculated
//                size = # of pages
PCB::PCB(JobSpec* new_job_ptr, int size)
{
  // cout << "In PCB" << endl;
  strcpy(my_class,"PCB");
  jobnumber = new_job_ptr->get_jobnumber();
  jobtime = new_job_ptr->get_jobtime();
  jobsize = new_job_ptr->get_jobsize();
  blockrate = new_job_ptr->get_blockrate();
  size_in_pages = size;
  strcpy(state,"ready");
  current_vpage = -1;
  blocktime = 0;
  pcb_page_table = new PageTable();
} // end PCB::PCB(JobSpec*,int)


//   Destructor:PCB::~PCB()
//   Purpose:   To destroy the receiver.
//   Pre:       Receiver is initialized.
//   Post:      Receiver is destroyed.
PCB::~PCB()
{
  delete pcb_page_table;
} // end PCB::~PCB()


//
// display
//


// Function: PCB::display()
// Purpose:  To display a representation of the receiver
//           at the computer screen with a header.
// Pre:      PCB is initalized and output = oldStuff
// Post:     output = oldStuff header PCB \n
void PCB::display()
{
  char ch;


  cout << endl;
  JobSpec::display();
  cout << setw(10) << " " << "Process size = " << size_in_pages;
  cout << "(pages)" << endl;
  cout << setw(10) << " " << "Current state: " << state << endl;
  cout << setw(10) << " " << "Virtual page to be executed: ";
  cout << setw(4) << current_vpage << endl;
  cout << setw(10) << " " << "Blocktime remaining: ";
  cout << setw(8) << blocktime << endl;
```

```
     pcb_page_table->display();
     cout << "STRIKE RETURN" << endl;
     cin.get(ch);
} // end PCB::display()



//
// access - modify
//


// Function: PCB::decr_jobtime(int time)
// Purpose:  To decrement the jobtime of a process to
//           simulate its execution.
// Pre:      receiver's jobtime = value
// Post:     jobtime = value - time
void PCB::decr_jobtime(int time)
{
   jobtime -= time;
} // end PCB::decr_jobtime(int time)


// GENERIC FUNCTION DESCRIPTIONS
// Function: PCB::get_????????()
// Purpose:  To return the value of ????????
// Pre:      ???????? = a value
// Post:     get_???????? = value, where ???????? is
//           a data member of the object


// Function: PCB::set_????????(new_value)
// Purpose:  To set the value of ???????? to value
// Pre:      ???????? has an initial value
// Post:     ???????? = new_value, where ???????? is
//           a data member of the object


int PCB::get_size_in_pages()
{
   return size_in_pages;
} // end


char* PCB::get_state()
{
   return state;
} // end


void PCB::set_state(string new_state)
{
   strcpy(state,new_state);
} // end PCB::set_state(string)

int PCB::get_current_vpage()
```

```
{
  return current_vpage;
} // end PCB::get_current_vpage()


void PCB::set_current_vpage(int vpage_num)
{
  current_vpage = vpage_num;
} // end PCB::set_current_vpage(int)


int PCB::get_blocktime()
{
  return blocktime;
} // end PCB::get_blocktime()


void PCB::set_blocktime(int btime)
{
 blocktime = btime;
} // end PCB::set_blocktime(int)


// Function:  PCB::decr_blocktime(int time)
// Purpose:   To decrement the receiver's blocktime.
// Pre:       receiver's blocktime = value
// Post:      blocktime = value - time
void PCB::decr_blocktime(int time)
{
 blocktime -= time;
} // end PCB::decr_blocktime(int)


// Function:  PCB::return_page_table_ptr()
// Purpose:   Return the address of the receiver's page table.
// Pre:       page_table_ptr has been initialized
// Post:      return_page_table_ptr() =
//            (PageTable*)pcb_page_table
PageTable* PCB::return_page_table_ptr()
{
  return pcb_page_table;
} // end PCB::return_page_table_ptr()


// Function:  PCB::check_for_blocked_IO()
// Purpose:   To test if a process will block for I/O in this
//            timeslice and should be placed on the blockq.
// Pre:       Receiver is initialized.
// Post:      check_for_blocked_IO() = TRUE or FALSE
boolean PCB::check_for_blocked_IO()
{
  if(random()<=blockrate)
    return TRUE;
  else
    return FALSE;
} // end PCB::check_for_blocked_IO()
```

```
// Function: PCB::check_for_new_current_vpage()
// Purpose:  To test if the receiver should continue
//           execution on a new page.
// Pre:      Receiver is initialized.
// Post:     check_for_new_page() = TRUE or FALSE
boolean PCB::check_for_new_current_vpage()
{
  if(random()>=((1.0/size_in_pages)+0.2))
    return TRUE;
  else
    return FALSE;
} // end PCB::check_for_new_current_vpage()



// Function: PCB::test_if_page_in_MM()
// Purpose:  To test if current_vpage is in MM by
//           testing the value of that page's presence_bit.
// Pre:      receiver's current_vpage = i
// Post:     return pcb_page_table->get_presence_bit() =
//           TRUE or FALSE
boolean PCB::test_if_page_in_MM()
{
  return pcb_page_table->get_presence_bit(current_vpage);
}// end  PCB::test_if_page_in_MM()



// Function: PCB::select_new_current_vpage()
// Purpose:  To select a new VM page in which the process will
//           continue execution.
// Pre:      current_vpage = i
// Post:     current_vpage = j, where j != i and
//           0 <= i <= size_in_pages
void PCB::select_new_current_vpage()
{
  int newpage;


  do{
    newpage = (int)(random()*size_in_pages);
  }
  while(current_vpage == newpage);
  current_vpage = newpage;
} // end PCB::select_new_current_vpage()



/* This is the implementation file of the PCBQ class


   This class implements a queue restricted in access to PCB
objects.   It exists in the OS simulation to provide for the
block and ready queue of an OS.  The block queue represents
processes waiting for I/O and each process is given the state
"blocked."  The ready queue represents processes able to execute
and waiting to obtain a time slice on the CPU.
*/
```

```cpp
#include "pcbq.h"


//
// display
//


// Function: PCBQ::display()
// Purpose:  To display a representation of the receiver
//           at the computer screen with a header.
// Pre:      PCBQ is initialized and output = oldStuff
// Post:     output = oldStuff header PCBQ \n
void PCBQ::display()
{
  cout << endl;
  cout << setw(30) << "PCB Queue" << endl;
  cout << endl;
  Queue::display();
}


//
// access - modify
//


// Function: PCBQ::enter(PCB* pcb_ptr)
// Purpose:  To restrict entry on the PCBQ to PCBs.
// Pre:      pcb_ptr is initialized
// Post:     PCBQ->rear() = pcb_ptr and returns 1 or
//           PCBQ is full and returns 0.
int PCBQ::enter(PCB* pcb_ptr)
{
  return Queue::enter(pcb_ptr);
} // end PCBQ::enter(PCB*)


// Function: PCBQ::search_q(int search_id,PCB*& proc_ptr)
// Purpose:  Search the queue for the PCB with
//           jobnumber = search_id.
// Pre:      search_id = i and proc_ptr = NIL
// Post:     If found return TRUE, and proc_ptr =
//           (PCB*) with jobnumber = i, else return
//           FALSE.
boolean PCBQ::search_q(int search_id,PCB*& proc_ptr)
{
  // cout << "In PCBQ::search_q" << endl;
  boolean repeatflag = FALSE;
  int repeat_jobnumber = -1;
  boolean cont = TRUE;


  if(size)
  {
    while(cont)
```

```
    {
      proc_ptr = (PCB*)front();
      if(repeatflag && (proc_ptr->get_jobnumber() ==
       repeat_jobnumber))
      {
        // cout << "A proc ID has been seen twice, stop search."
        << endl;
        cont = FALSE;
      }


      if(cont)
      {
        if(proc_ptr->get_jobnumber() == search_id)
        {
      // cout << "Proc found on PCBQ." << endl;
      return TRUE;
        }
        else //Proc ID != search_id
        {
      if(!repeatflag)
      {
        // cout << "First search_id not accepted, save as";
        // cout << " repeat marker." << endl;
        repeatflag = TRUE;
        repeat_jobnumber = proc_ptr->get_jobnumber();
      }
      rotate();
        } // end else
      } // end if(cont)
    } // end while
  } // end if(size)
  return FALSE;
} // end search_q




/* This is the implementation file for the PageTable class


   The class PageTable implements an array of page entries.  An
instance is used by a PCB object to record whether a virtual
page has been mapped into main memory, if it is in main memory
and if so, when.
*/



#include "pagetab.h"


//
// constructor - destructors
//


//   Constructor: PageTable::PageTable()
//   Purpose:     Initialize receiver to default values.
```

```cpp
//    Pre:         None
//    Post:        my_class = "PageTable" and receiver is
//                 initialized with default values
PageTable::PageTable()
{
  // cout << "In PageTable" << endl;
  strcpy(my_class,"PageTable");
  for(page** pptr=page_table;pptr<page_table+TABLESIZE;pptr++)
  {
     *pptr = new page;
     (*pptr)->page_frame_num = -1;
     (*pptr)->presence_bit = FALSE;
     (*pptr)->loadtime = 0;
  }
} // end PageTable::PageTable()


//    Destructor:PageTable::~PageTable()
//    Purpose:   To destroy the receiver.
//    Pre:       Receiver is initialized.
//    Post:      Receiver is destroyed.
PageTable::~PageTable()
{
  for(page** pptr=page_table;pptr<page_table+TABLESIZE;pptr++)
  {
    delete *pptr;
  }
} // end PageTable::~PageTable()


//
// display
//


// Function: PageTable::display()
// Purpose:  To display a representation of the receiver
//           at the computer screen with a header.
// Pre:      PageTable is initalized and output = oldStuff
// Post:     output = oldStuff header PageTable \n
void PageTable::display()
{
  int i = 0;
  cout << endl;
  cout.width(20);
  cout << "PageTable" << endl;
  cout << " page  pageframe present  loadtime(msec)" << endl;
  for(page** pptr=page_table;pptr<page_table+TABLESIZE;pptr++)
  {
    cout << setw(4) << i++;
    cout << setw(9) << (*pptr)->page_frame_num;
    if((*pptr)->presence_bit)
      cout << "     TRUE   ";
    else
      cout << "     FALSE ";
    cout << setw(14) << (*pptr)->loadtime << endl;
  }
} // end PageTable::display()
```

```
//
// access - modify
//


// GENERIC FUNCTION DESCRIPTIONS
// Function: PageTable::get_????????()
// Purpose:  To return the value of ????????
// Pre:      ???????? = a value
// Post:     get_???????? = value, where ???????? is
//           a data member of the object


// Function: PageTable::set_????????(new_value)
// Purpose:  To set the value of ???????? to value
// Pre:      ???????? has an initial value
// Post:     ???????? = new_value, where ???????? is
//           a data member of the object


int PageTable::get_page_frame_num(int index)
{
  return page_table[index]->page_frame_num;
} // end PageTable::get_page_frame_num(int)


void PageTable::set_page_frame_num(int index,int value)
{
  page_table[index]->page_frame_num = value;
} // end PageTable::set_page_frame_num(int,int)


boolean PageTable::get_presence_bit(int index)
{
  return page_table[index]->presence_bit;
} // end  PageTable::get_presence_bit(int)


void PageTable::set_presence_bit(int index,boolean value)
{
  page_table[index]->presence_bit = value;
} // end PageTable::set_presence_bit(int,value)


long PageTable::get_loadtime(int index)
{
  return page_table[index]->loadtime;
} // end  PageTable::get_loadtime(int)


void PageTable::set_loadtime(int index,long value)
{
 page_table[index]->loadtime = value;
} // end PageTable::set_loadtime(int,long)
```

INDEX

#ifndef preprocessor directive, 125

#include preprocessor directive, 6, 106

A

Access function, 115

Addressing, 169

Arguments, array, 73

Arithmetic assignment operators, 11

Arithmetic operators, 10

Array, 71
    implementation of binary trees, 323
    of dynamic objects, 170
    of objects, 114
    and pointers, 172

Assignment, 10
    of strings, 75

Automatic variables, 17

B

Base type, 166

Binary search tree, 283

break statement, 33, 48

C

case label, 32

char, 23

cin stream input, 7
    string input, 77

Class

BinaryTree, 315, 317

CharObj, 195, 207

constructor, 108

declaration, 103

destructor, 109

Element, 152, 188, 190

ElementSet, 181

FloatObj, 194, 201

Inputstr, 267, 270

IntObj, 155, 193, 197

List, 255, 257

member function definition, 110

Morpheme, 260, 263

PersonSet, 186

Queue, 274, 277

Sequence, 250, 252

specifications, 117

Stack, 280, 282

StringObj, 195, 204

Student, 104

Tree, 296, 302

Comments, 4

Comparison operators, 24

Component type, 72

Compound statement, 26

Concatenation of strings, 76

Constant declaration, 2

Constructor, 108

continue statement, 50

cout stream output, 8

ctype.h character functions, 49

D

Declaration, file, 147

default clause, 33